Machine Learning Programming Hands on

Dr. Uma Gajendragadkar

Dedication

To,

My Family

About Author

Uma Gajendragadkar, Ph.D. is a Machine Learning researcher, educator, and technology professional with extensive experience spanning academia and industry. With over 12 years of professional experience in Data Science, Machine Learning, Data Analytics, and Software Engineering, along with more than 15 years of teaching experience, she has dedicated her career to bridging the gap between theoretical concepts and real-world applications of computing technologies.

Dr. Gajendragadkar earned her Ph.D. in Computer Engineering from COEP, Savitribai Phule Pune University (formerly known as University of PUNE). She has worked on research and applied solutions in areas including Machine Learning, predictive analytics, Recommendation systems, Context sensitive systems, Search, Data Mining and data-driven problem solving.

As an educator, she has taught a broad range of subjects including Python Programming, Machine Learning, Advanced Databases, Information Retrieval, Databases etc. at undergraduate and graduate levels. Her teaching philosophy centers on making complex concepts simple, intuitive, and accessible to learners from diverse backgrounds. She believes that learning is most effective when students actively engage with concepts through experimentation, hands-on implementation, and real-world examples.

Through *Machine Learning Programming Hands-on: Learn with Python Libraries*, she combines academic knowledge, industry perspectives, and practical implementation techniques to help readers build a strong foundation in machine learning. Her goal is to make machine learning approachable and engaging by guiding readers through concepts with step-by-step explanations, examples, exercises, and hands-on coding experiences.

Preface

This book has three sections.

Section 1 introduces basic concepts in Machine Learning.

Section 2 covers various Machine Learning Libraries used for implementing Machine Learning solutions. These are Python based Machine Learning Libraries.

Section 3 covers the popularly used Machine learning Algorithms.

All datasets, downloadable notebooks, student worksheets, and instructor answer keys used in this book are available at:
[**Book Companion Repository**]-

https://github.com/UUGDR/Machine-Learning-Programming-Hands-on

Contents

SECTION 1

INTRODUCTION TO MACHINE LEARNING

Chapter 00: Before We Start

Before We Begin

Before we begin our journey into the fascinating field of Machine Learning, let us first ensure that our development environment is properly configured on your local machine.

A correctly configured environment will help you execute all examples, run experiments smoothly, and avoid unnecessary technical interruptions during learning.

You are required to complete the following setup:

- **Install Anaconda Distribution**

Download and install the latest version of the Anaconda distribution for your operating system (Windows, macOS, or Linux). Anaconda provides a comprehensive Python environment along with essential scientific computing libraries such as NumPy, Pandas, Matplotlib, and Scikit-learn.

- **Set Up Jupyter Notebook**

Jupyter Notebook is included within Anaconda. After installation, verify that Jupyter is functioning correctly by launching it from the Anaconda Navigator or by using the appropriate command:

```
jupyter notebook
```

Ensure that a notebook interface opens in your browser and that you are able to create and execute a new Python notebook.

- **Verify Python Environment**

Confirm that Python is properly installed and accessible. It is recommended that you use a dedicated conda environment for this course to manage dependencies efficiently.

- **Test Required Libraries**

Open a new notebook and test basic imports:

```
import numpy as np
import pandas as pd
import matplotlib.pyplot as plt
import sklearn
```

If no errors occur, your environment is ready.

Detailed, step-by-step installation instructions, along with screenshots, are provided in Appendix 1. Please carefully follow those instructions before proceeding further in this chapter.

Having your environment correctly configured will ensure that you can focus entirely on understanding the concepts rather than troubleshooting installation issues.

1. Chapter 01: What Is Machine Learning?

What Is Machine Learning?

Machine Learning is the science of teaching machines how to learn by themselves. Machine Learning represents the discipline of enabling computers to acquire knowledge autonomously. Machine learning is changing our world.

The reach of machine learning is so pervasive that you are likely to interact with it dozens of times daily without conscious awareness. From facial recognition systems that unlock your smartphone to biometric scanners that record your attendance, ML algorithms are woven into virtually every aspect of modern life.

As a specialized subset of artificial intelligence, machine learning empowers systems to absorb information from datasets and progressively enhance their performance. These systems employ various algorithms to examine data, detect recurring patterns, and generate forecasts.

Machine learning is an AI discipline that equips computers with the capability to discover patterns within datasets and generate decisions or predictions autonomously, rather than requiring explicit programming for each possible situation, essentially mimicking human experiential learning.

What Is Artificial Intelligence?

Artificial intelligence (AI) can be defined as the ability of machines to perform tasks that typically require human intelligence, such as learning, reasoning, problem-solving, and perception.

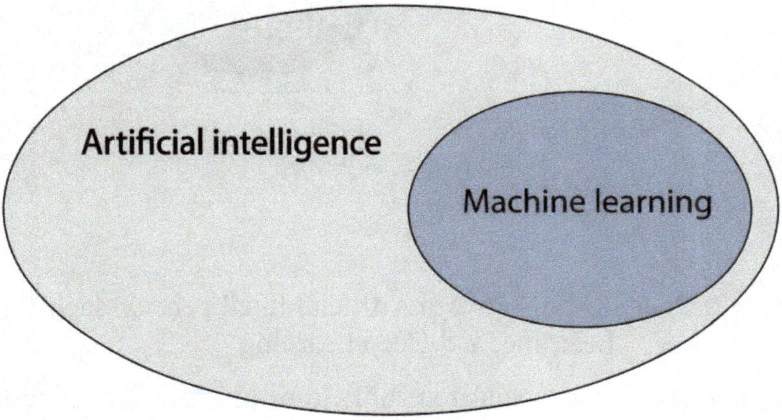

Figure 1-1: Relationship between Artificial Intelligence and Machine Learning

Machine Learning (ML) is a subset of Artificial Intelligence (AI) that focuses on enabling systems to learn from data and improve performance without being explicitly programmed. Instead of following fixed rules, machine learning algorithms identify patterns in data and use those patterns to make predictions or decisions in real-world applications such as recommendation systems, fraud detection, and medical diagnosis.

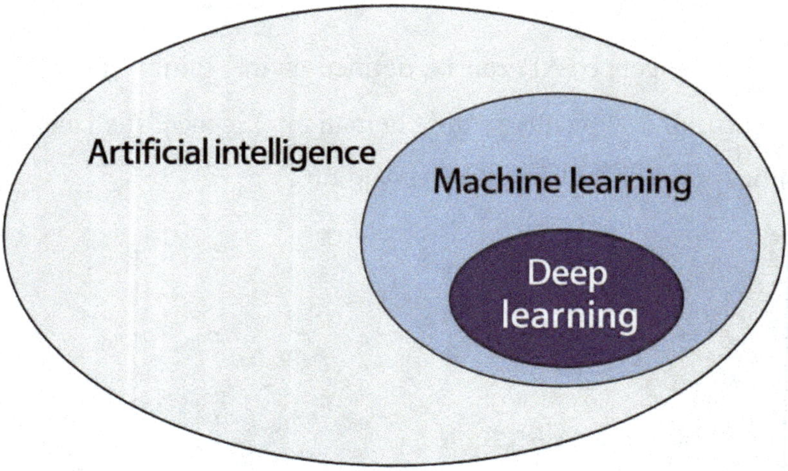

Figure 1-2: Relationship between Artificial Intelligence, Machine Learning, and Deep Learning

Deep Learning (DL) is a specialized subfield of Machine Learning that uses multi-layered neural networks to model complex patterns in large datasets. It is particularly effective for tasks involving images, speech, and natural language because it can automatically learn hierarchical features from raw data. Due to the availability of big data and high-performance computing, deep learning has become widely used in applications such as self-driving cars, voice assistants, image recognition, and language translation.

Humans vs. Machines

Figure 1-3: Humans vs. Machines

How Do Humans Think?

When we, as humans, need to make a decision based on our experience, how do we do it?

Humans think by learning from experience and applying that knowledge to new situations. When we need to make a decision, our brains naturally look for patterns based on what we have encountered before.

First, we recall past situations that are similar to the current one. Next, we derive certain rules or insights from those experiences, such as what worked well and what did not. Finally, we apply these learned rules to predict possible outcomes and choose the best course of action for the future.

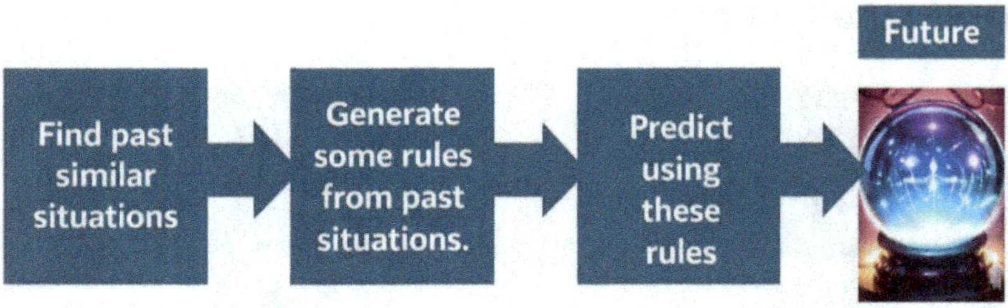

Figure 1-4: How Do Humans Think?

Machine learning (ML) teaches computers to learn from data and find patterns, just as humans learn from experience, so they can make predictions or decisions without being explicitly programmed for every single task. Instead of writing rules for every situation, you provide the computer with many examples, and it determines the rules itself, improving over time as it processes more data—just like a child learning to identify a cat after seeing many pictures of cats.

Machine learning is an area of artificial intelligence and computer science that includes supervised and unsupervised learning and involves the development of software and algorithms that can make predictions based on data.

Machine learning is utilized across various industries. In the field of data analytics, for example, it is used to make predictions based on trends and insights derived from data.

An example of the application of machine learning is the autonomous vehicle. Sensors around the vehicle generate thousands of data points, which are analyzed and processed to guide the vehicle toward its destination. Collective data from thousands of self-driving cars can be used to improve vehicle safety and prevent accidents.

Applications of Machine Learning

1. **Business Intelligence:** Machine learning models analyze large and complex datasets to uncover hidden patterns, trends, and anomalies. These insights help organizations make data-driven decisions and predict future business outcomes.
2. **Customer Relationship Management:** Machine learning algorithms study customer behavior, preferences, and interaction history to generate personalized recommendations. This improves customer engagement, retention, and overall satisfaction.
3. **Security:** Machine learning systems learn normal system behavior and detect deviations that may indicate cyber threats. By continuously learning from new attack patterns, they enhance threat detection and response.
4. **Human Resources:** Machine learning models analyze resumes, skills, and past hiring data to filter applications efficiently. They help identify candidates who best match job requirements while reducing manual effort.
5. **Supply Chain Management:** Machine learning models predict demand and optimize inventory levels using historical sales and logistics data. They also help streamline transportation and reduce

costs by learning efficient routing patterns.

6. **Natural Language Processing:** Machine learning models are trained on large text datasets to understand and process human language. They enable tasks such as sentiment analysis, language translation, and text summarization by learning linguistic patterns and context.
7. **Weather Prediction:** Machine learning models are trained on large volumes of historical and real-time weather data to identify patterns and trends. These models generate forecasts by learning how different atmospheric variables interact over time.
8. **Estimating Travel Times:** Machine learning algorithms analyze past traffic data, GPS signals, and current road conditions to predict travel durations. The system continuously improves its accuracy as it learns from new traffic patterns.
9. **Song Recommendation:** Machine learning systems learn from user behavior such as listening history, likes, and skips to model individual preferences. They use this learned information to recommend songs similar to those the user enjoys.
10. **Auto-Completing Sentences:** Machine learning language models learn statistical relationships between words from massive text datasets. Based on context, they predict the most likely next words in a sentence.

11. **Article Summarization:** Machine learning models are trained to recognize important sentences and key themes within text. They generate summaries by selecting or generating content that best represents the original article.

12. **Image Generation:** Machine learning models learn visual patterns from large image datasets paired with text descriptions. Using this learned knowledge, they generate new images that match the given prompts.

Machine Learning Terms

• **Model:** A mathematical representation learned from data that identifies patterns and can be used to make predictions or decisions.

• **Algorithm:** A defined set of steps or procedures used to train a model and solve a specific problem.

• **Feature:** An individual measurable property or characteristic of the data that the model uses as input.

• **Dataset:** A collection of data used to train, validate, and test machine learning models.

• **Training:** The process of teaching a model by feeding it data so it can learn patterns.

• **Label:** The correct output or target value associated with input data in supervised learning.

• **Supervised Learning:** A type of machine learning in which models learn from labeled data.

• **Unsupervised Learning:** A type of machine learning in which models discover patterns in unlabeled data.

• **Reinforcement Learning:** A learning approach in which an agent learns by interacting with an environment and receiving rewards or penalties.

• **Overfitting:** When a model performs well on training data but poorly on new, unseen data.

• **Underfitting:** When a model is too simple to capture underlying patterns in the data.

• **Training Data:** The portion of data used to train the model.

• **Test Data:** The portion of data used to evaluate the model's performance on unseen data.

• **Accuracy:** A metric that measures how often the model's predictions are correct.

• **Loss Function:** A mathematical function that measures how far a model's predictions are from the actual values.

• **Hyperparameters:** Settings defined before training that control how the model learns, such as the learning rate or number of layers.

What will you learn from This Book?

1. Machine learning concepts and core algorithms with practical implementation. This will give you a competitive edge, and you will be able to build upon the knowledge gained from this book to implement advanced algorithms later.
2. Python libraries such as Pandas, Scikit-learn, NumPy, Matplotlib, and Seaborn to analyze your data efficiently.
3. Linear Regression, Classification, Decision Trees, and other algorithms for building machine learning models.
4. How to solve classification and regression problems using machine learning techniques.
5. How to evaluate your machine learning models using appropriate evaluation metrics.
6. A solid understanding of important concepts such as Confusion Matrix, Precision, Recall, Accuracy, ROC curve, RMSE, overfitting, underfitting, and related evaluation techniques.

Summary

In this chapter, we began our journey into Machine Learning by understanding its fundamental idea: enabling machines to learn from data rather than being explicitly programmed for every possible scenario. We explored how machine learning represents a specialized subset of Artificial Intelligence and how Deep Learning further extends these capabilities through multi-layered neural networks.

We compared how humans learn from experience with how machines learn from data. Just as humans recall past experiences, derive insights, and apply learned rules to new situations, machine learning systems analyze historical data, identify patterns, and generate predictions for unseen data.

The chapter also examined the relationship between Artificial Intelligence, Machine Learning, and Deep Learning, clarifying how these fields are interconnected yet distinct in scope and methodology.

We discussed a wide range of real-world applications across industries such as business intelligence, customer relationship management, security, human resources, supply chain management, natural language processing, autonomous vehicles, weather forecasting, recommendation systems, and generative AI. These examples demonstrate how deeply embedded machine learning is in modern society.

In addition, we introduced essential machine learning terminology, including models, algorithms, features, datasets, supervised and unsupervised learning, reinforcement learning, overfitting, underfitting, training and test data, accuracy, loss functions, and hyperparameters. Understanding these foundational concepts is critical before progressing to algorithm design and implementation.

Finally, we outlined what you will gain from this book — a strong conceptual foundation, hands-on Python implementation skills, practical exposure to regression and classification models, and the ability to evaluate machine learning systems using appropriate performance metrics.

This chapter establishes the conceptual framework required to understand and implement machine learning algorithms in the chapters that follow.

Exercises

1. Explain in your own words how Machine Learning differs from traditional rule-based programming.
2. Describe the relationship between Artificial Intelligence, Machine Learning, and Deep Learning.
3. Compare how humans learn from experience with how machines learn from data.
4. Define the following terms:
    - Model
    - Algorithm
    - Feature
    - Dataset
    - Hyperparameter
5. List three applications of machine learning that you interact with daily. Briefly explain how data might be used in each case.

2. Chapter 02: Types of Machine Learning

Machine learning is broadly categorized into three main types:

- Supervised learning
- Unsupervised learning
- Reinforcement learning

These types differ in how they learn and make predictions. Supervised learning uses labeled data, unsupervised learning uses unlabeled data, and reinforcement learning learns through trial and error by interacting with an environment.

Introduction

Supervised Learning

In supervised learning, the machine learning model is trained using labeled data, where the correct output is already known. The model learns the relationship between inputs and outputs to make accurate predictions on new data.

Unsupervised Learning

In unsupervised learning, the model works with unlabeled data and tries to discover hidden patterns or structures on its own. It is commonly used for clustering, pattern discovery, and data exploration.

Reinforcement Learning

In reinforcement learning, an agent learns by interacting with an environment and receiving rewards or penalties for its actions. The goal is to learn an optimal strategy that maximizes long-term rewards through trial and error.

Let us first understand what labeled data and unlabeled data are.

Labeled Data vs. Unlabeled Data

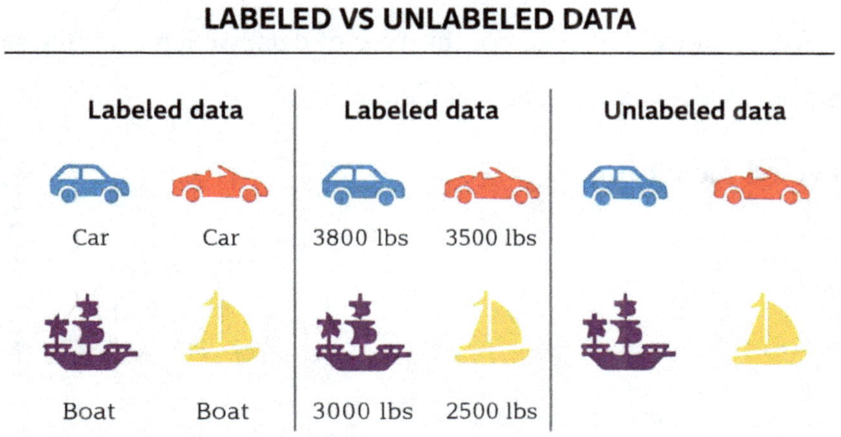

Figure 2-1: Labeled Data vs. Unlabeled Data

Labeled Data

Labeled data is a type of data in which each input is paired with a correct output or target value. It is commonly used in supervised learning to train models to make accurate predictions.

Unlabeled Data

Unlabeled data contains only input data without any associated output or target values. It is mainly used in unsupervised learning to discover patterns, relationships, or groupings within the data.

Types of Data

• **Numerical Data:** Any type of data that uses numbers, such as 4, 2.35, or –199. Examples include prices, sizes, or weights.

• **Categorical Data:** Any type of data that uses categories or states, such as male/female or cat/dog/bird. For this type of data, we have a finite set of categories associated with each data point.

Supervised Learning

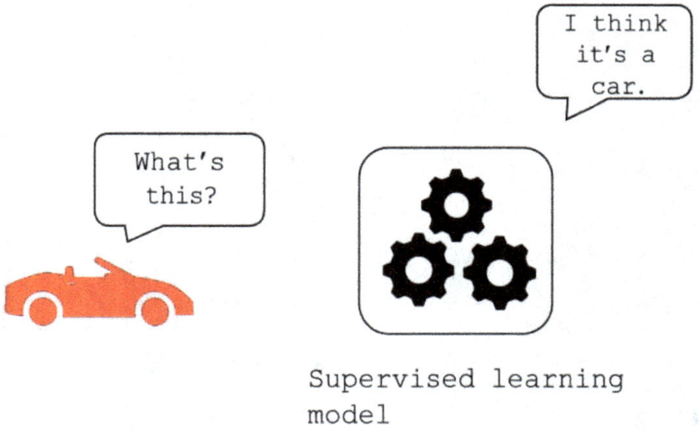

Figure 2-2: Supervised Learning

Supervised Machine Learning is based on supervision.

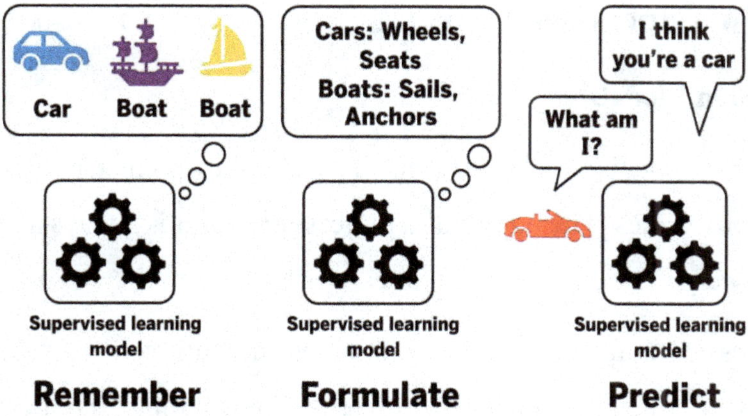

Figure 2-3: How Supervised Learning works

It works under guidance, where the model learns from examples that already have correct answers. In this approach, the machine is trained using a labeled dataset, meaning each input is paired with its expected output. Based on this training, the model learns the relationship between inputs and outputs and then uses that knowledge to make predictions on new, unseen data.

For example, consider a dataset containing labeled images of cars and boats. In the first step, the model is trained to recognize important features such as shape, size, wheels, windows, and overall structure (cars typically have wheels and windows, while boats have distinct shapes and no wheels). In the second step, a new image — such as a picture of a car — is given to the trained model. Finally, the model analyzes the image's features and predicts the correct output, identifying whether the object is a car or a boat based on what it learned during training.

Types of Supervised Learning

Regression Models

Regression models are used when the goal is to predict numerical or continuous values. The output of a regression model is always a number, such as weight, price, length, or time.

If the desired output consists of one or more continuous variables, the problem is called a regression problem. For example, predicting the length of a salmon based on its age and weight is a regression task because the output can take any numeric value within a range.

Examples of Regression Applications:

- **Stock market:** Predicting the future price of a stock using market trends and historical prices.
- **Healthcare:** Estimating a patient's recovery time or life expectancy based on medical history and symptoms.
- **Sales forecasting:** Predicting how much a customer is likely to spend based on demographics and past purchases.
- **Video platforms:** Predicting how long a user will watch a video based on viewing history and preferences.

Classification Models

Classification models are used when the goal is to predict categories or classes. The output of a classification model is a label, such as yes/no, true/false, or a specific category like car or boat.

In classification tasks, the data samples belong to two or more predefined classes. Using labeled data, the model learns how to assign the correct class to new, unseen inputs.

Example:

In handwritten digit recognition, each input image is assigned to one of a finite number of categories (digits 0–9). The model learns from labeled examples and predicts the correct digit for new images.

Supervised Learning Overview

Supervised learning algorithms are trained using labeled datasets, where each input is paired with a known output or target. During training, the model learns the relationship between input features and the target variable. Once trained, it can make accurate predictions on new, unseen data.

Common Supervised Learning Algorithms:

- Linear Regression
- Logistic Regression
- Decision Trees

- Random Forests
- Support Vector Machines (SVM)

Real-World Examples of Supervised Learning

- Predicting house prices based on size, location, and number of rooms.
- Email filtering, such as classifying emails as spam or not spam.
- Medical diagnosis, predicting whether a patient has a disease based on test results.

Regression Models: Predict Numbers

Regression models focus on predicting how much or how many.

- **Stock market:** Estimating stock prices using market indicators.
- **Medicine:** Predicting patient recovery time or treatment outcomes.
- **Retail:** Forecasting customer spending behavior.
- **Video recommendations:** Estimating how long a user will watch a video.

Classification Models: Predict a State or Category

Classification models predict outputs that belong to a finite set of classes. Many classification problems are binary (yes/no), while others involve multiple categories.

- **Sentiment analysis:** Classifying reviews as positive or negative.
- **Website analytics:** Predicting whether a user will click on a link.
- **Social networks:** Predicting whether two users will interact.
- **Video platforms:** Predicting whether a user will watch or skip a video.

Unsupervised Learning

Unsupervised learning is a type of machine learning in which the model learns from unlabeled or unstructured data. Unlike supervised learning, there are no predefined outputs or correct answers provided during training. The algorithm independently explores the data and discovers hidden patterns, structures, or relationships without human guidance.

In unsupervised learning, the focus is not on prediction accuracy but on understanding the data. These models are especially useful for descriptive modeling, data exploration, and pattern recognition.

Example of Unsupervised Learning

For example, if an algorithm is given a collection of images containing apples and bananas without any labels, it will analyze features such as shape, color, and size. Based on these similarities, the model will automatically group the images into separate clusters, even though it was never told which images represent apples or bananas.

Types of Unsupervised Learning

The main types of unsupervised learning are:

1. **Clustering**

   Clustering groups data points based on similarities and patterns within the data. Items that are similar are placed in the same group, while different items are placed in separate groups.

2. **Association**

   Association learning finds relationships or rules between variables in large datasets. It is commonly used to discover patterns such as items that frequently occur together.

3. **Dimensionality Reduction**

   Dimensionality reduction decreases the number of input features while preserving important information. It helps simplify data, improve performance, and make visualization easier.

These techniques help machines analyze unlabeled data, discover hidden patterns, and gain meaningful insights without predefined outputs.

Unsupervised Learning – Clustering

Clustering is the most widely used technique in unsupervised learning. In this approach, the model groups data points based on similarities and differences within the dataset. Data points that are similar to each other are placed in the same cluster, while dissimilar points are placed in different clusters.

In clustering, machines are not given any labels or categories in advance. Instead, they are instructed to find hidden patterns and organize the data in a meaningful way.

Example:

Consider a group of images containing various fruits. The model receives these images without any information about their names or types. By analyzing visual features such as color, shape, and texture, the algorithm groups similar fruits together, forming

clusters such as apples in one group and bananas in another.

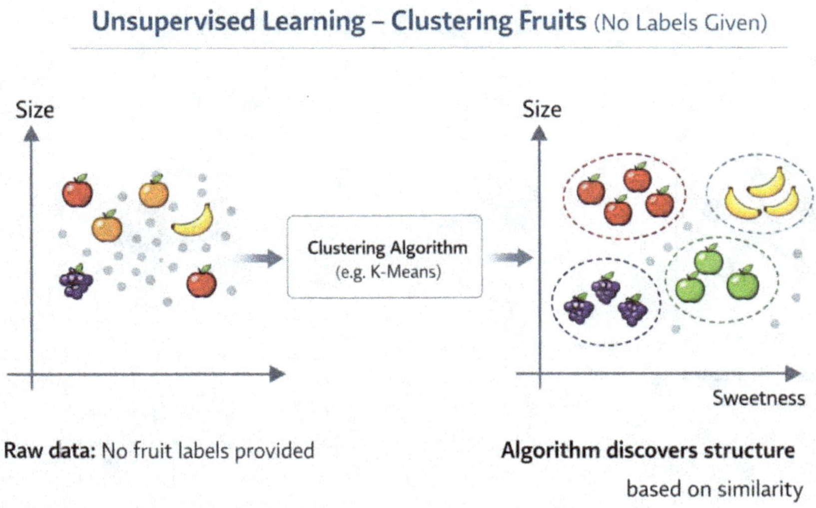

Figure 2-4: Unsupervised Learning

Why Unsupervised Learning Is Useful

Unsupervised learning is particularly effective when working with large datasets where labeling data is difficult, expensive, or time-consuming. It helps in discovering unknown patterns, identifying customer segments, detecting anomalies, and reducing data complexity.

In summary, unsupervised learning analyzes unlabeled data to reveal meaningful structures and relationships, making it a powerful tool for data exploration and insight generation.

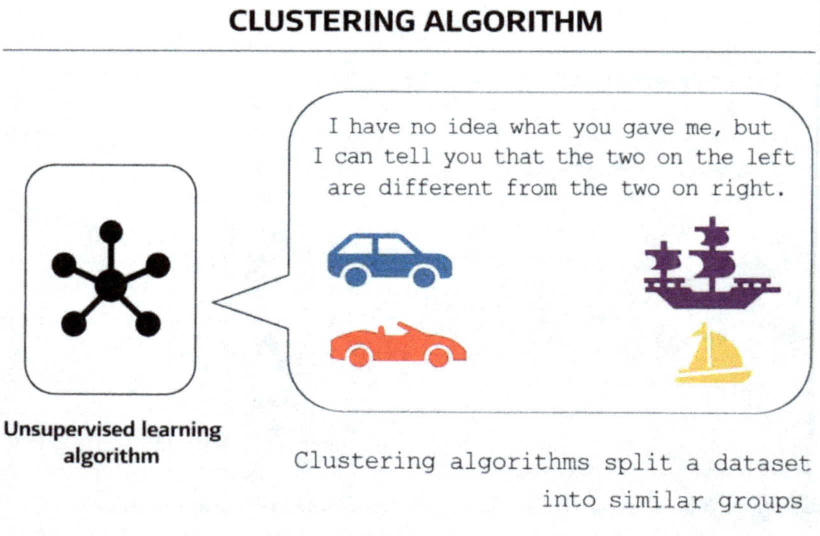

Figure 2-5: Clustering Algorithm

Clustering Examples

- **Market segmentation:** Dividing customers into groups based on demographics and purchasing behavior for targeted marketing strategies.
- **Genetics:** Clustering species into groups based on gene similarity.
- **Medical imaging:** Segmenting images to study different tissue types.
- **Video recommendations:** Grouping users based on demographics and viewing history to suggest relevant videos.

Types of Clustering Algorithms

- **K-means clustering:** Groups data points by selecting random centroids and iteratively adjusting them until optimal clusters are formed.
- **Hierarchical clustering:** Groups the closest data points first and continues merging clusters until well-defined groups are formed.
- **Density-Based Spatial Clustering (DBSCAN):** Groups data points in high-density areas and labels isolated points as noise.
- **Gaussian Mixture Models (GMM):** Assign fractions of membership of a data point to multiple clusters. For example, if there are clusters A, B, and C, a point could belong 60% to A, 25% to B, and 15% to C.

Association

Association rule mining is a rule-based technique used to identify meaningful relationships among data items in large datasets. In unsupervised learning, these algorithms discover frequent if–then patterns (called association rules) that reveal correlations, co-occurrences, and hidden connections between different data objects without using labeled data.

Dimensionality Reduction

Dimensionality reduction is an unsupervised learning method that focuses on decreasing the number of features or dimensions in a dataset. It helps make complex data easier to understand and process while preserving most of the important information.

This technique works by identifying and retaining the most significant features and removing redundant, irrelevant, or noisy data. Common algorithms such as Principal Component Analysis (PCA) and Singular Value Decomposition (SVD) are widely used to reduce data complexity without significantly affecting the quality or meaning of the original dataset.

Reinforcement Learning

Reinforcement learning (RL) is a type of machine learning in which an agent learns how to make decisions by interacting with its environment and receiving feedback in the form of rewards or penalties. Through repeated trial and error, the agent learns which actions lead to the best outcomes.

This approach trains systems to choose actions that maximize long-term rewards, similar to how humans learn from experience. Actions that move the agent closer to its goal are reinforced, while actions that lead to poor outcomes are gradually avoided.

How Reinforcement Learning Works

Reinforcement learning operates using a feedback-driven process in which an AI agent interacts with its environment, takes actions, and learns from the results of those actions. Over time, the agent improves its behavior by learning which actions lead to better outcomes.

In this approach, the agent receives rewards for desirable actions and penalties for undesirable ones, with the overall objective of maximizing cumulative rewards. Unlike supervised learning, reinforcement learning does not rely on labeled datasets; instead, the agent learns entirely from its own experiences. This learning process closely resembles how humans learn in everyday life — for example, a child learns what is right or wrong through repeated experiences.

Example:

In a game-playing scenario, the game itself represents the environment, each move corresponds to a state, and the agent's goal is to achieve a high score. The agent receives feedback after each action in the form of rewards or penalties, which helps it learn better strategies over time.

Types of Reinforcement Learning

Model-Based Reinforcement Learning:

In model-based reinforcement learning, the agent builds an internal representation of the environment. This model helps predict the outcomes of actions and supports planning and decision-making in advance.

Example: Dynamic programming, where a complete model of the environment is used to determine the optimal policy.

Model-Free Reinforcement Learning:

Model-free reinforcement learning does not require prior knowledge of the environment. The agent learns directly through interaction and trial and error, updating its strategy based on feedback.

Example: Algorithms such as Q-learning and SARSA, which learn optimal policies by estimating action values from experience.

Applications of Reinforcement Learning

Video Games:

Reinforcement learning has been successfully applied to gaming, where agents can achieve or exceed human-level performance. Famous examples include AlphaGo and AlphaGo Zero.

Resource Management:

Reinforcement learning is used to optimize resource allocation and scheduling, helping systems minimize delays and improve efficiency.

Research such as "Resource Management with Deep Reinforcement Learning" demonstrates its effectiveness in complex scheduling tasks.

Robotics:

In robotics, reinforcement learning enables machines to learn control strategies and adapt to real-world environments. It is widely used in industrial and manufacturing settings to make robots more autonomous and intelligent.

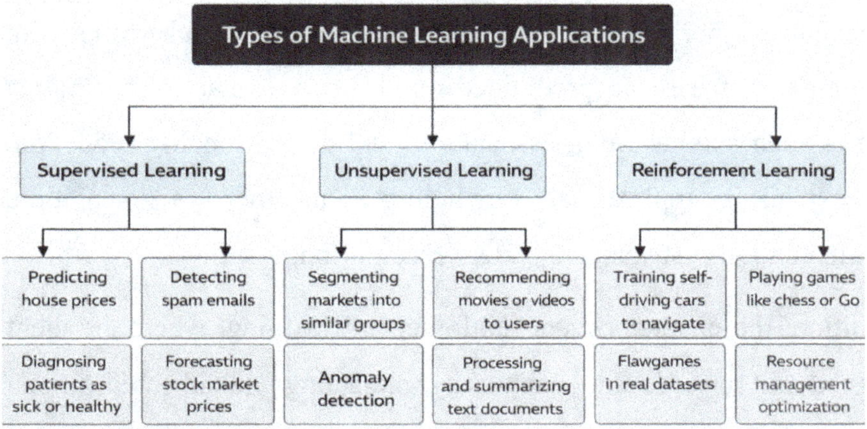

Figure 2-6: Various Applications of Machine Learning

The above diagram illustrates various applications grouped by different types of machine learning.

Summary

This chapter introduces the major types of machine learning: supervised learning, unsupervised learning, and reinforcement learning. It explains how supervised learning uses labeled data, where input data is provided along with correct output labels, to make predictions and classifications. The chapter also discusses its subtypes, such as classification and regression, along with applications like spam detection, medical diagnosis, and price prediction.

The chapter further describes unsupervised learning, which works with unlabeled data where no predefined outputs are available. It explores subtypes such as clustering, association, and dimensionality reduction, and explains applications including customer segmentation, recommendation systems, and pattern recognition.

In addition, the chapter covers reinforcement learning, where an agent learns through rewards and penalties by interacting with an environment. It discusses different reinforcement learning methods and applications such as robotics, self-driving cars and gaming.

Exercises

Exercise 1 – Classify Machine Learning Applications

Objective:

Read each scenario below and identify the most appropriate type of machine learning used. Choose from:

- Supervised Learning (Regression or Classification)
- Unsupervised Learning
- Reinforcement Learning

Scenarios:

1. Estimating house prices using features such as area, number of rooms, and location.
2. Forecasting today's stock prices based on previous prices and market indicators.
3. Identifying whether an email is spam or legitimate using email content and sender information.
4. Classifying images as faces or animals based on pixel values.
5. Analyzing long documents and generating a concise summary of the content.
6. Suggesting movies or videos to users on platforms like YouTube or Netflix based on viewing history.

7. Designing chatbots that communicate with users and respond to questions.
8. Training autonomous vehicles to navigate city roads without human control.
9. Predicting whether a patient is healthy or sick based on medical test results.
10. Dividing customers into similar groups using factors such as location, spending habits, and interests.
11. Training systems to play strategy games such as chess or Go.

Instructions for Students:

- Identify whether the task involves labeled data, unlabeled data, or learning through interaction and feedback.
- Specify the learning type and, where applicable, mention whether it is regression or classification.

Tip: If the output is a number, think regression. If the output is a category, think classification. If the system learns by trial and error, think reinforcement learning.

Exercise 2 – Define and Differentiate

a) What is Machine Learning?

b) Explain the difference between:

- Supervised learning

- Unsupervised learning
- Reinforcement learning

Exercise 3 – Label vs. No Label

Why is labeled data required in supervised learning but not in unsupervised learning? Give one real-world example for each.

Exercise 4 – True or False

State whether the following statements are True or False. Justify your answers.

(a) Clustering algorithms require target variables.
(b) Reinforcement learning always uses historical datasets.
(c) Classification is a supervised learning task.
(d) Dimensionality reduction is an unsupervised technique.

Exercise 5 – Choose the Right Approach

You are given a dataset with 1 million records, but only 2% are labeled.

- Which type of machine learning would you prefer?
- Explain why.

Exercise 6 – Reinforcement Learning Components

Identify and explain the following components with an example:

- Agent
- Environment

- Action
- Reward
- Policy

Exercise 7 – Short Case Studies

1. Healthcare Case

A hospital wants to:

- Predict whether a patient will develop diabetes.
- Discover unknown patterns among patients.

a) Identify the machine learning type for each task.
b) Name one suitable algorithm for each.

2. E-Commerce Case

An online platform wants to:

- Recommend products.
- Detect unusual buying behavior.

Identify the learning type used for each problem and explain your reasoning.

SECTION 2

TOOLS TO IMPLEMENT MACHINE LEARNING

3. Chapter 03: Pandas

Learning Objectives

After reading this chapter, you will be able to:

1. Understand Pandas and its role in data analysis
2. Work with Series and DataFrame structures
3. Load and inspect datasets from CSV, Excel, and JSON files
4. Select, filter, and index data using loc and iloc
5. Handle missing values and clean datasets
6. Perform data transformation and manipulation
7. Merge and combine datasets using merge() and concat()

Pandas: Python Data Analysis Library

Pandas is an open-source, BSD-licensed Python library that provides fast, flexible, and easy-to-use data structures for data manipulation and analysis. It is one of the most widely used libraries in data science, machine learning, and analytics. Pandas was created by Wes McKinney in 2008 to make data analysis in Python more efficient and intuitive.

What is Pandas?

Pandas is a powerful Python library designed to work with structured, tabular, and labeled data. It provides high-level data structures that make data cleaning, transformation, and analysis simple and efficient. Pandas is commonly used for data preprocessing before applying machine learning algorithms. It plays a critical role in the data science workflow, especially when working with datasets from spreadsheets, CSV files, databases, and APIs.

Why Pandas Is Important for Machine Learning

- Helps clean and preprocess raw data
- Makes feature selection and transformation easier
- Integrates seamlessly with NumPy, Matplotlib, and Scikit-learn
- Enables efficient handling of large datasets

Pandas is often the first library used in any machine learning pipeline.

Installation:

To install Pandas in Jupyter Notebook, use the following command:

```
!pip install pandas
```

Importing:

To import the Pandas library into your code, use the following command:

```
import pandas as pd
```

The alias "pd" is a standard convention and is used throughout most Pandas code.

Pandas Data Structures

Pandas Series

A Series is a one-dimensional labeled array capable of holding any data type, such as integers, floats, strings, or objects. Each value in a Series has an associated index. A Series can be thought of as a single column in a table.

Example:

```
import pandas as pd


x = [9, 3, 12]
sr = pd.Series(x)
print(sr)
```

Pandas DataFrame

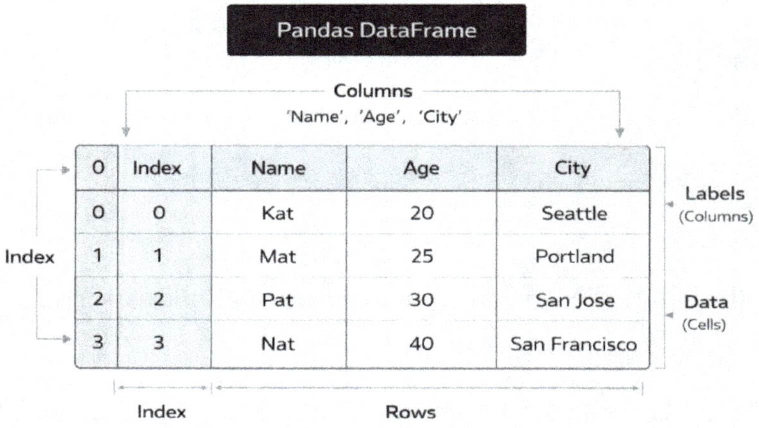

Figure 3-1: Pandas Dataframe

A DataFrame is a two-dimensional data structure that organizes data into rows and columns, similar to a spreadsheet or SQL table. Each column can have a different data type. Both rows and columns are labeled. In Pandas, most real-world datasets are represented as DataFrames.

Types of Data Pandas Can Handle

Pandas is ideal for working with tabular data, including:

- CSV files
- Excel spreadsheets
- SQL tables
- JSON data
- Time-series data

Reading and Writing Data in Pandas

Pandas supports many file formats and data sources out of the box. Functions used to read data typically start with read_*, while functions used to save data start with to_*.

Common Read Functions

- read_csv()
- read_excel()
- read_json()
- read_sql()

Pandas is ideal for tabular data (from spreadsheets, CSV files, or databases). In Pandas, a data table is called a DataFrame.

Reading and Writing Data in Pandas

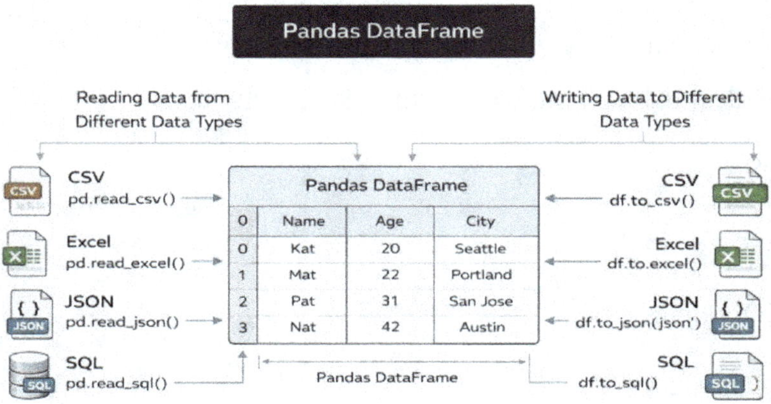

Figure 3-2: Reading and Writing Pandas DataFrame

Pandas supports integration with many file formats and data sources out of the box (CSV, Excel, SQL, JSON). Importing data from each of these data sources is handled by functions with the prefix read_*. Similarly, the to_* methods are used to store data.

Creating a DataFrame

To create a DataFrame, we use the DataFrame method from Pandas on data stored in a Python dictionary.

```
import pandas as pd

carsdataset = {
  'cars': ["Ferrari", "Honda", "Toyota"],
  'color': ["Green", "Blue", "Silver"]
}

df = pd.DataFrame(carsdataset)
print(df)
```

Reading Data from CSV

CSV (Comma-Separated Values) is one of the most common and simplest file formats used to store tabular data. Pandas makes it very easy to read data from a CSV file and convert it into a DataFrame for analysis.

To read a CSV file in Pandas, we use the read_csv() function. This function loads the data from the CSV file into a DataFrame, where the data is organized in rows and columns and can be easily explored, cleaned, and analyzed.

Once the data is loaded, you can view the first few rows using df.head() and check the structure of the dataset using df.info(). Reading data from CSV is usually the first step in data analysis and machine learning workflows because most real-world datasets are stored in CSV format.

```
import pandas as pd

df = pd.read_csv('data.csv')
print(df.to_string())
```

Reading a JSON File

JSON (JavaScript Object Notation) is a widely used data format for storing and exchanging structured data, especially in web applications and APIs. Pandas provides built-in support for reading JSON data and converting it into a DataFrame for easy analysis.

To read data from a JSON file in Pandas, we use the read_json() function. This function loads the JSON content into a DataFrame, organizing the data into rows and columns that can be easily manipulated and analyzed.

```
import pandas as pd

df = pd.read_json('data.json')
print(df.to_string())
```

After loading the data, you can inspect the DataFrame using methods like df.head() and df.info(). Reading data from JSON files is especially useful when working with API responses, web data, or nested data structures in real-world applications.

Reading an Excel File

Excel files are commonly used to store and share structured data in rows and columns. Pandas provides simple and powerful functions to read Excel files and convert them into a DataFrame for further analysis.

To read data from an Excel file in Pandas, we use the read_excel() function. This function loads the data from an Excel spreadsheet into a DataFrame, making it easy to explore, clean, and analyze the data using Pandas operations.

```
import pandas as pd

# Read from the first sheet
df = pd.read_excel("furniture.xlsx")

# Read from a specific sheet by name or index
df_sheet2 = pd.read_excel("furniture.xlsx", sheet_name="Sheet2")
df_sheet_index_1 = pd.read_excel("furniture.xlsx", sheet_name=1)

# Read specific furniture related columns only
df_specific_cols = pd.read_excel(
    "furniture.xlsx",
    usecols=["Price", "Category", "Material", "Sales"]
)
```

Once the data is loaded, you can preview the dataset using df.head() and check column data types with df.info(). Reading data from Excel files is especially useful when working with business reports, spreadsheets, and data collected from manual processes.

Writing Data to CSV and Excel

After cleaning, analyzing, or transforming data in Pandas, it is often necessary to save the results for further use or sharing. Pandas provides easy-to-use functions to write DataFrame data to different file formats, such as CSV and Excel.

To write a DataFrame to a CSV file, we use the to_csv() function. This saves the data in a simple text format that can be opened in spreadsheet tools or used by other applications.

CSV

```
import pandas as pd

# Create sample data
data = {
    "col1": [1, 2, 3],
    "col2": ["A", "B", "C"]
}

# Create DataFrame
df = pd.DataFrame(data)

# Export to CSV without row index
df.to_csv("furniture.csv", index=False)
```

Excel

To write a DataFrame to an Excel file, we use the to_excel() function. This is useful when sharing results with users who work primarily with Excel.

```
import pandas as pd


# ===============================
# Create Sample Data
# ===============================
data = {
    'col1': [1, 2],
    'col2': [3, 4]
}


# ===============================
# Create DataFrame
# ===============================
df = pd.DataFrame(data)


# ===============================
# Export DataFrame to Excel File
# ===============================
df.to_excel(
    'furniture.xlsx',
    sheet_name='Sheet1',
    index=False
)
```

Writing data to CSV and Excel allows you to store processed data, share results with others, and integrate Pandas workflows with other tools and systems.

Viewing Data

After loading data into a Pandas DataFrame, the first step is to explore and understand the dataset. Pandas provides several simple and useful functions to view data and inspect its structure.

The head() function displays the first few rows of the DataFrame, helping you quickly understand what the data looks like. Similarly, the tail()

function shows the last few rows. To get an overall summary of the dataset, info() provides details such as column names, data types, and non-null values, while describe() gives statistical insights for numerical columns.

df.head()

df.tail()

df.info()

df.describe()

```
import pandas as pd

df = pd.read_csv('data.csv')

# View first 5 rows
df.head()

# View last 5 rows
df.tail()

# Get information about the DataFrame
df.info()
```

Viewing data is an essential step before performing data cleaning, analysis, or machine learning, as it helps identify missing values, incorrect data types, and potential issues early in the workflow.

Data Cleaning

Data cleaning is a crucial step in any data analysis or machine learning workflow. Real-world data is often messy, incomplete, or inconsistent, and Pandas provides powerful tools to clean and prepare data before analysis.

Using Pandas, we can handle missing values, remove duplicate records, fix incorrect data types, and standardize data formats. Functions like isnull(), dropna(), fillna(), and drop_duplicates() help ensure the dataset is accurate and reliable.

Clean data leads to better insights and more accurate machine learning models. Spending time on data cleaning helps reduce errors and improves the overall quality of analysis and predictions.

1) Handling Null Values

Null values are common in real-world datasets and can occur due to missing information, data collection errors, or incomplete records. Handling these missing values correctly is an important part of data cleaning in Pandas.

Pandas provides several methods to identify and manage null values. We can detect missing data using isnull() or isna(), remove rows or columns containing null values using dropna(), or replace null values with a specific value such as zero, the mean, or a placeholder using fillna().

Proper handling of null values ensures data consistency and improves the performance and accuracy of data analysis and machine learning models.

Remove Rows with NULLs:

In some cases, rows containing null or missing values may not be useful for analysis or machine learning. Pandas allows us to easily remove such rows to ensure the dataset contains only complete and reliable records.

The dropna() function is used to remove rows that contain one or more null values. By default, it drops any row where at least one column has a missing value, helping to maintain data quality.

```
import pandas as pd

df = pd.read_csv('data.csv')
new_df = df.dropna()
print(new_df)
```

Removing rows with null values simplifies data processing and prevents errors during analysis or model training, especially when missing data cannot be meaningfully replaced.

Replace NULLs with a specific value:

```
df.fillna(450, inplace=True)
```

Slicing DataFrames

Slicing a DataFrame means selecting specific rows, columns, or individual values from the dataset. Pandas provides flexible and easy-to-use methods to slice data, making it simple to work with only the data you need.

You can slice rows using index positions, select specific columns by their names, or access a particular cell using row and column labels. Methods such as loc[], iloc[], and column indexing are commonly used for slicing DataFrames. Slicing helps focus on relevant subsets of data, making analysis faster and more efficient, especially when working with large datasets.

Creating a Sample DataFrame for Slicing

```
import pandas as pd

player_data = [
    ['Kat', 28, 68, 6200000],
    ['Pat', 31, 74, 7100000],
    ['Nat', 26, 70, 5400000],
    ['Mat', 34, 82, 8300000],
    ['Max', 29, 76, 6900000],
    ['Maggie', 37, 73, 7600000],
    ['Olga', 24, 80, 5800000]
]

df = pd.DataFrame(player_data, columns=['Name', 'Age', 'ID', 'Salary'])
print(df)
```

Slicing Rows

Slicing rows means selecting specific rows from a DataFrame based on their position or index. This is useful when you want to analyze only a portion of the dataset instead of the entire DataFrame.

Pandas provides methods such as iloc[] for position-based slicing and loc[] for label-based slicing. These methods allow you to extract single rows or a range of rows easily.

```
df1 = df.iloc[0:5]  # first 5 rows
print(df1)
```

Slicing Columns

Slicing columns means selecting one or more columns from a DataFrame to work with specific features or attributes. This is commonly done when you want to analyze or process only certain variables in the dataset.

In Pandas, columns can be selected using column names, either individually or as a list. You can also use loc[] to select columns along with specific rows.

```
df1 = df.iloc[:, 0:5]  # first 5 columns
print(df1)
```

Selecting a Specific Cell

Selecting a specific cell in a Pandas DataFrame means accessing a single value at the intersection of a particular row and column. This is useful when you need to inspect, update, or analyze an individual data point.

Pandas provides methods such as loc[] (label-based) and iloc[] (position-based) to access a specific cell easily.

```
salary = df.iloc[1, 4]  # 2nd row, 5th column
print("Specific Cell Salary:", salary)
```

Boolean Filtering

Boolean filtering is used to select rows from a DataFrame that meet specific conditions. It allows you to filter data based on logical expressions, making it easy to focus on relevant records.

In Pandas, boolean conditions are created using comparison operators and passed inside square brackets. You can also combine multiple conditions using logical operators such as & (and), | (or), and ~ (not).

```
# ==============================
# Filter Data Based on Salary
# ==============================

data = df[df['Salary'] > 60000]  # rows where Salary > 60000

print("\nFiltered Data based on Salary > 60000:\n", data)
```

Boolean filtering helps narrow down datasets for analysis, reporting, and machine learning by selecting only the rows that satisfy given criteria.

Joining DataFrames

Joining DataFrames is used to combine data from multiple tables based on a common column or index. This is especially useful when related information is stored in separate DataFrames and needs to be analyzed together.

In Pandas, the join() method allows you to merge DataFrames using their index or a key column. It supports different types of joins such as left, right, inner, and outer joins.

```
import pandas as pd

data1 = {
    "name": ["Bella", "Harry", "Maggie"],
    "age": [40, 50, 20]
}

data2 = {
    "Education": ["Ph.D", "M.S", "B.S"]
}

df1 = pd.DataFrame(data1)
df2 = pd.DataFrame(data2)

newdf = df1.join(df2)
print(newdf)
```

Joining DataFrames helps create a unified dataset, making analysis more complete and meaningful by bringing related data into a single DataFrame.

Merging DataFrames

Merging DataFrames is used to combine two or more DataFrames based on one or more common columns. It is similar to SQL joins and is commonly used when datasets share a common key.

In Pandas, the merge() function allows you to specify the join column and the type of join, such as inner, left, right, or outer. This provides flexibility in how the data is combined.

```
import pandas as pd

# Employees DataFrame
data1 = {
    'EmployeeID': ['K123', 'K300', 'K240', 'K444', 'K555'],
    'Name': ['Bella', 'Harry', 'Maggie', 'Kat', 'Nancy'],
    'DeptID': ['Sales', 'Marketing', 'Accounts', 'Training', 'IT']
}

employees = pd.DataFrame(data1)
```

```
# Departments DataFrame
data2 = {
    'DeptID': ['K123', 'K555', 'K444'],
    'DeptName': ['Sales', 'IT', 'Training']
}

departments = pd.DataFrame(data2)

# Merge
merged_df = pd.merge(employees, departments)
print(merged_df)
```

Merging DataFrames helps integrate related datasets into a single structure, enabling more detailed analysis and better insights.

Concatenating DataFrames

Concatenating DataFrames is used to stack or combine multiple DataFrames along rows or columns. It is commonly applied when datasets have the same structure and need to be combined into a single DataFrame.

In Pandas, the concat() function allows you to join DataFrames either vertically (row-wise) or horizontally (column-wise). This is useful when appending new data or combining datasets collected at different times.

Below is a simple example.

First, we create two DataFrames with the same structure.

```
import pandas as pd

df1 = pd.DataFrame({
    "Name": ["Kat", "Mat"],
    "Age": [20, 22],
    "City": ["Seattle", "Portland"]
})

df2 = pd.DataFrame({
    "Name": ["Pat", "Nat"],
    "Age": [33, 43],
    "City": ["San Jose", "San Francisco"]
})
```

Now, we concatenate the two DataFrames row-wise using pd.concat().

```
df_concat = pd.concat([df1, df2], ignore_index=True)
print(df_concat)
```

This will give us below output.

Name	**Age**	**City**
Kat	20	Seattle
Mat	22	Portland
Pat	33	San Jose
Nat	43	San Francisco

Table 3-1

Concatenating DataFrames helps organize data efficiently by bringing similar datasets together, making analysis and data processing easier.

Exercise: Mini Project

Learning Outcome

After completing the exercise, students will be able to:

- Load and manipulate datasets using Pandas
- Clean and filter real-world data

- Prepare data for machine learning workflows

Objective: Apply Pandas concepts to a real dataset.

Tasks:

- Load a CSV dataset of your choice
- Handle missing values
- Select relevant columns
- Apply filtering conditions
- Save the cleaned dataset

Hands-On Pandas Exercise

In this hands-on exercise, you will practice the nine most common Pandas operations on a CSV dataset called cars.csv. You will write and run code in Jupyter Notebook, observe the output, and answer short questions.

Dataset: cars.csv (Place it in the same folder as your notebook, or provide the correct path)

Learning Outcomes

- Load a CSV file into a Pandas DataFrame.
- Inspect the shape, columns, and sample rows of a DataFrame.
- Filter rows using boolean conditions, .loc, and .query.
- Select columns and create new derived columns.

- Handle missing values using .isna(), .dropna(), and .fillna().
- Compute grouped summary statistics using .groupby() and .agg().
- Sort data using .sort_values().
- Create a second DataFrame and merge/concatenate it with the original.
- Use .apply() to transform data with a custom function.

Rules

- Do not hard-code column names unless you confirm they exist in your copy of cars.csv.
- If you are unsure which columns are numeric or categorical, inspect df.dtypes.
- Keep your code readable: use meaningful variable names, comments, and clean output.

Starter Cell (Run First)

Create one cell at the top of your notebook and run it before attempting the steps:

```
import pandas as pd
import numpy as np
pd.set_option('display.max_columns', 50)
```

Step 1 — Read the Data (pd.read_csv)

Tasks:

1. Load cars.csv into a DataFrame named df.
2. Print df.shape.
3. Print df.columns as a Python list.

Questions:

A) How many rows and columns does the dataset have?

B) List three column names you think will be useful later (write them here).

Code Skeleton (Fill In)

```
# TODO Load cars.csv
# df = ...

# TODO Inspect basic structure
# print(...)
# print(...)
```

Step 2 — View Data (.head() and .tail())

Tasks:

1. Display the first five rows using df.head().
2. Display the last five rows using df.tail().
3. Use df.sample(5, random_state=0) to view five random rows.

Questions:

A) Do you notice any missing values? If yes, in which columns?

B) Are there columns that appear categorical (text) versus numeric?

Code Skeleton (Fill In)

```
# TODO head
# TODO tail
# TODO sample
```

Step 3 — Filter Rows (.loc and .query)

Tasks:

1. Pick **one** numeric column (e.g., a column with dtype int or float).
2. Create a filtered DataFrame with rows above a threshold (e.g., > median).
3. Perform the same filtering once with .loc and once with .query() (two approaches).
4. Print the number of rows before and after filtering.

Hint: Use df.select_dtypes(include='number').columns to find numeric columns.

Questions:

A) Which column did you filter on?

B) What threshold did you use, and why (median/mean/fixed value)?

Code Skeleton (Fill In)

```
# TODO choose a numeric column dynamically
# num_cols = ...
# col = ...

# TODO compute threshold (for example, median)
# thr = ...

# TODO filter with loc
# df_loc = ...

# TODO filter with query (watch out for spaces in column names)
# df_q = ...
```

Step 4 — Select Columns (df[[...]] and Create a New Column)

Tasks:

1. Select 2–4 columns and store them in df_small.
2. Create a **new derived column** in df_small (e.g., a normalized value or ratio).
3. Show df_small.head().

Hint: If you don't know what to select, start with one categorical and one numeric column.

Questions:

A) Which columns did you select, and why?

B) What does your derived column represent?

Code Skeleton (Fill In)

```
# TODO pick columns
# cols = [...]
# df_small = df[cols].copy()

# TODO create a derived column
# df_small["new_feature"] = ...

# TODO display
```

Step 5 — Handle Missing Values (.isna(), .dropna(), .fillna())

Tasks:

1. Compute missing values per column using df.isna().sum().
2. Create df_drop = df.dropna() and compare row counts.
3. Create df_fill by filling numeric NaNs with the median and categorical NaNs with 'Unknown'.

Questions:

A) Which columns had the most missing values?

B) After dropping NaNs, how many rows remained?

C) Why might filling be better than dropping in some cases?

Code Skeleton (Fill In)

```
# TODO missing counts
# missing = ...

# TODO dropna
# df_drop = ...

# TODO fillna (numeric median, categorical 'Unknown')
# df_fill = ...
```

Step 6 — Group and Aggregate (.groupby() and .agg())

Tasks:

1. Pick one categorical column to group by (e.g., brand, origin, type).
2. Compute at least two aggregations on a numeric column (mean, median, count, min, max).
3. Sort the result by one metric (descending).

Questions:

A) Which grouping column did you use?

B) What interesting pattern do you observe from the group summary?

Code Skeleton (Fill In)

```
# TODO choose group column
# group_col = ...

# TODO choose numeric target column
# value_col = ...

# TODO group and aggregate
# summary = ...
```

Step 7 — Sort Data (.sort_values())

Tasks:

1. Sort the full DataFrame by one numeric column (descending).
2. Show the top 10 rows after sorting (only a few columns).
3. Sort by **two columns** (e.g., primary numeric descending, secondary categorical ascending).

Questions:

A) What are the top three rows after sorting? Any surprises?

B) When would multi-column sorting be useful?

Code Skeleton (Fill In)

```
# TODO choose sort columns
# col1 = ...
# df_sorted = ...

# TODO show top 10
```

Step 8 — Merge Datasets (.merge() or .concat())

Tasks:

1. Create a key column called car_id = df_fill.index (or use reset_index()).
2. Create a second DataFrame named df_extra with columns:
   - car_id
   - A synthetic column such as price_usd or owner_count Generate values using NumPy random values with a fixed seed.
3. Merge df_fill and df_extra on car_id (left join).
4. Verify the merged DataFrame has the expected number of rows.

Questions:

A) What is the difference between a left join and an inner join?

B) Why did we create a key column for merging?

Code Skeleton (Fill In)

```
# TODO create key
# df_keyed = ...

# TODO create df_extra
# df_extra = ...

# TODO merge
# df_merged = ...
```

Step 9 — Apply Functions (.apply())

Tasks:

1. Write a function that converts one numeric column into a category:
   Example bins: Low / Medium / High based on quantiles.
2. Use .apply() (or pd.cut()) to create a new categorical column.
3. Show the value counts of the new category column.

Questions:

A) Why might we convert continuous values into bins?

B) When is .apply() slower than vectorized operations?

Code Skeleton (Fill In)

```
# TODO choose numeric column
# col = ...

# TODO define function and apply
# def label(x): ...
# df_merged["..."] = df_merged[col].apply(label)

# TODO value_counts
```

Extension Challenges (Optional)

1. **Visualization:** Create a histogram of one numeric column and a bar chart of group means.
2. **Feature Engineering:** Create two additional derived features and justify them.
3. **Data Quality:** Identify outliers (IQR method) and report how many you found.
4. **Mini-Report (5–8 sentences):** Summarize what you learned and one challenge you faced.

Summary

Pandas is a powerful open-source library in Python designed for data manipulation and analysis. It provides flexible and efficient data structures that make it easy to work with structured data such as tables, spreadsheets, and time-series datasets. Built on top of NumPy, Pandas combines high performance with ease of use, making it a fundamental tool in data science and analytics.

The core data structures in pandas are the Series (one-dimensional) and DataFrame (two-dimensional). A DataFrame allows users to organize data into rows and columns, similar to a table, and supports operations like filtering, sorting, grouping, and merging datasets. These capabilities help in transforming raw data into meaningful insights.

Pandas offers a wide range of functions for handling missing data, performing statistical analysis, and reshaping datasets. It also supports reading from and writing to various file formats such as CSV, Excel, and SQL databases, which makes it highly versatile for real-world applications. Integration with tools like Jupyter Notebook further enhances its usability by enabling interactive data exploration and visualization.

Overall, Pandas simplifies complex data operations and improves productivity for analysts, researchers, and developers. Its intuitive syntax and rich functionality make it an essential library for anyone working with data in Python.

References

1. W. McKinney, *Python for Data Analysis*, 2nd ed. Sebastopol, CA, USA: O'Reilly Media, 2017.
2. W. McKinney, "Data Structures for Statistical Computing in Python," in *Proceedings of the 9th Python in Science Conference (SciPy 2010)*, Austin, TX, USA, 2010, pp. 51–56.
3. pandas Development Team, "pandas documentation," [Online]. Available: https://pandas.pydata.org/docs/
4. NumPy Developers, "NumPy documentation," [Online]. Available: https://numpy.org/doc/
5. M. Heydt, *Learning Pandas*. Birmingham, U.K.: Packt Publishing, 2016.

4. Chapter 04: Numpy

Learning Objectives

After reading this chapter you will be able to:

1. Understand the purpose of NumPy and its advantages over Python lists for numerical computing.
2. Create and manipulate multi-dimensional arrays using core NumPy functions.
3. Perform efficient mathematical and statistical operations on arrays.
4. Apply indexing, slicing, and filtering techniques for data manipulation.

NumPy – Numerical Computing with Python

NumPy is a library for the Python programming language that adds support for large, multidimensional arrays and matrices, along with a large collection of high-level mathematical functions to operate on these arrays. It is a powerful Python library used for working with numerical data. It provides fast and efficient data structures and mathematical functions that are essential for data analysis, scientific computing, and machine learning.

In 2005, Travis Oliphant created NumPy by incorporating features of the competing Numarray into Numeric, with extensive modifications. NumPy is open-source software and has many contributors.

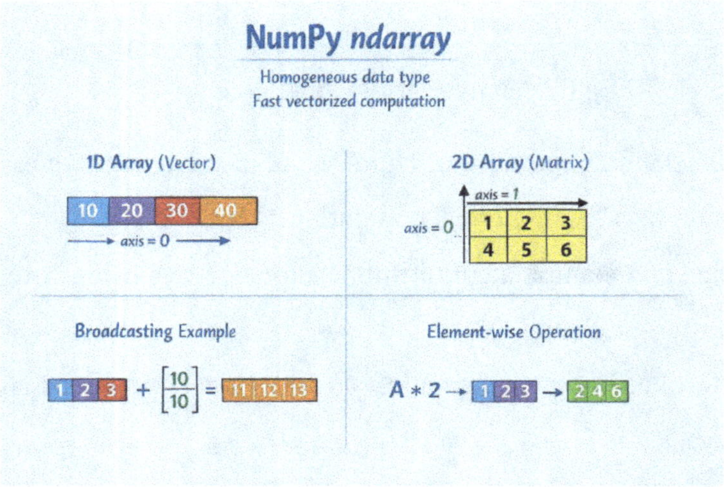

Figure 4-1: Numpy

Why Use NumPy?

- Much faster than Python lists
- Supports multi-dimensional arrays
- Provides built-in mathematical and statistical functions
- Efficient memory usage
- Essential for machine learning and deep learning

NumPy helps us work with numbers efficiently and at scale. In Python, lists serve the purpose of arrays, but they are slow to process. NumPy provides an array object that is up to 50 times faster than traditional Python lists. The array object in NumPy is called ndarray. It comes with many supporting functions that make working with ndarrays very easy. Arrays are frequently used in data science, where speed and efficient resource usage are critical.

Installation of NumPy

Install NumPy in Jupyter Notebook using the following command:

```
!pip install numpy
```

Import NumPy

To import NumPy, use the following statement:

```
import numpy as np
```

NumPy Arrays

The core data structure in NumPy is the ndarray (N-dimensional array).

Creating a NumPy Array

```
arr = np.array([10, 20, 30, 40])
print(arr)
```

Output:

[10 20 30 40]

Unlike Python lists, NumPy arrays store elements of the same data type, making operations faster and more efficient.

NumPy Array vs Python List

Feature	Python List	NumPy Array
Speed	Slow	Very Fast
Data Type	Mixed	Same Type
Math Operations	Manual	Built-in
ML Usage	Limited	Widely Used

Table 4-1

Creating Arrays Using Built-in Functions

Zeros Array

np.zeros(5)

Output:

[0. 0. 0. 0. 0.]

Ones Array

np.ones(4)

Output:

[1. 1. 1. 1.]

Range of Numbers

np.arange(1, 10)

Output:

[1 2 3 4 5 6 7 8 9]

Multi-Dimensional Arrays

2D Array (Matrix)

```
arr2d = np.array([
    [10, 20, 30],
    [40, 50, 60]
])
print(arr2d)
```

Output:

```
[[10 20 30]
 [40 50 60]]
```

Used heavily in machine learning datasets and image data.

Shape and Size of an Array

arr2d.shape

Output:

(2, 3)

arr2d.size

Output:

6

Basic Mathematical Operations

Element-wise Operations

```
a = np.array([10, 20, 30])
b = np.array([1, 2, 3])
a + b
```

Output:

[11 22 33]

a * b

Output:

[10 40 90]

No loops are required – NumPy handles operations internally.

Statistical Functions

```
data = np.array([20, 22, 33, 43])
np.mean(data)
```

Output:

29.5

np.max(data)

Output:

43

np.min(data)

Output:

20

Indexing and Slicing

Accessing Elements

```
arr = np.array([10, 20, 30, 40])
arr[2]
```

Output:

30

Slicing

arr[1:3]

Output:

[20 30]

Boolean Filtering

```
ages = np.array([20, 22, 33, 43])
ages[ages > 25]
```

Output:

[33 43]

Very useful in data filtering and machine learning preprocessing.

Reshaping Arrays

```
arr = np.arange(1, 7)
arr.reshape(2, 3)
```

Output:

```
[[1 2 3]
 [4 5 6]]
```

NumPy in Machine Learning

NumPy is used to:

- Store feature matrices
- Perform matrix multiplication
- Normalize data
- Implement algorithms efficiently

Most machine learning models internally operate on NumPy arrays.

Example:

```
import numpy

arr = numpy.array([10, 20, 30, 40, 50])
print(arr)
```

Create a Two Dimensional Array

```
import numpy as np

arr = np.array([[10, 20, 30], [40, 50, 60]])
print(arr)
```

Array Indexing

```
import numpy as np

arr = np.array([10, 20, 30, 40])
print(arr[0])
```

Slicing an Array

Slice elements from index 1 to index 5 from the following array:

```
import numpy as np

arr = np.array([1, 2, 3, 4, 5, 6, 7])
print(arr[1:5])
```

Sorting a Numeric Array

```
import numpy as np

arr = np.array([30, 20, 40, 10])
print(np.sort(arr))
```

Sorting an Alphabetical Array

```
import numpy as np

arr = np.array(["kiwi", "berry", "pear"])
print(np.sort(arr))
```

Summary

NumPy forms the backbone of scientific computing in Python by providing a fast, flexible, and memory-efficient way to work with numerical data. This chapter introduced **NumPy arrays** as the core data structure and demonstrated how they enable **vectorized computation**, eliminating slow Python loops while making code more expressive and closer to mathematical notation. Key concepts—such as array creation, indexing and slicing, broadcasting, shape manipulation, and basic linear algebra operations—were discussed with practical examples to build intuition.

Hands-On Exercises for NumPy

Exercise 1: Create an Array

Create a NumPy array with values: 10, 20, 30, 40, 50.

Exercise 2: Statistical Analysis

Using NumPy, find the **mean**, **maximum**, and **minimum** of the array: [20, 22, 33, 43].

Exercise 3: Boolean Filtering

From the array [10, 25, 30, 45, 60], filter values greater than 30.

Exercise 4: Reshape

Create an array from 1 to 12 and reshape it into a 3 × 4 matrix.

Exercise 5: Real-World Thinking

Store ages of students in a NumPy array and calculate:

- Average age
- Oldest student
- Youngest student

Exercise 6: Creating NumPy Arrays

Create NumPy arrays for the following:

a) A 1D array containing numbers from 1 to 10

b) A 2D array with shape (3, 3) containing all zeros

c) A 3 × 3 identity matrix

Hint: Use np.array(), np.zeros(), np.eye()

Exercise 7: Array Properties

Given the array:

arr = np.array([[10, 20, 30], [40, 50, 60]])

Find: shape, number of dimensions, total number of elements, and data type.

Exercise 8: Indexing and Slicing

Using the array:

arr = np.array([5, 10, 15, 20, 25, 30])

a) Access the third element

b) Slice elements from index 1 to 4

c) Get the last two elements

Exercise 9: Mathematical Operations

Given:

a = np.array([2, 4, 6])

b = np.array([1, 3, 5])

Perform: element-wise addition, element-wise multiplication, and square each element of a.

Exercise 10: Statistical Functions

Create an array of exam scores:

scores = np.array([72, 85, 90, 68, 88, 76])

Find: mean, max, min, and standard deviation.

Exercise 11: Boolean Indexing

Using the same scores array:

a) Select scores greater than 80

b) Count how many scores are less than 75

Exercise 12: Reshaping Arrays

Create an array with values from 1 to 12 and:

a) Reshape it into a 3 × 4 matrix

b) Reshape it into a 2 × 6 matrix

Exercise 13: Random Numbers

Generate:

a) An array of 10 random numbers between 0 and 1

b) A 4 × 4 matrix of random integers between 10 and 50

Hint: Use np.random.rand() and np.random.randint()

Exercise 14: Aggregations Along Axis

Given:

data = np.array([[10, 20, 30], [40, 50, 60], [70, 80, 90]])

a) Find the sum of each row

b) Find the mean of each column

Exercise 15: Mini Practical Task

Create a NumPy array representing daily temperatures for a week:

temps = np.array([72, 75, 78, 80, 77, 74, 73])

a) Find the average temperature

b) Find the hottest and coldest day (values)

c) Increase all temperatures by 2 degrees

References

1. Harris, C. R., Millman, K. J., van der Walt, S. J., Gommers, R., Virtanen, P., Cournapeau, D., Oliphant, T. E. (2020). Array programming with NumPy. *Nature*, 585, 357–362. https://doi.org/10.1038/s41586-020-2649-2
2. Oliphant, T. E. (2006). *A guide to NumPy*. Trelgol Publishing.
3. Oliphant, T. E. (2007). Python for scientific computing. *Computing in Science & Engineering*, 9(3), 10–20. https://doi.org/10.1109/MCSE.2007.58
4. Van der Walt, S., Colbert, S. C., & Varoquaux, G. (2011). The NumPy array: A structure for efficient numerical computation. *Computing in Science & Engineering*, 13(2), 22–30. https://doi.org/10.1109/MCSE.2011.37
5. NumPy Developers. (2024). *NumPy documentation*. https://numpy.org/doc/
6. Wes McKinney (2022). *Python for Data Analysis* (3rd ed.). O'Reilly Media.
7. Virtanen, P., Gommers, R., Oliphant, T. E., et al. (2020). SciPy 1.0: Fundamental algorithms for scientific computing in Python. *Nature Methods*, 17, 261–272. https://doi.org/10.1038/s41592-019-0686-2

5. Chapter 05: Scikit Learn Library

Learning Objectives

After reading this chapter, you will be able to:

1. Understand the role of Scikit-Learn in machine learning workflows
2. Apply built-in algorithms for classification and regression tasks
3. Perform data splitting, training, and testing of models
4. Evaluate models using standard performance metrics

What is Scikit-Learn?

Scikit-Learn is a popular Python library for machine learning that offers simple tools for **classification, regression, clustering, and dimensionality reduction**.

It is one of the most widely used machine learning libraries in Python. Built on top of **NumPy, SciPy, and Matplotlib**, it provides a simple and efficient way to implement machine learning algorithms for a variety of tasks.

Also known as **Sklearn**, Scikit-Learn is an open-source Python library designed to simplify the implementation of machine learning models. It provides a wide range of tools for **data preprocessing, model selection,**

and evaluation, making it a preferred choice for both beginners and professionals.

1. Scikit-Learn Features

- Provides simple and efficient tools for predictive data analysis.
- Accessible to everyone and reusable in various contexts.
- Built on **NumPy, SciPy, and Matplotlib**.
- Open source and commercially usable under the BSD license.

The Scikit-Learn project started as **scikits.learn**, a Google Summer of Code project by French data scientist **David Cournapeau** in 2007.

Scikit-Learn focuses on modeling data. Some of the most popular groups of models provided by Sklearn include:

- **Supervised learning algorithms:** Linear Regression, Support Vector Machine, Decision Tree, etc.
- **Unsupervised learning algorithms:** Clustering, Factor Analysis, Principal Component Analysis, and unsupervised neural networks.
- **Clustering models:** Used for grouping unlabeled data.
- **Cross-validation:** Evaluates the accuracy of supervised models on unseen data.
- **Dimensionality reduction:** Reduces the number of attributes in data; helpful for summarization, visualization, and feature

selection.

- **Ensemble methods:** Combine predictions of multiple supervised models.
- **Feature extraction:** Extract meaningful attributes from image and text data.
- **Feature selection:** Identify the most useful attributes for creating supervised models.

Why Use Scikit-Learn?

- Easy to learn and use
- Consistent and beginner-friendly API
- Supports most common machine learning algorithms
- Strong documentation and community support
- Widely used in industry and academia

Installing Scikit-Learn

To install Scikit-Learn in Jupyter Notebook, use the following command:

```
!pip install scikit-learn
```

Importing Scikit-Learn

Scikit-Learn is usually imported by importing specific modules as needed.

```
from sklearn import datasets
from sklearn.model_selection import train_test_split
```

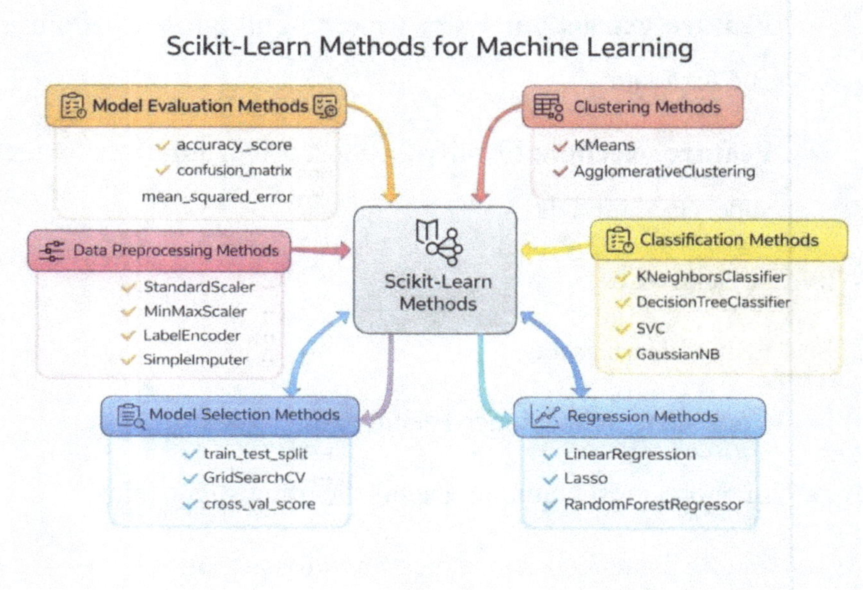

Figure 5-1: Scikit-Learn Methods

2. Data Preprocessing Methods

Machine learning models are highly sensitive to data quality. Scikit-Learn provides preprocessing utilities to **clean, transform, and prepare data** before modeling.

2.1 Feature Scaling

Many algorithms perform better when features are on the same scale.

StandardScaler

- Centers data to **mean = 0** and **variance = 1**
- Useful for algorithms such as **SVM, KNN, and Logistic Regression**

```
from sklearn.preprocessing import StandardScaler

scaler = StandardScaler()
X_scaled = scaler.fit_transform(X)
```

MinMaxScaler

Scales features to a fixed range (usually 0 to 1)

```
from sklearn.preprocessing import MinMaxScaler

scaler = MinMaxScaler()
X_scaled = scaler.fit_transform(X)
```

2.2 Encoding Categorical Data

LabelEncoder

Converts categorical labels into numeric form

```
from sklearn.preprocessing import LabelEncoder

encoder = LabelEncoder()
y_encoded = encoder.fit_transform(y)
```

2.3 Handling Missing Values

SimpleImputer

Replaces missing values using mean, median, or most frequent value

```
from sklearn.impute import SimpleImputer

imputer = SimpleImputer(strategy='mean')
X_filled = imputer.fit_transform(X)
```

3. Supervised Learning Methods

Supervised learning algorithms learn from labeled data, where the output is known.

3.1 Classification Methods

Classification predicts discrete class labels.

KNeighborsClassifier (KNN)

Classifies based on nearest neighbors

```
from sklearn.neighbors import KNeighborsClassifier

model = KNeighborsClassifier(n_neighbors=5)
model.fit(X_train, y_train)
```

DecisionTreeClassifier

Uses decision rules learned from data

Easy to interpret

```
from sklearn.tree import DecisionTreeClassifier

model = DecisionTreeClassifier()
model.fit(X_train, y_train)
```

Support Vector Classifier (SVC)

Finds the optimal separating hyperplane

```
from sklearn.svm import SVC

model = SVC(kernel='linear')
model.fit(X_train, y_train)
```

GaussianNB

Probabilistic classifier based on Bayes' theorem

```
from sklearn.naive_bayes import GaussianNB

model = GaussianNB()
model.fit(X_train, y_train)
```

3.2 Regression Methods

Regression predicts continuous numerical values.

LinearRegression

Models a linear relationship between input and output

```
from sklearn.linear_model import LinearRegression

model = LinearRegression()
model.fit(X_train, y_train)
```

Lasso Regression

Performs feature selection using L1 regularization

```
from sklearn.linear_model import Lasso

model = Lasso(alpha=0.1)
model.fit(X_train, y_train)
```

RandomForestRegressor

Ensemble method using multiple decision trees

```
from sklearn.ensemble import RandomForestRegressor

model = RandomForestRegressor(n_estimators=100)
model.fit(X_train, y_train)
```

4.Unsupervised Learning Methods

Unsupervised learning discovers patterns in unlabeled data.

Clustering Methods

KMeans

Groups data into K clusters based on similarity

```
from sklearn.cluster import KMeans

kmeans = KMeans(n_clusters=3)
clusters = kmeans.fit_predict(X)
```

Agglomerative Clustering

Hierarchical clustering approach

```
from sklearn.cluster import AgglomerativeClustering

model = AgglomerativeClustering(n_clusters=3)
labels = model.fit_predict(X)
```

Dimensionality Reduction

Principal Component Analysis (PCA)

Reduces number of features while retaining variance

```
from sklearn.decomposition import PCA

pca = PCA(n_components=2)
X_reduced = pca.fit_transform(X)
```

5. Model Selection Methods

Model selection ensures better generalization to unseen data.

train_test_split

Splits data into training and testing sets

```
from sklearn.model_selection import train_test_split

X_train, X_test, y_train, y_test = train_test_split(
    X, y, test_size=0.2, random_state=42)
```

Summary

In this chapter, we explored **Scikit-learn**, one of the most powerful and widely used libraries for implementing machine learning models in Python. It provides a simple and consistent interface to build, train, and evaluate models efficiently.

The chapter introduced key supervised learning algorithms such as **linear regression** for prediction and **classification models** like logistic regression and decision trees.

Overall, this chapter provided a strong foundation for implementing machine learning models using Scikit-learn, enabling learners to move from theoretical understanding to practical application in real-world data science problems.

Exercise

Hands-On Scikit-Learn Basic Exercise

Learning Objectives

By the end of this exercise, students will be able to:

- Import Scikit-Learn correctly
- Load a built-in dataset
- Split data into training and testing sets
- Train a basic machine learning model
- Make predictions
- Evaluate model accuracy

You may not fully understand every concept presented in this exercise at this stage. However, as you progress through the upcoming chapters and build your foundational knowledge, the purpose and methodology of this exercise will become clear.

Prerequisites

- Python installed
- Basic Python syntax
- Familiarity with NumPy and Pandas (optional)

Exercise 1: Import Required Libraries

Task: Import scikit-learn modules required for a simple ML task.

```
import numpy as np
import pandas as pd

from sklearn.datasets import load_iris
from sklearn.model_selection import train_test_split
from sklearn.linear_model import LogisticRegression
from sklearn.metrics import accuracy_score
```

Question:

What is the purpose of train_test_split?

Exercise 2: Load the Dataset

We will use the Iris dataset, which is included in scikit-learn.

```
iris = load_iris()

X = iris.data
y = iris.target
```

Tasks:

Print the shape of X

Print the first 5 rows of X

Print the target labels y

```
print(X.shape)
print(X[:5])
print(y[:5])
```

Question:

How many features does the Iris dataset have?

Exercise 3: Split the Dataset

Split the dataset into training and testing data.

```
X_train, X_test, y_train, y_test = train_test_split(
    X, y, test_size=0.2, random_state=42
)
```

Tasks:

Print the shape of X_train

Print the shape of X_test

Question:

Why do we keep some data aside for testing?

Exercise 4: Create the Model

Create a Logistic Regression model.

```
model = LogisticRegression(max_iter=200)
```

Question:

Is the model trained at this step? (Yes / No)

Exercise 5: Train the Model

Fit the model using training data.

```
model.fit(X_train, y_train)
```

Question:

Which data is used for learning — training or testing?

Exercise 6: Make Predictions

Use the trained model to predict the test data.

```
y_pred = model.predict(X_test)
```

Tasks:

Print the first 10 predicted values

Print the first 10 actual values

```
print(y_pred[:10])
print(y_test[:10])
```

Exercise 7: Evaluate the Model

Calculate accuracy of the model.

```
accuracy = accuracy_score(y_test, y_pred)
print("Model Accuracy:", accuracy)
```

References

1. Pedregosa, F., Varoquaux, G., Gramfort, A., Michel, V., Thirion, B., Grisel, O., et al. (2011). *Scikit-learn: Machine learning in Python. Journal of Machine Learning Research (JMLR), 12,* 2825–2830.
2. Scikit-Learn Developers. *Scikit-Learn: Machine Learning in Python – Official Documentation.* Retrieved from https://scikit-learn.org/stable/

6. Chapter 06: Matplotlib Library

Learning Objectives

After reading this chapter, you will be able to:

1. Understand the basics of data visualization using Matplotlib
2. Create common plots such as line, bar, and scatter plots
3. Customize plots using labels, titles, and legends
4. Visualize trends and patterns in datasets

Data Visualization Using Matplotlib

1. Introduction

Matplotlib is one of the most widely used Python libraries for data visualization. It was originally developed by **John D. Hunter** and is an open-source library distributed under a BSD-style license.

Matplotlib provides powerful tools for creating both **two-dimensional (2D)** and **three-dimensional (3D)** plots, with especially strong support for 2D visualizations. It enables users to create:

- Publication-quality plots
- Interactive visualizations with zooming and panning
- Highly customizable charts (colors, labels, layouts, styles)

Matplotlib plots can be exported to multiple file formats such as **PNG, PDF, SVG**, and can be embedded seamlessly into **Jupyter Notebook, JupyterLab**, and graphical user interfaces.

Matplotlib works closely with **NumPy**, making it a strong open-source alternative to MATLAB for numerical computing and visualization.

2. Installing Matplotlib in Jupyter Notebook

To install Matplotlib in a Jupyter Notebook environment, use the following command:

!pip install matplotlib

Once installed, the library can be imported and used directly within notebook cells.

3. Importing Matplotlib

Matplotlib's plotting functionality is mainly accessed through the **pyplot** module, which provides a MATLAB-like interface.

The alias **plt** is conventionally used to keep code concise and readable.

4. Simple Line Plot

A line plot is one of the most basic and commonly used plots. It shows the relationship between two variables by connecting data points with straight lines.

Example: Simple Line Plot

```
import matplotlib.pyplot as plt

x = [1, 2, 3, 4]
y = [2, 4, 6, 8]

plt.plot(x, y)
plt.show()
```

This plot shows how y changes linearly with respect to x.

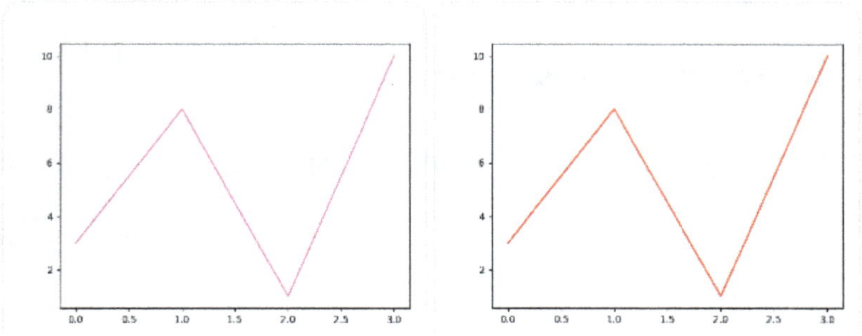

Figure 6-1: Line Plot

5. Drawing a Line Between Two Points

Matplotlib can also be used to draw a line between just two points, which is useful for illustrating slopes or relationships.

```
plt.plot([1, 3], [2, 6])
plt.show()
```

6. Line Plot with Labels

Labels help explain what each axis represents and make the plot easier to understand.

```
plt.plot(x, y)
plt.xlabel("X Axis")
plt.ylabel("Y Axis")
plt.show()
```

7. Plot with Title, Labels, and Grid

Adding a title and grid improves readability, especially for reports and presentations.

```
plt.plot(x, y)
plt.title("Simple Line Plot")
plt.xlabel("X Values")
plt.ylabel("Y Values")
plt.grid(True)
plt.show()
```

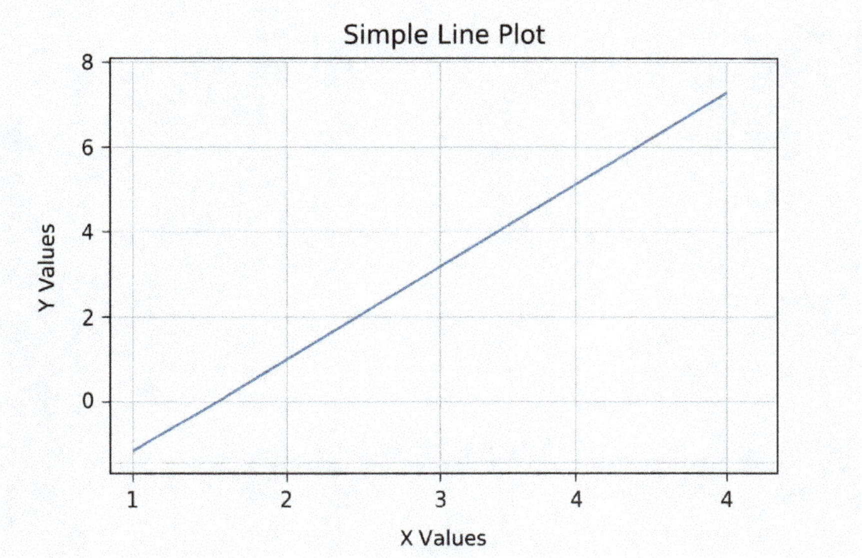

Figure 6-2: Simple Line Plot

8. Histogram

A histogram is used to visualize the distribution of numerical data. It groups values into intervals called bins, and displays the frequency of values in each bin.

In simple terms:

X-axis → data ranges (bins)

Y-axis → frequency of values

Example: Histogram

```
import matplotlib.pyplot as plt
import numpy as np

data = np.random.randn(1000)

plt.hist(data, bins=20)
plt.xlabel("Value")
plt.ylabel("Frequency")
plt.title("Histogram Example")
plt.show()
```

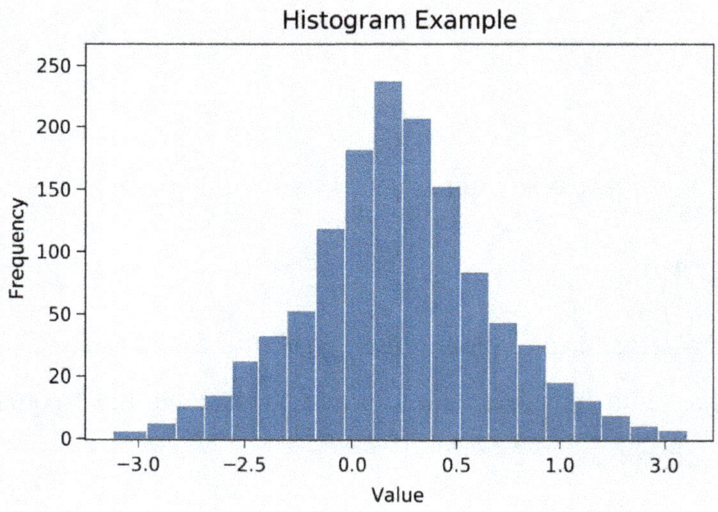

Figure 6-3: Histogram

9. Pie Chart

A pie chart is used to represent proportions or percentages of a whole.

Example: Pie Chart

```
labels = ['Python', 'Java', 'C++', 'Others']
sizes = [40, 30, 20, 10]

plt.pie(sizes, labels=labels, autopct='%1.1f%%')
plt.title("Programming Language Usage")
plt.show()
```

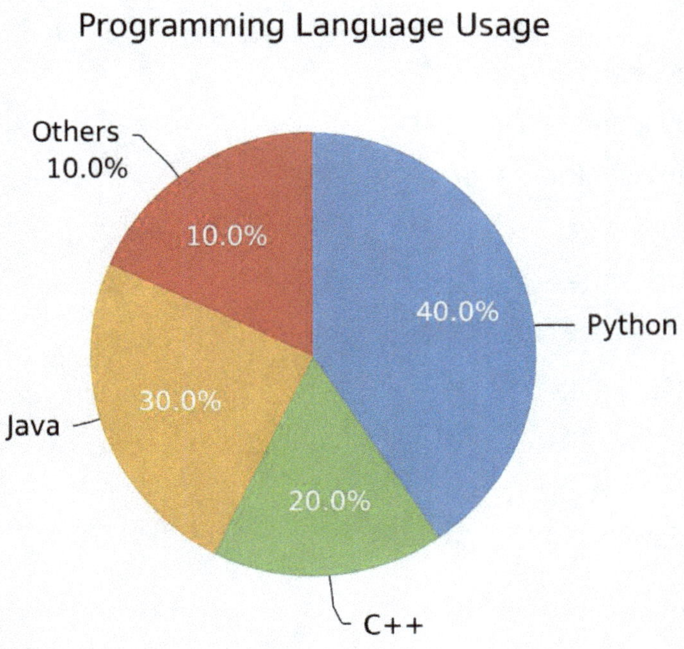

Figure 6-4: Pie Chart

10. 3D Scatter Plot Using Matplotlib

A three-dimensional scatter plot represents data points using three coordinates (X, Y, Z). This type of plot is useful when analyzing relationships among three variables.

```
from mpl_toolkits.mplot3d import Axes3D
import matplotlib.pyplot as plt
import numpy as np

fig = plt.figure()
ax = fig.add_subplot(111, projection='3d')

x = np.random.rand(50)
y = np.random.rand(50)
z = np.random.rand(50)

ax.scatter(x, y, z)
ax.set_xlabel("X Axis")
ax.set_ylabel("Y Axis")
ax.set_zlabel("Z Axis")

plt.show()
```

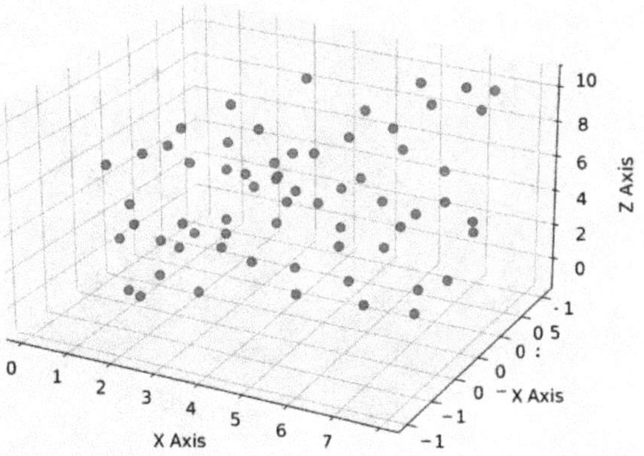

Figure 6-5: 3D Scatter Plot

11. Three-Dimensional Bar Graph

A 3D bar graph extends the bar chart into three dimensions and is useful for visualizing multi-variable categorical data.

```
from mpl_toolkits.mplot3d import Axes3D
import numpy as np
import matplotlib.pyplot as plt

fig = plt.figure()
ax = fig.add_subplot(111, projection='3d')

x = np.arange(5)
y = np.zeros(5)
z = np.zeros(5)
dx = dy = np.ones(5)
dz = [3, 7, 1, 5, 9]

ax.bar3d(x, y, z, dx, dy, dz)
plt.show()
```

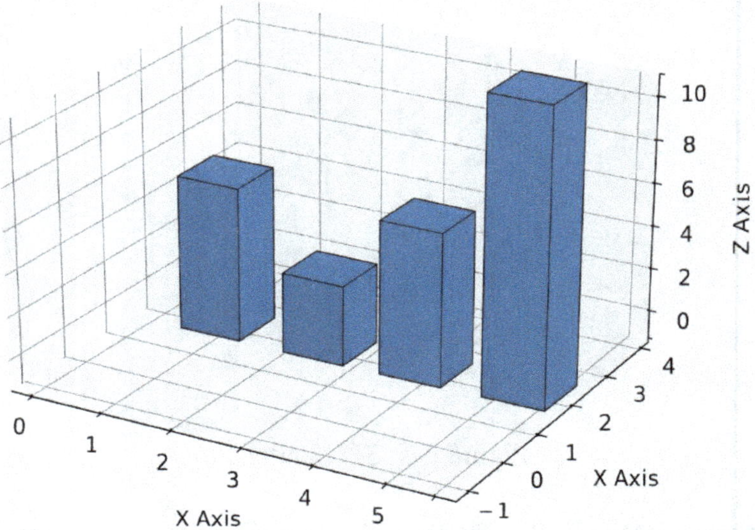

Figure 6-6: 3D Bar Graph

Summary

Matplotlib is a foundational visualization library in Python that supports:

- **2D and 3D plotting**
- **Statistical visualizations**
- **Interactive and publication-quality graphics**

Understanding Matplotlib is essential for **data analysis, machine learning, and scientific computing**, as visualization plays a critical role in **interpreting data** and **communicating insights**.

Exercises

Hands-On Practice Exercise for Matplotlib

Dataset Used in This Lab

We will use a small **"cars" dataset** containing:

- **speed:** Car speed (mph)
- **dist:** Stopping distance (feet)

You Will:

- Install Matplotlib
- Import required libraries
- Load the cars dataset
- Create a **bar chart, histogram, and pie chart**

Exercise 1 — Install Matplotlib

Task:

Run the installation command inside your Jupyter Notebook cell:

```
!______ install matplotlib
```

Exercise 2 — Import Required Libraries

Complete the import statements.

```
import ______ as pd
import ___________.pyplot as plt
```

Exercise 3 — Load the Cars Dataset

Run the code below to create the dataset.

```
from io import StringIO

data = StringIO(
"""speed,dist
4,2
4,10
7,4
7,22
8,16
9,10
10,18
10,26
11,17
11,28
12,14
12,20
13,26
13,34
14,46
15,26
15,36
16,32
16,40
17,32
17,40
18,42
18,56
19,76
20,48
20,52
22,84
23,92
24,93
24,120
"""
)

cars = pd.read_csv(________)
```

Task 1

Display the first 5 rows.

```
cars._______()
```

Task 2

Display the dataset shape.

```
print(cars._______)
```

Exercise 4 — Create Speed Groups

Complete the bins and labels code.

```
bins = [___, ___, ___, ___, ___]
labels = ["0-10", "11-15", "16-20", "21+"]

cars["speed_group"] = pd._______(cars["speed"], bins=bins, labels=labels)
```

Exercise 5 — Compute Average Distance Per Speed Group

Complete the groupby statement.

```
group_avg = cars._______("speed_group")["dist"]._______()
group_avg
```

Exercise 6 — Draw a Bar Chart

Complete the plotting code.

```
plt.figure(figsize=(6,4))
plt._______(group_avg.index, group_avg.values)
plt.title("______________________________")
plt.xlabel("______________________________")
plt.ylabel("______________________________")
plt.show()
```

Exercise 7 — Draw Histogram of Speed

Fill in the missing parts.

```
plt.figure(figsize=(6,4))
plt._______(cars["_______"], bins=__)
plt.title("______________________________")
plt.xlabel("______________________________")
plt.ylabel("______________________________")
plt.show()
```

Exercise 8 — Draw Pie Chart

Step 1: Count number of cars in each group.

```
group_counts = cars["_______"]._______().sort_index()
group_counts
```

Step 2: Plot the pie chart.

```
plt.figure(figsize=(6,6))
plt._______(
    group_counts.values,
    labels=group_counts.index,
    autopct="______"
)
plt.title("________________________________")
plt.show()
```

Bonus Challenge — Scatter Plot

Complete the scatter plot.

```
plt.figure(figsize=(6,4))
plt._______(cars["________"], cars["________"])
plt.title("______________________________")
plt.xlabel("______________________________")
plt.ylabel("______________________________")
plt.grid(_____)
plt.show()
```

Reflection Questions

1. Why do we create speed groups before plotting a bar chart?
2. What does a histogram show that a bar chart does not?
3. When would you prefer a pie chart over a bar chart?
4. What relationship do you observe between speed and stopping distance?

References

1. Hunter, J. D. (2007). *Matplotlib: A 2D graphics environment. Computing in Science & Engineering.*
2. Matplotlib Documentation. Retrieved from https://matplotlib.org/
3. McKinney, W. *Python for Data Analysis.* O'Reilly Media.

7. Chapter 07: Seaborn

Learning Objectives

After reading this chapter, you will be able to:

1. Understand the basics of data visualization using Matplotlib
2. Create common plots such as line, bar, and scatter plots
3. Customize plots using labels, titles, and legends
4. Visualize trends and patterns in datasets ·

Data Visualization Using Seaborn

1. Introduction

Seaborn is a **high-level Python data visualization library** built on top of Matplotlib. It provides a simpler interface for drawing **statistical graphics** and integrates seamlessly with **Pandas DataFrames**.

While Matplotlib focuses on **low-level plotting control**, Seaborn emphasizes:

- **Statistical relationships**
- **Cleaner default styles**
- **Faster exploratory data analysis (EDA)**

Seaborn is especially useful in **data science** and **machine learning workflows**, where understanding **distributions, relationships, and patterns** is critical.

2. Installing and Importing Seaborn

Installation

We can install the Seaborn library in Jupyter Notebook using the following command:

```
!pip install seaborn
```

Importing Seaborn

For importing Seaborn, we have to use below code.

```
import seaborn as sns
import matplotlib.pyplot as plt
```

Seaborn automatically applies visually appealing themes.

```
sns.set(style="whitegrid")
```

3. Built-in Datasets in Seaborn

Seaborn provides several built-in datasets useful for learning and experimentation.

```
data = sns.load_dataset("tips")
```

Common datasets include:

tips

iris

titanic

penguins

4. Scatter Plot (Relationship Between Two Variables)

A scatter plot is used to visualize relationships between two numerical variables and optionally a categorical variable.

Example

```
sns.scatterplot(data=data, x="total_bill", y="tip", hue="sex")
plt.title("Total Bill vs Tip")
plt.show()
```

Use case:

Detect trends, correlations, clusters, and outliers.

5. Histogram (Distribution of Data)

A histogram shows how data is distributed across bins.

Example

```
sns.histplot(data=data, x="total_bill", bins=20, kde=True)
plt.title("Distribution of Total Bill")
plt.show()
```

Why Seaborn is better than Matplotlib here:

Automatic KDE (density curve)

Cleaner styling

Less code

6. Box Plot (Detecting Spread and Outliers)

A box plot visualizes:

Median

Quartiles

Outliers

Example

```
sns.boxplot(data=data, x="day", y="total_bill")
plt.title("Total Bill by Day")
plt.show()
```

7. Bar Plot (Aggregated Statistics)

A bar plot represents aggregated values, typically the mean.

Example

```
sns.barplot(data=data, x="day", y="tip")
plt.title("Average Tip by Day")
plt.show()
```

8. Heatmap (Correlation Analysis)

A heatmap is commonly used to visualize correlation matrices.

Example

```
corr = data.corr(numeric_only=True)
sns.heatmap(corr, annot=True, cmap="coolwarm")
plt.title("Correlation Heatmap")
plt.show()
```

Use case:

Feature selection, multicollinearity detection.

9. Seaborn vs Matplotlib (Conceptual Comparison)

Aspect	Seaborn	Matplotlib
Level	High-level	Low-level
Statistical plots	Excellent	Limited
Default styling	Clean	Basic
DataFrames	Native support	Manual

Figure 7-1: Seaborn vs Matplotlib

10. When to Use Seaborn

Use Seaborn when:

Performing exploratory data analysis

Visualizing statistical relationships

Working with Pandas DataFrames

You want publication-ready plots quickly

Summary

Seaborn Simplified Visualizations

Seaborn simplifies complex statistical visualizations by:

- **Reducing boilerplate code**

- **Improving aesthetics**
- **Integrating naturally with Pandas**

It is an essential tool for **data scientists, analysts, and ML practitioners** for rapid insight generation.

Exercises

1. How is Seaborn different from Matplotlib?
2. Why are box plots useful in data analysis?

Hands-On

1. Create a scatter plot between total_bill and tip using Seaborn.
2. Plot a histogram for total_bill with KDE enabled.
3. Create a bar plot showing average tip by gender.

Applied

1. Use a box plot to analyze spending behavior across days.
2. Generate a heatmap for a dataset and identify strongly correlated features.

Hands-On Practice: Jupyter Notebook

The accompanying codebase includes a **Jupyter Notebook** for hands-on practice. In this exercise, you will learn how to **import the Seaborn library, load datasets, and generate various types of plots**. Follow the **step-by-step instructions**, execute each command in sequence, and observe how data is transformed into meaningful visualizations.

Objective

In this lab, you will learn how to:

- Install and import the Seaborn library
- Load the built-in **Iris dataset**
- Inspect the dataset
- Prepare the environment for visualization

We will use the **Iris dataset** to explore Seaborn's functionality.

Step 1 — Install Seaborn Library

Install the Seaborn package (if not already installed).

Run the following command in a Jupyter Notebook cell:

```
!pip install seaborn
```

Step 2 — Import Required Libraries

Import necessary libraries for plotting.

```
from matplotlib import pyplot as plt
import seaborn as sns
```

Step 3 — Enable Inline Plotting

Ensure plots are displayed inside the Jupyter Notebook.

```
%matplotlib inline
```

Step 4 — Load the Iris Dataset

Load the built-in Iris dataset available in Seaborn.

```
iris = sns.load_dataset("iris")
```

Step 5 — Display Top Rows of Dataset

Inspect the first few rows of the dataset.

```
iris.head()
```

Step 6 — Explore Dataset Structure (Optional but Recommended)

Display dataset shape:

```
iris.shape
```

Display dataset summary:

```
iris.describe()
```

Step 7 — Check Unique Species

```
iris["species"].unique()
```

Step 8 — Ready for Visualization

At this point:

- **Seaborn is installed**
- **Libraries are imported**
- **Dataset is loaded**
- **Data is inspected**

You are now ready to create Seaborn visualizations, such as:

- **Scatter plots**
- **Pair plots**
- **Histograms**
- **Box plots**

Exercise 2 Draw a Pair plot

```
# Load the Iris dataset
iris_data = sns.load_dataset("iris")

# Create a pairplot with species as hue
sns.pairplot(data=iris_data, hue="species", height=3)

# Display the plot
plt.show()
```

Exercise 3 Draw a Box Plot

```
# Create a new figure with specified size
plt.figure(figsize=(10, 8))

# Draw boxplot for all numerical features in the Iris dataset
sns.boxplot(data=iris)

# Display the plot
plt.show()
```

Exercise 4 – Draw a violin plot

```
# Define custom colors for each species
species_colors = ["#78C850",  # Setosa
                  "#F08030",  # Versicolor
                  "#6890F0"]  # Virginica

# Create a violin plot for numerical features
plt.figure(figsize=(10, 8))
sns.violinplot(data=iris, palette=species_colors)

# Display the plot
plt.show()
```

Exercise 5 – Draw a Histogram

```
# Exercise 5 - Draw a Histogram

# 1) Plot histogram of petal length from Iris dataset with KDE curve
plt.figure(figsize=(8, 5))
sns.histplot(data=iris, x="petal_length", kde=True)

plt.title("Distribution of Petal Length (Iris Dataset)")
plt.xlabel("Petal Length")
plt.ylabel("Frequency")
plt.show()


# 2) Plot histogram using another built-in dataset (Penguins)

# Load the Penguins dataset
penguins = sns.load_dataset("penguins")

# Create histogram for flipper length
plt.figure(figsize=(8, 5))
sns.histplot(data=penguins, x="flipper_length_mm", kde=True)

plt.title("Distribution of Flipper Length (Penguins Dataset)")
plt.xlabel("Flipper Length (mm)")
plt.ylabel("Frequency")
plt.show()
```

Exercise 6 – Draw a Swarm Plot

```
# Exercise 6 – Draw a Swarm Plot

# Create a new figure
plt.figure(figsize=(8, 6))

# Draw swarm plot of Petal Length across different species
sns.swarmplot(
    data=iris,
    x="species",
    y="petal_length",
    palette=species_colors
)

# Add title and labels
plt.title("Petal Length Distribution Across Species")
plt.xlabel("Species")
plt.ylabel("Petal Length")

# Display the plot
plt.show()
```

Exercise 7 – Draw a Bar Plot

```
# Exercise 7 - Draw a Bar Plot

# Create a new figure
plt.figure(figsize=(8, 6))

# Draw bar plot showing average body mass across islands
sns.barplot(
    data=penguins,
    x="island",
    y="body_mass_g"
)

# Add title and labels
plt.title("Average Body Mass by Island")
plt.xlabel("Island")
plt.ylabel("Body Mass (g)")

# Display the plot
plt.show()
```

Exercise 8 – Draw a Heatmap Plot

```
# Exercise 8 – Draw a Heatmap Plot

# Compute correlation matrix of numerical features
correlation_matrix = iris.corr()

# Create a new figure
plt.figure(figsize=(8, 6))

# Draw heatmap with annotations
sns.heatmap(
    data=correlation_matrix,
    annot=True,
    square=True,
    cmap="coolwarm"
)

# Add title
plt.title("Correlation Heatmap of Iris Dataset")

# Display the plot
plt.show()
```

References

1. Waskom, M. (2021). *Seaborn: Statistical Data Visualization. Journal of Open Source Software.*
2. Seaborn Documentation https://seaborn.pydata.org/
3. Pearson, K. (1895). *Notes on Regression and Inheritance. Proceedings of the Royal Society of London.*
4. McKinney, W. (2017). *Python for Data Analysis.* O'Reilly Media.

SECTION 3

MACHINE LEARNING ALGORITHMS

- **Chapter 08 – Linear Regression**
- **Chapter 09 – Classification**
- **Chapter 10 – Training and testing ML models**
- **Chapter 11 – Naive Bayes Theorem**
- **Chapter 12 – Decision Trees**
- **Chapter 13 – Neural Networks**
- **Chapter 14 – K-Nearest Neighbors (KNN)**
- **Chapter 15 – Support Vector Machines (SVM)**
- **Chapter 16 - Unsupervised Algorithms**
- **Chapter 17 – Reinforcement Learning**

8. Chapter 08: Linear Regression

Learning Objectives

After reading this chapter, you will be able to:

1. Formulate linear regression models to represent relationships between variables.
2. Interpret regression coefficients and understand their real-world meaning.
3. Compute model parameters using the least squares method.
4. Evaluate regression performance using metrics such as MSE, RMSE, and R^2.
5. Implement linear regression using Scikit-Learn for real-world prediction tasks.

Introduction

Regression and classification tasks fall under the category of Supervised Machine Learning. Supervised Machine Learning is a technique in which models are trained using labeled data, meaning that both input features and their corresponding output values are provided during training.

Linear Regression is a supervised learning algorithm that determines the best-fitting straight line between independent variables and a dependent variable. It models the linear relationship between these variables to make predictions. Linear Regression is also considered a statistical method used to predict a continuous dependent (target) variable based on one or more independent variables.

Types of Linear Regression

- **Simple linear regression:** This involves predicting a dependent variable based on a single independent variable.
- **Multiple linear regression:** This involves predicting a dependent variable based on multiple independent variables.
- **Polynomial linear regression:** This involves predicting a dependent variable based on a polynomial relationship between independent and dependent variables.

Application Areas

- **Prediction**: Estimating future values based on historical data.
- **Forecasting**: Predicting trends over time.
- **Causal Relationships**: Determining how changes in one variable affect another.

Linear Regression

A Linear Regression model's main aim is to find the best-fitting linear line and the optimal values of intercept and coefficients such that the error is minimized. Error is the difference between the actual value and predicted value, and the goal is to reduce this difference.

Equation of linear regression

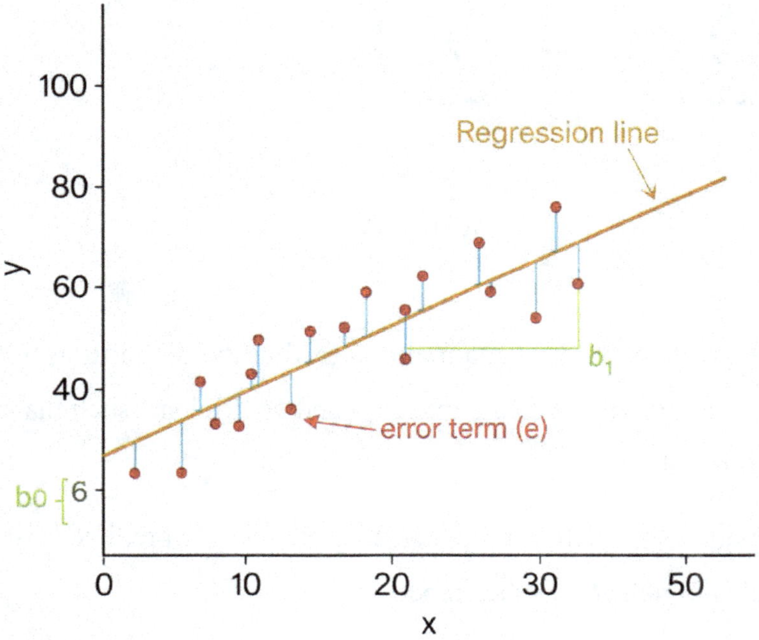

Figure 8-1 : Linear Regression

$$y = b_o + b_1 x$$

y is the dependent variable.

x is the independent variable

b_o is the intercept, b_1 is coefficient or slope

Mathematical Approach:

$$\sum e_i^2 = \sum (Y_i - \hat{Y}_i)^2$$

Figure 8-2

A Linear Regression model's main aim is to find the best fitting linear line and the optimal values of the intercept and coefficients such that the error is minimized.

Error is the difference between the actual value and the predicted value, and the goal is to reduce this difference.

The vertical distance between a data point and the regression line is known as the error or residual. Each data point has one residual, and the sum of all the differences is known as the sum of residuals/errors.

Error

Mathematical Approach:

Residual/Error = Actual values – Predicted Values

Sum of Residuals/Errors = Σ (Actual – Predicted Values)

Square of Sum of Residuals/Errors = $(\Sigma\ (\text{Actual} - \text{Predicted Values}))^2$

Assumptions of Linear Regression

Linearity: It states that the dependent variable Y should be linearly related to independent variables. This assumption can be checked by plotting a scatter plot between both variables.

A regression line can represent either a Positive Linear Relationship or a Negative Linear Relationship.

Positive Linear Relationship

If the dependent variable increases on the Y-axis and the independent variable progress on X-axis, then such a relationship is termed a Positive linear relationship.

$$y = a_0 + a_1 x$$

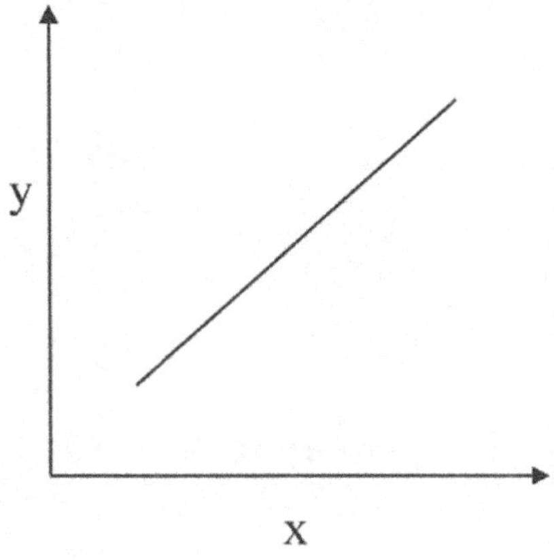

Figure 8-3: Positive Linear Relationship

Negative Linear Relationship

If the dependent variable decreases on the Y-axis while the independent variable increases on the X-axis, we refer to this relationship as a negative linear relationship.

$$y = -a_0 + a_1 x$$

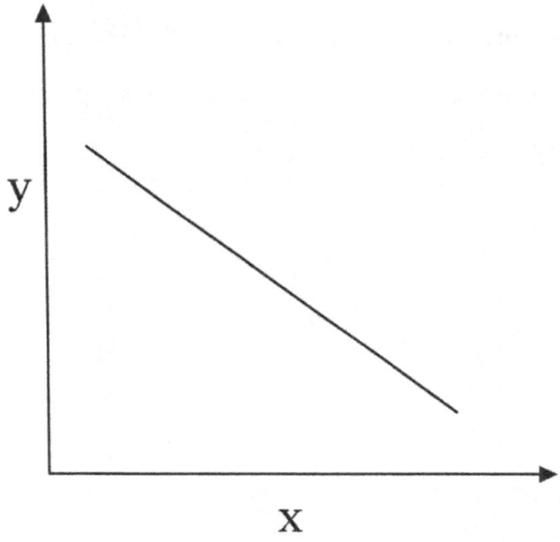

Figure 8-4: Negative Linear Relationship

Evaluation Metrics for Linear Regression

The most used metrics are :

Coefficient of Determination or R-squared (R2)

Root Mean Squared Error (RSME) and Residual Standard Error (RSE)

Coefficient of Determination or R-Squared (R2)

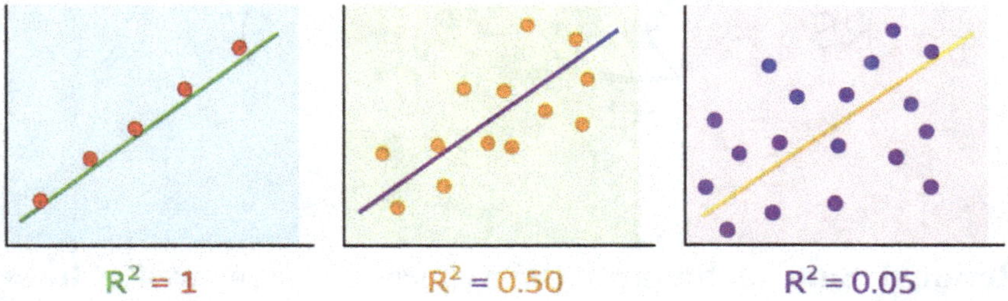

Figure 8-5

R-squared is a number that explains the amount of variation that is explained/captured by the developed model. It always ranges between 0 & 1. Overall, the higher the value of R-squared, the better the model fits the data.

Mathematically it can be represented as,

$$R^2 = 1 - \frac{RSS}{TSS}$$

Residual sum of Squares (RSS) is defined as the sum of squares of the residual for each data point in the plot/data. It is the measure of the difference between the expected and the actual observed output.

$$\text{RSS} = \sum_{i=1}^{n} (y_i - b_0 - b_1 x_i)^2$$

The **Residual Sum of Squares (RSS)** measures how well a **linear regression model** fits the observed data.

It calculates the **total squared error** between:

- the **actual values** (y_i), and
- the **values predicted by the model** ($b_0 + b_1 x_i$).

  Here,

- y_i - Actual observed value of the dependent variable for the i-th data point
- x_i - Input (independent variable) value for the i-th observation
- b_0 - Intercept of the regression line (value of y when $x = 0$)
- b_1 - Slope of the regression line (change in y per unit change in x)
- $(y_i - b_0 - b_1 x_i)$ - **Residual (error)** the difference between actual and predicted values

- $(\quad\cdot)^2$ - Squaring ensures all errors are positive and penalizes large errors
- $\sum_{i=1}^{n}$ - Adds the squared errors over all n observations

RSS tells us **how far the regression line is from the actual data points**.

- **Smaller RSS** → better model fit
- **Larger RSS** → poorer model fit

Total Sum of Squares (TSS) is defined as the sum of errors of the data points from the mean of the response variable. Mathematically TSS is,

$$TSS = \sum_{i=1}^{n} \left(y_i - -\overline{y}\right)^2$$

Where,

y_i= i-th observed value

$\bar{y}$= mean of all observed values

n= total number of observations

TSS measures the total variability in the data before applying any model.

The significance of R-squared is shown by the following figures,

Residual Sum of Squares | Linear regression

Root Mean Squared Error

The Root Mean Squared Error is the square root of the variance of the residuals. It specifies the absolute fit of the model to the data i.e. how close the observed data points are to the predicted values. Mathematically it can be represented as

$$RMSE = \sqrt{\frac{1}{n}\sum_{i=1}^{n}\left(y_i^{Actual} - y_i^{Predicted}\right)^2}$$

Where,

y_i^{actual}= true (observed) value

$y_i^{\text{predicted}}$= model-predicted value

n= number of data points

We can explain step by step the above equation

1. **Error (Residual):**

$$e_i = y_i^{\text{actual}} - y_i^{\text{predicted}}$$

2. **Square the errors:**

$$e_i^2$$

3. **Mean of squared errors (MSE):**

$$\text{MSE} = \frac{1}{n}\sum_{i=1}^{n} e_i^2$$

4. **Square root → RMSE:**

$$\text{RMSE} = \sqrt{\text{MSE}}$$

Mean Absolute Error (MAE)

MAE is a statistical and machine learning metric used to evaluate the average size of prediction errors, regardless of whether the errors are positive or negative. It measures the accuracy of continuous predictions by calculating the average absolute difference between actual values and predicted values.

Key Features of MAE

Formula:

$$MAE = \frac{1}{n}\sum_{i=1}^{n}|y_i - \hat{y}_i|$$

Where:

- (n) = total number of observations
- $\sum$ = summation symbol, meaning all errors are added together
- $|y_i - \hat{y}_i|$ = absolute error between the actual value and the predicted value

A smaller MAE value indicates better model accuracy, while an MAE of 0 means the predictions are perfectly accurate.

Advantages of MAE

- **Less sensitive to outliers:** Unlike Mean Squared Error (MSE) or Root Mean Squared Error (RMSE), MAE does not square error values, so large errors have less impact.
- **Easy to interpret:** The error is expressed in the same units as the original data, making it straightforward to understand.
- **Useful for continuous data:** Commonly applied in regression problems to assess prediction performance.

Overfitting and Underfitting in Linear Regression

Overfitting

Overfitting happens when a machine learning model performs very well on the training data but fails to perform well on new or unseen data. An overfitted model learns not only the important patterns in the data but also the noise. Because of this, it gives inaccurate predictions when new data is introduced and does not generalize well. In simple terms, the model becomes too specific to the training data.

Underfitting

Underfitting occurs when a model performs poorly on both the training data and the test data. An underfitted model is too simple and fails to capture the underlying patterns present in the data. This usually happens when:

- The model is trained for too little time
- The model is overly simple
- There is insufficient or poor-quality data

Underfitted models cannot learn properly and therefore produce inaccurate predictions during training as well as testing.

Bias and Variance

Bias

Bias refers to the error introduced by making overly simple assumptions in the learning algorithm.

- Models with high bias are too simple.
- They fail to capture complex patterns in the data.
- This leads to poor performance on both training and test datasets.

For example, many linear models have high bias. They are:

- Fast to train
- Easy to understand
- Less flexible

Because of this, they often perform poorly on complex problems. In simple words, bias represents errors caused by wrong assumptions made by the model.

Variance

Variance measures how sensitive a model is to changes in the training data.

- A model with high variance changes significantly when the training data changes slightly.
- Such models memorize the training data instead of learning

general patterns.

Ideally, a good model should:

- Learn the underlying relationship between inputs and outputs
- Not change drastically when trained on a different dataset

High variance models tend to overfit, while low variance models generalize better.

Overfitting simplified

When a model learns every detail and noise in the training data, it becomes overfitted. The model starts treating noise as meaningful patterns, which reduces its performance on unseen data.

How to reduce overfitting:

- Use cross-validation
- Collect more relevant and clean data
- Remove unnecessary features using feature selection
- Apply regularization techniques

Underfitting simplified

Underfitting occurs when a model is unable to learn meaningful patterns from the training data and also fails to generalize to test data.

This usually happens when the model has:

- High bias

- Low variance

Such models show:

- Low training accuracy
- Very low testing accuracy

How to reduce underfitting:

- Increase model complexity
- Add more meaningful features
- Remove noise from the data

Key Takeaway

- Overfitting → Model is too complex and learns noise
- Underfitting → Model is too simple and misses patterns
- Bias → Error due to simplicity
- Variance → Error due to sensitivity to data changes

A good machine learning model finds the right balance between bias and variance.

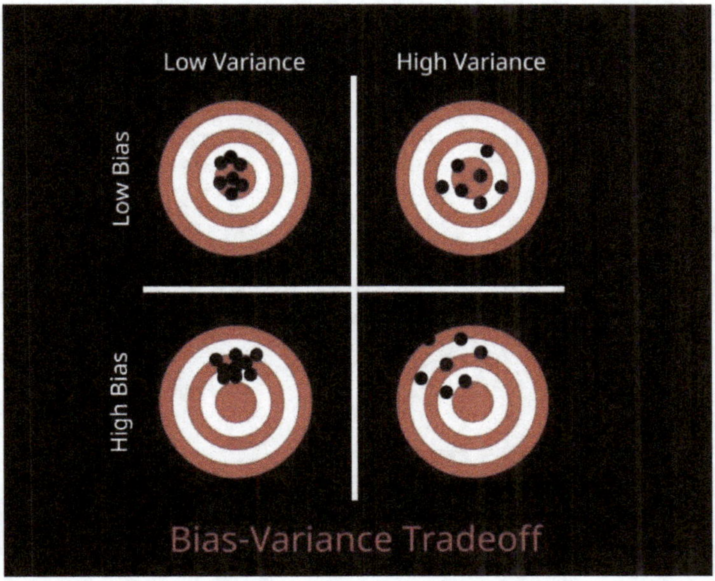

Figure 8-6: Bias Variance Tradeoff

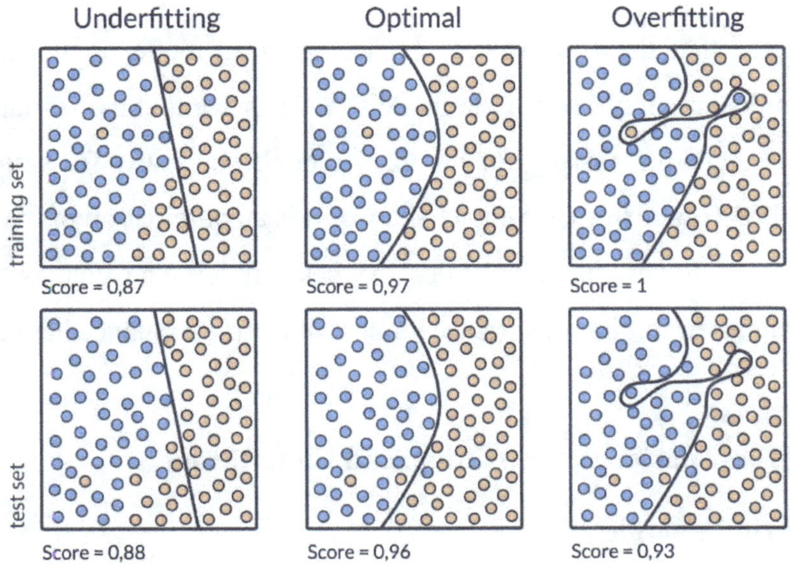

Figure 8-7: Underfitting and Overfitting

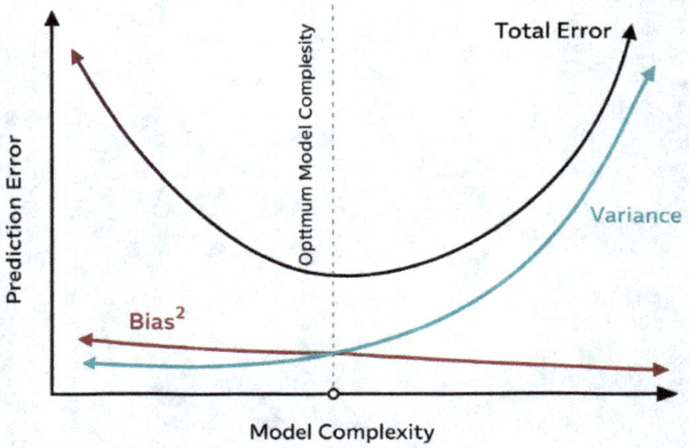

Figure 8-8: Bias Variance Tradeoff Curve

On the X-axis we have Model Complexity. On the Y-axis we have Error.

We can see that the Bias Curve (↓) decreases as model complexity increases. It starts high for simple models. We can see that the Variance Curve (↑) increases sharply for complex models. It is low for simple models. The Total Error Curve is U-shaped. It is a combination of bias + variance. The lowest point indicates the best model. The goal is not minimum bias or minimum variance alone, but the right balance between them.

Linking Bias, Variance, Overfitting, and Underfitting

Real-World Examples

1) House Price Prediction

Underfitting (High Bias)

- **Model:** Predicts house price using only the number of bedrooms.
- **Problem:**
  - Ignores location, size, age, and amenities.
  - Poor predictions on both training and test data.
- **Result:** Too simple → Underfitting.

Overfitting (High Variance)

- **Model:** Uses dozens of features like wall color, owner name, zip+4 code, and exact construction date.
- **Problem:**
  - Perfect on training data.
  - Fails badly on new houses.
- **Result:** Too complex → Overfitting.

Good Fit (Balanced)

- **Model uses:** Location, square footage, bedrooms, and age.
- Learns real patterns.
- Performs well on unseen houses.
- **Result:** Balanced bias and variance.

2) Exam Preparation Analogy

Underfitting

- Student studies only definitions.
- Fails to solve application problems.

Overfitting

- Student memorizes exact previous exam questions.
- Fails when questions are slightly changed.

Good Fit

- Student understands concepts + practices problems.
- Can handle new questions.

Machine learning models behave the same way.

3) Email Spam Detection

High Bias Model

- **Rule:** "If email contains 'offer', mark as spam."
- Misses many spam emails.
- Incorrectly flags useful emails.

High Variance Model

- Memorizes exact spam emails.
- Fails when spammers slightly change wording.

Balanced Model

- Learns general spam patterns.
- Works well on new emails.

Multiple Linear Regression Example

Linear Regression for Cucumber Yield

Linear regression can be used to understand the relationship between **fertilizer usage and cucumber yield**. Researchers often study how different nutrients such as **nitrogen (N), phosphorus (P), and potassium (K)** influence the growth and productivity of cucumber crops.

Since multiple factors affect crop yield at the same time, **multiple linear regression** is commonly used to model their combined impact.

A simple linear regression equation for cucumber yield can be written as:

$$\text{Total Cucumber Yield} = b_0 + b_1 \times b_2 \times \text{Nitrogen}$$
$$+ b_2 \times \text{Phosphorus} + b_3 \times \text{Potassium}$$

Explanation of Terms

- **(b_0)** (Intercept):
  Represents the expected cucumber yield when no fertilizer is applied.

- **(b_1, b_2, b_3)** (Coefficients):
  Represent how much the cucumber yield changes for a one-unit increase in nitrogen, phosphorus, and potassium, respectively, while keeping other factors constant.

This model helps farmers and researchers:

- Understand which fertilizer has the **most impact** on cucumber yield
- Predict yield based on fertilizer levels
- Optimize fertilizer use to improve production and reduce waste

Assume we collect the following data from a cucumber farm.

Observation	Nitrogen (kg)	Phosphorus (kg)	Potassium (kg)	Cucumber Yield (tons)
1	50	30	40	18
2	60	35	45	21
3	70	40	50	25
4	80	45	55	28
5	90	50	60	32

Table 8-1

Assume the trained model gives the following coefficients:

- $b_0 = 2$
- $b_1 = 0.18$
- $b_2 = 0.12$
- $b_3 = 0.10$

Final Regression Equation

$$\boxed{\text{Total Cucumber Yield} = 2 + 0.18N}$$

Prediction Example

For a farm using:

- Nitrogen = 70 kg
- Phosphorus = 40 kg
- Potassium = 50 kg

$$\begin{aligned} \text{Yield} &= 2 + (0.18 \times 70) + (0.12 \times 40) + (0.10 \times 50) \\ &= 2 + 12.6 + 4.8 + 5 \\ &= \mathbf{24.4\ tons} \end{aligned}$$

Below is an **original, conceptual visualization** showing how linear regression fits cucumber yield data.

Exercise 1: Prediction (Easy)

Using the regression equation

$$y = 16 + 1.2x$$

1. Predict the yield when:
   - (a) $(x = 12)$
   - (b) $(x = 28)$

Exercise 2: Residual Calculation (Medium)

For $(x = 20)$, the **actual observed yield** is **42 tons**.

1. Compute the predicted value $\hat{y}$
2. Calculate the **error (residual)**:

$$e = y - \hat{y}$$

Exercise 3: Conceptual Questions (Easy)

Answer in one or two lines:

1. What does the slope (b_1) represent?
2. What does a positive slope indicate?
3. What happens to the regression line if $(b_1 = 0)$?

Exercise 4: Model Understanding (Medium)

1. If the intercept (b_0) is negative, does the model become invalid? Explain.
2. Can linear regression capture non-linear relationships? Why or why not?

Exercise 5: Error and Fit (Interview-Style)

1. What is a **residual** in linear regression?
2. How is RSS related to residuals?
3. What does a high RSS indicate about the model?

Bonus Exercise (Advanced)

Given the residuals for three observations:

Observation	Residual (e)
1	2
2	−1
3	3

Table 8-2

1. Compute the **sum of squared errors**:

$$\sum e_i^2$$

Python Exercise: Linear Regression (Hands-on)

Starter Dataset

We will model the relationship between:

- **x:** Fertilizer amount (kg)
- **y:** Crop yield (tons)

```
import numpy as np

x = np.array([5, 10, 15, 20, 25, 30, 35])
y = np.array([22, 28, 35, 40, 46, 52, 58])
```

Exercise 1: Fit a Regression Line Using NumPy

Task

1. Use np.polyfit() to find the best-fit line $y = b_0+b_1x$
2. Print the slope and intercept

```
b1, b0 = np.polyfit(x, y, 1)   # slope, intercept
print("Intercept (b0):", b0)
print("Slope (b1):", b1)
```

Question:
Is your slope close to ~1.2 and intercept close to ~16? Why might it differ slightly?

Exercise 2: Make Predictions

Task

Predict the yield when fertilizer is **x = 18 kg**.

```
x_new = 18
y_pred = b0 + b1 * x_new
print("Predicted yield at x=18:", y_pred)
```

Question:
What does this prediction mean in real-life farming terms?

Exercise 3: Plot Scatter + Regression Line

Task

Plot:

- Scatter points
- Best-fit regression line

```
import matplotlib.pyplot as plt

plt.figure(figsize=(7,5))
plt.scatter(x, y)
plt.plot(x, y_hat)
plt.xlabel("Fertilizer (kg)")
plt.ylabel("Yield (tons)")
plt.title("Linear Regression: Fertilizer vs Yield")
plt.show()
```

Question:
Are points close to the line? What does that indicate?

Hands-On Implementation Exercise of Linear Regression

Problem Statement

Real-World Business Scenario

Predicting Employee Salaries Based on Experience

A mid-sized technology company is reviewing its compensation strategy to ensure fair and competitive salary structures. The Human Resources (HR) department has historical data containing employees' years of professional experience and their corresponding annual salaries.

Management would like to answer the following business questions:

- How strongly does work experience influence salary?
- Can we build a predictive model to estimate salary for a candidate based on years of experience?
- Is the current salary structure aligned with a consistent growth trend?
- How accurate would such a predictive model be for decision-making?

As a Data Scientist, you are tasked with developing a Linear Regression model using the historical Salary dataset provided in the company's data repository (included in the codebase with this book).

Your Responsibilities

You must:

- Load and explore the dataset to understand its structure.
- Prepare the data for modeling.
- Split the data into training and testing subsets.
- Build and train a Linear Regression model using Scikit-learn.
- Generate salary predictions for unseen data.
- Evaluate the model using appropriate regression metrics:
    - Mean Absolute Error (MAE)
    - Mean Squared Error (MSE)
    - Root Mean Squared Error (RMSE)
    - R^2 Score
- Visualize the regression line and interpret the relationship between experience and salary.

Business Objective

The final model should help HR:

- Estimate fair compensation for new hires.
- Forecast salary growth patterns.
- Identify inconsistencies or outliers in existing salary structures.

- Support data-driven compensation decisions.

Expected Outcome

By completing this exercise, you will simulate a real-world analytics workflow commonly performed in business environments:

- Problem understanding
- Data exploration
- Model development
- Model evaluation
- Business interpretation

This exercise demonstrates how machine learning can transform raw organizational data into actionable business insights.

What will you learn?

In this project, you will learn how to:

- Load the Salary dataset
- Prepare data for Machine Learning
- Build a Linear Regression model using Scikit-learn
- Make predictions
- Evaluate model performance
- Visualize results using plots

This Jupyter Notebook is included in the codebase that accompanies this book. Follow the steps carefully and complete each code cell.

Step 1 — Import Required Libraries

Task: Import NumPy, Pandas, Matplotlib, and the required Scikit-learn modules.

YOUR CODE HERE

```
import ____ as np
import ____ as pd
import matplotlib.pyplot as ____

from sklearn.model_selection import ____
from sklearn.linear_model import ____
from sklearn.metrics import ____, ____, ____
```

Step 2 — Load the Salary Dataset

Task: Load the Salary dataset from the codebase folder (example: Salary_Data.csv).

Expected columns (commonly used):

- YearsExperience
- Salary

YOUR CODE HERE

```
df = pd.____("____")   # e.g., "Salary_Data.csv"
df.____()
```

Checkpoint: Display the first 5 rows.

YOUR CODE HERE

Step 3 — Explore the Dataset

Task: Check:

- shape of dataset
- column names
- missing values
- basic statistics

YOUR CODE HERE

```
print("Shape:", df.____)

print("\nColumns:", df.____.tolist())

print("\nMissing values:\n", df.____().____())

df.____()
```

Step 4 — Define Features (X) and Target (y)

Task:

- Set **X** = YearsExperience
- Set **y** = Salary

Hint: In scikit-learn, X should be 2D.

YOUR CODE HERE

```
X = df[[ "____" ]]      # YearsExperience
y = df["____"]          # Salary

print("X shape:", X.____)
print("y shape:", y.____)
```

Step 5 — Split Dataset into Training and Test Sets

Task: Split the data into:

- training set
- test set

Use a reasonable test size (example: 20% or 30%) and set a random state.

YOUR CODE HERE

```
X_train, X_test, y_train, y_test = ____(
    ____, ____,
    test_size=____,
    random_state=____
)

print(X_train.shape, X_test.shape)
```

Step 6 — Train the Linear Regression Model

Task:

1. Create the Linear Regression model
2. Train (fit) it on training data

YOUR CODE HERE

```
model = ____()
model.____(X_train, y_train)

print("Intercept:", model.____)
print("Coefficient:", model.____[0])
```

Step 7 — Make Predictions

Task:
Predict salaries for the test set.

YOUR CODE HERE

```
y_pred = model.____(X_test)

pd.DataFrame({
    "YearsExperience": X_test["____"].values,
    "ActualSalary": y_test.values,
    "PredictedSalary": y_pred
}).____()
```

Checkpoint: Display first 5 predictions.

YOUR CODE HERE

Step 8 — Evaluate the Model

Task: Compute model performance using:

- MAE (Mean Absolute Error)
- MSE (Mean Squared Error)
- RMSE (Root Mean Squared Error)
- R^2 Score

YOUR CODE HERE

```
mae = ____(y_test, y_pred)
mse = ____(y_test, y_pred)
rmse = np.____(mse)
r2 = ____(y_test, y_pred)

print("MAE :", mae)
print("MSE :", mse)
print("RMSE:", rmse)
print("R^2 :", r2)
```

Visualization Section

Step 9 — Scatter Plot of Actual Data

Task: Create a scatter plot of:

- YearsExperience (X-axis)
- Salary (Y-axis)

YOUR CODE HERE

```
plt.____(figsize=(7, 5))
plt.____(df["____"], df["____"])
plt.title("______________________________")
plt.xlabel("______________________________")
plt.ylabel("______________________________")
plt.____()
```

Step 10 — Plot Regression Line (Train Set)

Task:
Plot:

- training points as scatter
- regression line using model predictions on X_train

YOUR CODE HERE

```
plt.figure(figsize=(7, 5))
plt.scatter(X_train["____"], y_train, label="____")

y_train_line = model.predict(____)
plt.plot(X_train["____"], y_train_line, label="____")

plt.title("______________________________")
plt.xlabel("______________________________")
plt.ylabel("______________________________")
plt.legend()
plt.show()
```

Step 11 — Plot Regression Line (Test Set)

Task:
Plot:

- test points as scatter
- regression line (same trained model)

YOUR CODE HERE

```
plt.figure(figsize=(7, 5))
plt.scatter(X_test["____"], y_test, label="____")

X_line = X_test.sort_values(by="____")
y_line = model.predict(____)

plt.plot(X_line["____"], y_line, label="____")

plt.title("______________________________")
plt.xlabel("______________________________")
plt.ylabel("______________________________")
plt.legend()
plt.show()
```

Step 12 — Residual Plot (Optional but Recommended)

Task:

1. Compute residuals = y_test − y_pred
2. Plot residuals vs predicted values
3. Add a horizontal reference line at y = 0

YOUR CODE HERE

```
residuals = ____ - ____


plt.figure(figsize=(7, 5))
plt.scatter(____, residuals)
plt.axhline(0)
plt.title("______________________________")
plt.xlabel("______________________________")
plt.ylabel("______________________________")
plt.show()
```

Mini Exercises

Exercise A

What does the **slope** of the regression line represent in this dataset?

Exercise B

If the model has a **high R^2**, what does it indicate?

Exercise C

What happens if the dataset contains outliers? How can it affect the regression line?

Optional Challenge

1. Try changing the test size (example: 0.2 → 0.3).
2. Retrain the model and compare the evaluation metrics.
3. Write your conclusion in 2–3 lines.

Summary

Linear Regression is one of the most fundamental and widely used Supervised Machine Learning algorithms for predictive analysis. Linear regression helps establish a relationship between dependent and independent variables by fitting a straight line through the data points.

We learned how the algorithm uses mathematical equations to model relationships and predict continuous values such as sales, prices, temperature, or profit. The concepts of slope, intercept, and the regression line were introduced to understand how changes in input variables affect output values.

We also studied the process of building a linear regression model, including data collection, preprocessing, training, testing, and model evaluation. Important performance metrics such as Mean Absolute Error (MAE), Mean Squared Error (MSE), and Root Mean Squared Error (RMSE) were discussed to evaluate model accuracy.

Finally, we implemented Linear Regression using Python and Scikit-learn, visualized regression lines and prediction results, and understood practical applications of regression models in solving real-world problems. Linear regression serves as an important foundation for learning more advanced machine learning techniques.

Exercises

Exercise 1 —

1. What is Linear Regression?
2. What is the difference between simple and multiple linear regression?
3. What does the coefficient (slope) represent?
4. What is the role of the intercept?
5. What is the objective function minimized in Linear Regression?

Exercise 2 — Mathematical Understanding

Given: $y = 3x + 5$

1. What is the slope?
2. What is the intercept?
3. Predict y when $x = 10$
4. If slope increases, what happens to the line?

Exercise 3 — Hands-On Coding

Fill in the blanks:

```
from sklearn.linear_model import __________
from sklearn.model_selection import __________

X = df[["__________"]]
y = df["__________"]

X_train, X_test, y_train, y_test = __________(
    X, y, test_size=0.2, random_state=42
)

model = __________()
model.__________(X_train, y_train)

y_pred = model.__________(X_test)
```

Exercise 4 — Model Evaluation

1. What is Mean Squared Error (MSE)?
2. What is R^2 Score?
3. When is $R^2 = 1$?
4. What does a low R^2 indicate?

Exercise 5 — Multiple Linear Regression

Fill in the blanks:

```
X = df[["____", "____", "____"]]
y = df["____"]

model.____(X, y)

pred = model.____([[1800, 3, 2]])
```

Exercise 6

1. If coefficient of Area = 200, what does it mean?
2. If coefficient of Age is negative, what does it mean?
3. Why normalize features?

References

1. D. C. Montgomery, E. A. Peck, and G. G. Vining, *Introduction to Linear Regression Analysis*, 5th ed. Hoboken, NJ, USA: Wiley, 2012.
2. N. R. Draper and H. Smith, *Applied Regression Analysis*, 3rd ed. New York, NY, USA: Wiley, 1998.
3. G. James, D. Witten, T. Hastie, and R. Tibshirani, *An Introduction to Statistical Learning: With Applications in R*, 2nd ed. New York, NY, USA: Springer, 2021.
4. T. Hastie, R. Tibshirani, and J. Friedman, *The Elements of Statistical Learning*, 2nd ed. New York, NY, USA: Springer, 2009.
5. C. M. Bishop, *Pattern Recognition and Machine Learning*. New York, NY, USA: Springer, 2006.
6. K. P. Murphy, *Machine Learning: A Probabilistic Perspective*. Cambridge, MA, USA: MIT Press, 2012

    A. E. Hoerl and R. W. Kennard, "Ridge regression: Biased estimation for nonorthogonal problems," *IEEE Trans. Autom. Control*, vol. 15, no. 1, pp. 55–67, Feb. 1970.

7. D. L. Donoho, "Compressed sensing," *IEEE Trans. Inf. Theory*, vol. 52, no. 4, pp. 1289–1306, Apr. 2006.
8. T. Zhang, "Sparse recovery with orthogonal matching pursuit under RIP," *IEEE Trans. Inf. Theory*, vol. 57

9. Chapter 09: Classification

Learning Objectives

After reading this chapter, you will be able to:

1. Differentiate between classification and regression problems.
2. Construct and interpret confusion matrices for model evaluation.
3. Calculate accuracy, precision, recall, and F1-score.
4. Analyze classification performance using ROC curves and AUC.
5. Implement classification models using Scikit-learn on real datasets.

What is Classification?

Classification is a task that involves using algorithms to assign data points to predefined categories or classes. It is a type of supervised learning where a model learns from labeled data to predict the class label for new, unseen data. Classification models can be binary, predicting between two classes, or multiclass, predicting between more than two classes.

Classification Fundamentals

- **Predictive Modeling:** Classification is a predictive modeling task where the goal is to predict the class label of a data point based on its features.

- **Supervised Learning:** It falls under supervised learning, meaning the model learns from a labeled dataset where the correct class labels are provided.
- **Categorization:** Classification algorithms are used to categorize data into predefined groups or classes.

Types of Classification

Binary Classification Model

Binary classification problems predict a binary outcome, which is one of two possible classes.

Examples:

- "Is this a cat or a dog?"
- "Is this email spam or not spam?"
- "Will the customer buy this product?"
- "Is this product a book or a farm animal?"

Multiclass Classification Model

Multiclass classification problems allow you to generate predictions for multiple classes. This means predicting one of more than two outcomes.

Examples:

- "Is this a cat, a dog, or a bird?"

- "Is this product a book, movie, or clothing?"
- "Is this movie a romantic comedy, documentary, or thriller?"
- "Is this a mobile, a laptop, or a desktop?"

How Classification Works

- **Training:** The model is trained on a labeled dataset, learning to identify patterns and relationships between features and class labels.
- **Prediction:** Once trained, the model can predict the class label of new, unseen data points by applying the learned patterns.
- **Evaluation:** The performance of the classification model is evaluated using metrics like accuracy, precision, recall, and F1 score.

Examples of Classification

Disease Diagnosis: Assigning a diagnosis to a patient based on observed characteristics like age, blood pressure, and the presence or absence of certain symptoms.

Spam Detection: Classifying emails as spam or not spam.

Image Recognition: Classifying images into categories like cats, dogs, and birds.

Risk Assessment: Classifying individuals into risk categories based on their financial or health profiles.

Churn Forecast: Predicting if a customer will churn or not.

Classification Algorithms

Some of the classification algorithms are

1) Logistic Regression
2) K Nearest Neighbor
3) Decision Tree
4) Support Vector Machine
5) Naive Bayes

Logistic Regression

Logistic regression works by fitting a line or curve to a set of data points. The line or curve represents the relationship between the independent variables, which are the features you use to predict the outcome, and the dependent variable, which is the outcome you are trying to predict.

The logistic function is used to transform the output of the line or curve into a probability. The logistic function is a sigmoid function, which means that it has a characteristic S shape. This shape allows the logistic regression model to predict probabilities that range from 0 to 1.

Advantages of Logistic Regression

1. It is a simple and easy-to-understand algorithm.

2. It can be used to solve a variety of problems, including binary classification and multiclass classification.

3. It can be used to provide probabilities for the predicted outcome.

4. It is relatively efficient to train and deploy.

Disadvantages of Logistic Regression

1. It can be sensitive to outliers.

2. It can be computationally expensive to train for large datasets.

3. It may not be able to capture complex relationships between the independent variables and the dependent variable.

Overall, logistic regression is a powerful machine learning algorithm that can be used to solve a variety of problems. It is a good choice for beginners because it is relatively simple to understand and implement.

Logistic Regression Assumptions

- **Binary Target:** In the case of binary logistic regression, the target variables must always be binary, and the desired outcome is represented by 1.

- **No Multicollinearity:** There should not be any multicollinearity in the model, which means the independent variables must be independent of each other.

- **Feature Selection:** We must include meaningful variables in our model.

- **Sample Size:** We should choose a large sample size for logistic regression.

Binary Logistic Regression Model

The simplest form of logistic regression is binary or binomial logistic regression, in which the target or dependent variable can have only two possible types, either 1 or 0. It allows us to model a relationship between multiple predictor variables and a binary or binomial target variable.

$$f(x) = \frac{1}{1 + e^{-x}}$$

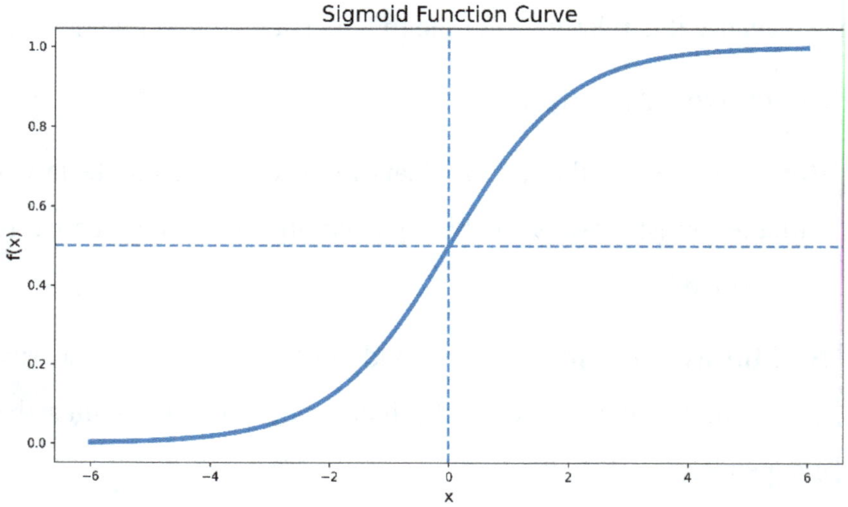

Figure 9-1: Sigmoid Function Curve

Sigmoid Function

The sigmoid function, also known as the logistic function, produces a smooth S-shaped curve that transforms any real-valued input into an output between 0 and 1. Because of this property, it is widely used to model probabilities in binary classification problems.

- Behavior at the Extremes: As the input value approaches positive infinity, the predicted output (y) approaches 1. Conversely, as the input moves toward negative infinity, the predicted output (y) approaches 0.
- Classification Threshold: A common decision rule is to use 0.5 as the cutoff. If the sigmoid output is greater than 0.5, the instance is classified as 1 (YES); if it is less than 0.5, it is classified as 0 (NO).
- Probabilistic Interpretation: The sigmoid output can be interpreted as a probability. For example, an output value of 0.75 indicates a 75% probability that a patient has a particular condition.

Classification Evaluation Criteria

Confusion Matrix

A **confusion matrix** is a performance evaluation tool used in classification problems to compare **predicted labels** with **actual labels**.

- **True Positives (TP)**: Cases where the model correctly predicts the positive class.

- **True Negatives (TN)**: Cases where the model correctly predicts the negative class.
- **False Positives (FP)**: Cases where the model incorrectly predicts a positive class when it is actually negative (Type I error).
- **False Negatives (FN)**: Cases where the model incorrectly predicts a negative class when it is actually positive (Type II error).

The confusion matrix forms the basis for calculating key evaluation metrics such as **Accuracy, Precision, Recall, and Specificity**, and helps identify whether a model is making more false alarms or missing actual positive cases.

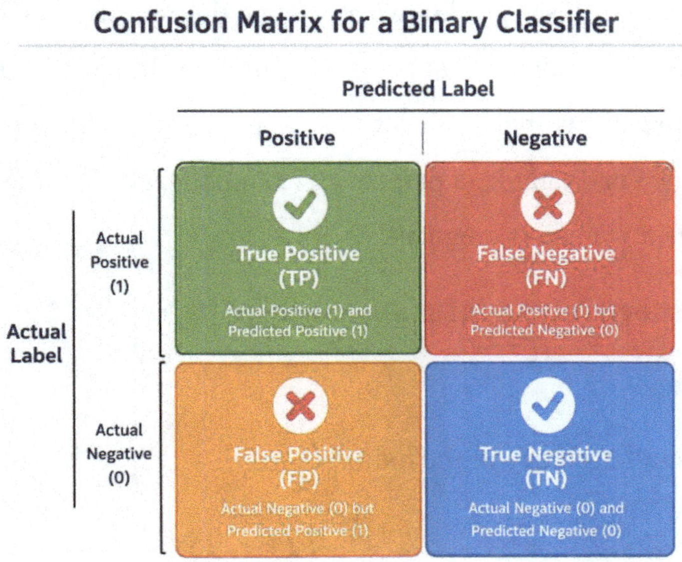

Figure 9-2: Confusion Matrix

True Positives (TP) represent the number of instances where a model correctly predicted the positive class. Essentially, TP indicates the model accurately identified cases that truly belong to the positive class.

True Negatives (TN) represent the number of negative examples that were correctly classified as negative by a model. Essentially, it's the count of instances where the model predicted "no" and the actual outcome was also "no".

A false positive (FP), also known as a Type I error, means concluding that something is true when it is actually false. This is also referred to as a "false alarm".

A false negative (FN), also known as a Type II error, occurs when a test fails to detect a condition that is actually present. In simpler terms, it's when a test result wrongly indicates that something is not the case when it actually is. For example, a pregnancy test might show negative results even though a woman is pregnant.

How to interpret a confusion matrix:

1. **Accuracy -**

   The overall accuracy of the model,

$$\text{Accuracy} = \frac{TP + TN}{TP + TN + FP + FN}$$

   Accuracy measures the overall correctness of a model by calculating the proportion of all predictions—both positive and negative—that are correctly classified. It indicates how often the model makes the right decision across all classes.

2. **Precision -**

   The ability of the model to avoid false positives, calculated as

$$\text{Precision} = \frac{TP}{TP + FP}$$

Precision measures how many of the predicted positive cases are actually correct. It focuses on the quality of positive predictions.

3. **Recall (Sensitivity) -**

The ability of the model to identify all relevant instances

$$\text{Recall} = \frac{TP}{TP + FN}$$

Recall (Sensitivity) measures how many of the actual positive cases are correctly identified by the model. It focuses on capturing all positives.

4. **Specificity -**

The ability of the model to correctly identify negative instances

$$\text{Specificity} = \frac{TN}{TN + FP}$$

Specificity measures how many of the actual negative cases are correctly identified. It focuses on correctly rejecting negatives.

Below is a simple numeric example with step-by-step calculations for Accuracy, Precision, Recall, and Specificity.

Example Confusion Matrix Values

True Positives (TP) = 40`

True Negatives (TN) = 50

False Positives (FP) = 10

False Negatives (FN) = 20

Total samples = 40 + 50 + 10 + 20 = **120**

1. Accuracy

$$\text{Accuracy} = \frac{TP + TN}{TP + TN + FP + FN}$$

$$= \frac{40 + 50}{40 + 50 + 10 + 20} = \frac{90}{120} = 0.75\ (75\%)$$

2. Precision

$$\text{Precision} = \frac{TP}{TP + FP}$$

$$= \frac{40}{40 + 10} = \frac{40}{50} = 0.80\ (80\%)$$

3. Recall (Sensitivity)

$$\text{Recall} = \frac{TP}{TP + FN}$$

$$= \frac{40}{40 + 20} = \frac{40}{60} = 0.67\ (66.7\%)$$

4. Specificity

$$\text{Specificity} = \frac{TN}{TN + FP}$$

$$= \frac{50}{50 + 10} = \frac{50}{60} = 0.83\ (83.3\%)$$

Summary Table

Metric	Value
Accuracy	75%
Precision	80%
Recall	66.7%
Specificity	83.3%

Table 9-1

Hands On Real World Classification Project

Problem Statement

Real-World Business Scenario

Early Prediction of Heart Disease Using Machine Learning

Cardiovascular disease remains one of the leading causes of mortality worldwide. Early detection of heart disease significantly improves treatment outcomes, reduces emergency hospitalizations, and lowers long-term healthcare costs. However, identifying high-risk patients based on multiple clinical indicators can be complex and time-consuming for healthcare providers.

A leading healthcare network has collected historical patient data that includes demographic, clinical, and lifestyle-related variables such as age, blood pressure, cholesterol levels, heart rate, and other diagnostic measurements. The organization aims to leverage this data to develop a Machine Learning–based predictive system that can identify patients at high risk of developing heart disease in the near future.

Business Objective

The goal of this project is to design and develop a predictive classification model that can:

- Identify patients who are most likely to develop heart disease.

- Assist physicians in early intervention and preventive care planning.
- Improve clinical decision-making efficiency.
- Optimize resource allocation within healthcare facilities.
- Reduce emergency cardiac incidents through proactive monitoring.

The final system should function as a clinical decision-support tool, providing risk assessments that help healthcare professionals make informed medical decisions.

Role of the Data Scientist

As a Data Scientist, your responsibilities include:

- Understanding the clinical problem and defining prediction objectives.
- Exploring and preprocessing the provided heart disease dataset.
- Selecting and training appropriate classification models.
- Evaluating model performance using suitable metrics (accuracy, precision, recall, F1-score, ROC-AUC).
- Interpreting results within a healthcare context.
- Ensuring that the model aligns with ethical, regulatory, and safety standards.

Risk, Ethical, and Regulatory Considerations

In healthcare applications, predictive accuracy alone is not sufficient. Because the system directly impacts patient health and well-being, ethical responsibility and regulatory compliance are critical.

1. Patient Privacy and Data Protection (HIPAA Compliance)

Healthcare data contains highly sensitive information protected under regulations such as:

- HIPAA (Health Insurance Portability and Accountability Act) in the United States.
- GDPR (for international data processing contexts).

Key Requirements:

- Remove or anonymize personally identifiable information (PII/PHI).
- Restrict and monitor data access.
- Encrypt stored and transmitted data.
- Follow the "minimum necessary" data usage principle.

Non-compliance can result in legal penalties, reputational damage, and loss of patient trust.

2. Data Security Risks

Healthcare systems are frequent targets of cyberattacks. Risks include:

- Unauthorized access to patient data.
- Data breaches.
- Model extraction or adversarial attacks.

Mitigation strategies include:

- Secure cloud infrastructure.
- Role-based access control (RBAC).
- Regular security audits.
- Secure deployment practices.

3. Bias and Fairness

Machine learning models can unintentionally reflect biases present in historical healthcare data.

Potential Sources of Bias:

- Underrepresentation of certain ethnic or socioeconomic groups.
- Gender imbalance.
- Unequal access to healthcare resources.

Consequences may include unequal model performance across populations, leading to inaccurate treatment recommendations.

Mitigation approaches:

- Perform subgroup performance analysis

- Use fairness evaluation metrics
- Ensure representative training data
- Conduct bias audits before deployment

Healthcare systems must promote equitable outcomes across all patient groups.

4. Clinical Risk: False Positives and False Negatives

In medical diagnosis, prediction errors have serious consequences.

False Positives:

- Healthy patients incorrectly flagged as high risk.
- May lead to anxiety and unnecessary diagnostic procedures.
- **False Negatives:** High-risk patients incorrectly classified as low risk
- Can delay treatment and increase mortality risk.

Therefore, evaluation metrics such as sensitivity (recall) and specificity must be carefully balanced according to clinical priorities.

5. Accountability and Human Oversight

The predictive model must serve as a decision-support system, not as a replacement for medical professionals. Clinical judgment remains essential.

Healthcare providers must:

- Interpret model outputs.
- Consider patient context.
- Make final treatment decisions.

Human oversight ensures responsible and ethical use of AI in medicine.

6. Regulatory Approval and Clinical Validation

Before real-world deployment, predictive systems may require:

- Internal validation.
- External validation using independent datasets.
- Institutional Review Board (IRB) approval.
- Regulatory review (e.g., FDA clearance if applicable).

Comprehensive documentation should include:

- Data sources.
- Model methodology.
- Validation results.
- Risk mitigation procedures.
- Monitoring and retraining plans.

7. Continuous Monitoring and Model Drift

Healthcare environments evolve over time due to:

- Changing patient demographics.
- New treatment protocols.
- Emerging diseases.

Models must be continuously monitored to detect performance degradation and retrained when necessary.

Ethical Guiding Principles

The development and deployment of healthcare machine learning systems should align with:

- **Beneficence** – Promote patient well-being.
- **Non-maleficence** – Avoid causing harm.
- **Justice** – Ensure fairness and equity.
- **Autonomy** – Respect patient privacy and rights.

Patient safety must always take priority over predictive performance.

Conclusion

Developing a heart disease prediction model represents a powerful application of Machine Learning in healthcare. However, it is not merely a technical exercise. It requires:

- Strong clinical understanding
- Ethical responsibility
- Fairness evaluation
- Regulatory compliance

- Ongoing monitoring

When designed and deployed responsibly, such predictive systems can transform healthcare by enabling early detection, improving treatment outcomes, and supporting data-driven clinical decision-making — ultimately saving lives while maintaining patient trust and regulatory integrity.

Example Implementation

(Note - *This sample exercise does not consider all the factors discussed in our case study)

Heart Disease Prediction (Binary Classification)

Learning Objectives

- Load a real-world healthcare dataset from UCI
- Prepare features and binary target variable
- Handle missing values appropriately
- Train a Logistic Regression classifier
- Evaluate using confusion matrix, precision/recall, and ROC-AUC
- Understand healthcare risk tradeoffs and limitations

Real-World Scenario

A clinic wants to screen patients for elevated risk of coronary artery disease using routinely collected medical measurements. The goal is to develop a predictive model that estimates the probability of heart disease and helps clinicians decide which patients may require additional testing.

IMPORTANT: This example Notebook is for educational purposes only and must not be used for real medical diagnosis.

Dataset Information

Dataset: UCI Heart Disease Dataset (Cleveland subset commonly used)

- **Target variable:** num (0–4)
- **For this lab, convert to binary:**
  - 0 = No heart disease
  - 1 = Presence of heart disease (values 1–4)

Step 1: Import Libraries

Fill in the blanks:

```
import numpy as _____
import pandas as _____
from sklearn.model_selection import __________
from sklearn.preprocessing import __________
from sklearn.linear_model import __________
from sklearn.metrics import __________, __________, __________
```

Step 2: Load Dataset

```
# Use ucimlrepo to fetch dataset (id=45)
heart = fetch_ucirepo(id=_____)
X_raw = heart.data._______
y_raw = heart.data._______
```

Step 3: Define Binary Target

```
# Convert target to binary (0 vs 1-4)
y_num = y_raw.iloc[:, 0]
y = (y_num >= _____).astype(int)
```

Step 4: Data Cleaning

```
# Replace '?' with NaN and convert columns to numeric
X = X_raw.replace('?', np.nan)
X[col] = pd.to_numeric(X[col], errors='_____')

# Use SimpleImputer with strategy = '_________'
```

Step 5: Train-Test Split

```
# Use 80/20 split and stratify by y
train_test_split(X, y, test_size=____, random_state=42, stratify=____)
```

Step 6: Feature Scaling

```
# Use StandardScaler and fit only on training data
scaler = _________()
X_train_scaled = scaler._________(X_train)
X_test_scaled = scaler._________(X_test)
```

Step 7: Train Logistic Regression

```
# Logistic Regression models probability using sigmoid function
clf = LogisticRegression(max_iter=_____, class_weight=_____)
clf.fit(__________, __________)
```

Step 8: Model Evaluation

```
# Compute
confusion_matrix(_____, _____)
classification_report(_____, _____)
roc_auc_score(_____, _____)
```

Plot ROC curve using matplotlib.

Reflection Questions

1. Why is this model not ready for real clinical use?
2. What are the risks of false positives and false negatives?
3. What bias or fairness issues might arise?
4. What additional validation would be required?

Summary

Classification is an important Supervised Machine Learning technique used to predict categorical outcomes by assigning data into predefined classes or categories. Unlike regression, which predicts continuous values, classification predicts discrete labels such as Yes/No, Spam/Not Spam, or Disease/No Disease.

We learned different types of classification problems, including binary classification, multiclass classification. Important concepts such as training data, testing data, decision boundaries, and class labels were introduced to understand the classification process.

The chapter also covered model evaluation techniques using metrics such as Accuracy, Precision, Recall, F1-Score, and Confusion Matrix to measure the performance of classification models. These metrics help in understanding the strengths and weaknesses of a model.

Finally, we implemented classification algorithms using Python and Scikit-learn and observed how classification techniques are applied in real-world applications such as email filtering, medical diagnosis, fraud detection, customer segmentation, and sentiment analysis. Classification forms a fundamental building block for many advanced machine learning applications.

Exercises

- What is the difference between:
  - Classification and regression?
  - Binary and multi-class classification?
- Give three real-world examples of classification problems.
- What is the role of the target variable in classification?

Evaluation Metrics

Given a confusion matrix:

	Predicted 0	**Predicted 1**
Actual 0	80	20
Actual 1	10	90

Table 9-2

Compute:

A. Accuracy

B. Precision

C. Recall

D. F1-score

E. False Positive Rate

5. What does ROC-AUC measure?
6. Why is accuracy misleading for imbalanced datasets?
7. In disease screening, should we prefer high precision or high recall? Why?

References

1. Janosi, A., Steinbrunn, W., Pfisterer, M., & Detrano, R. (1989). Heart Disease. UCI Machine Learning Repository.
2. Scikit-learn Documentation: LogisticRegression, roc_auc_score.
3. American Medical Association. (2021). *Augmented intelligence in health care policy*. AMA Policy H-480.940.
4. Centers for Disease Control and Prevention (CDC). (2023). *Heart disease facts*. https://www.cdc.gov/heartdisease
5. European Parliament and Council of the European Union. (2016). *General Data Protection Regulation (GDPR)*. Regulation (EU) 2016/679.
6. Esteva, A., Kuprel, B., Novoa, R. A., Ko, J., Swetter, S. M., Blau, H. M., & Thrun, S. (2017). Dermatologist-level classification of skin cancer with deep neural networks. *Nature*, 542, 115–118. https://doi.org/10.1038/nature21056
7. Food and Drug Administration (FDA). (2021). *Artificial intelligence and machine learning (AI/ML)-enabled medical devices action plan*. U.S. FDA.
8. Goodfellow, I., Bengio, Y., & Courville, A. (2016). *Deep learning*. MIT Press.
9. Health Insurance Portability and Accountability Act of 1996 (HIPAA), Pub. L. No. 104–191, 110 Stat. 1936 (1996).
10. London, A. J. (2019). Artificial intelligence and black-box medical decisions: Accuracy versus explainability. *Hastings Center Report*, 49(1), 15–21.
11. Obermeyer, Z., Powers, B., Vogeli, C., & Mullainathan, S. (2019). Dissecting racial bias in an algorithm used to manage the health of populations. *Science*, 366(6464), 447–453. https://doi.org/10.1126/science.aax2342
12. Rajkomar, A., Dean, J., & Kohane, I. (2019). Machine learning in medicine. *New England Journal of Medicine*, 380, 1347–1358.
13. Rudin, C. (2019). Stop explaining black box machine learning models for high stakes decisions and use interpretable models instead. *Nature Machine Intelligence*, 1, 206–215.

14. Topol, E. (2019). *Deep medicine: How artificial intelligence can make healthcare human again*. Basic Books.
15. World Health Organization (WHO). (2021). *Ethics and governance of artificial intelligence for health: WHO guidance*. World Health Organization.
16. Barocas, S., Hardt, M., & Narayanan, A. (2019). *Fairness and machine learning: Limitations and opportunities*.
17. Lundberg, S. M., & Lee, S.-I. (2017). A unified approach to interpreting model predictions (SHAP). *Advances in Neural Information Processing Systems*, 30.
18. Mitchell, T. M. (1997). *Machine learning*. McGraw-Hill.

10. Chapter 10: Training and Testing ML Models

Learning Objectives

After reading this chapter, you will be able to:

1. Differentiate between overfitting and underfitting and analyze their impact on model generalization.
2. Compute and interpret key classification performance metrics, including TPR (Recall), FPR, Precision, and F1 Score.
3. Analyze the effect of the classification threshold on model performance and understand the trade-off between Precision and Recall.
4. Interpret ROC curves and AUC values to evaluate and compare classification models, including those in imbalanced datasets.
5. Select an optimal classification threshold based on application-specific requirements and apply evaluation techniques to improve model performance.

Training and Testing ML Models

Overfitting and Underfitting are two crucial concepts in machine learning and are the prevalent causes for the poor performance of a machine learning model.

Underfitting

Model Comparison: Underfitting Vs Good Fit

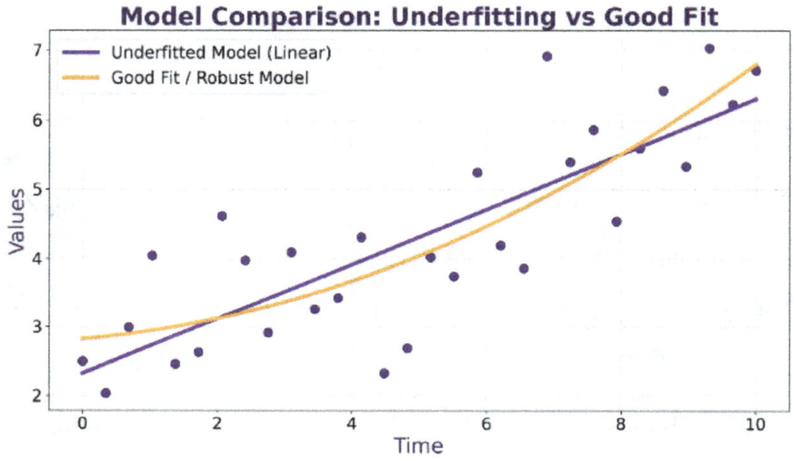

Figure 10-1: Underfitting vs Good Fit

Underfitting occurs when a model has high bias and low variance. Such a model is too simple or too generic and does not predict accurate results. Such models need more training time or more input features to consider.

A model that is underfit cannot establish a dominant trend in the data, therefore making accurate predictions very challenging. It does not perform well on new data. Underfitting happens when we oversimplify our model.

Overfitting

Model Comparison: Overfitting Vs Good Fit

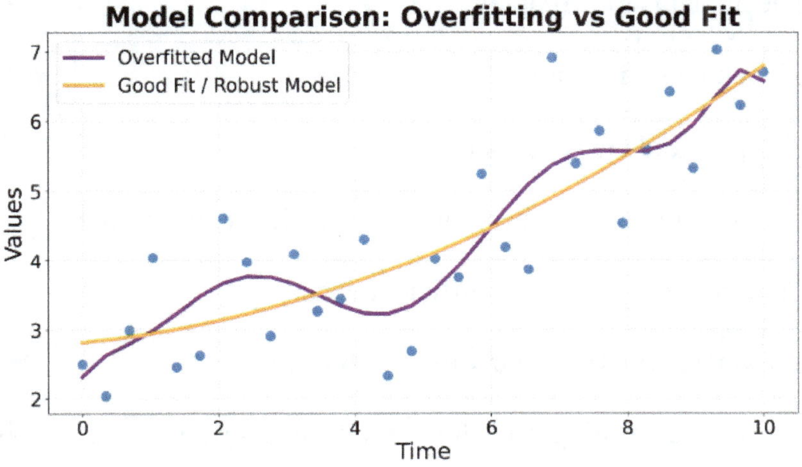

Figure 10-2: Overfitting vs Good Fit

Overfitting is the opposite of underfitting and refers to a model with low bias and high variance. Overfitting is a problem because it takes in all of the outliers or inconsistent data and will try to match that with the new data being given to the model. Overfitting happens when we overcomplicate our model. We don't want to underfit or overfit. We want our ML model to generalize well.

How to handle Overfitting

Reasons for Overfitting

1. Data used for training is not cleaned and contains noise (garbage values) in it.

2. The model has a high variance.
3. The size of the training dataset used is not enough.
4. The model is too complex.

Ways to Tackle Overfitting

1. Using K-fold cross-validation.
2. Using regularization techniques such as Lasso and Ridge.
3. Training the model with sufficient data.

Creating datasets for training/testing/validating

Normally, we use existing data for training and testing datasets—but sometimes we might need to have a third set, a validation set, to use to make decisions on which model to use. If you need to break your data into three sets—it is best to use either a 60/20/20 split or an 80/10/10 split between training/testing/validation data.

K fold cross validation

K-fold cross-validation is a technique used to evaluate the performance of a machine learning model by splitting the dataset into k subsets, or folds. The model is trained on k-1 folds and tested on the remaining fold, and this process is repeated k times, with each fold used as the test set once. This provides a more robust estimate of the model's generalization ability compared to a single train-test split.

Regularization

Regularization is a technique that does not require the use of testing data. Instead, it measures performance and complexity with two different error functions and adds them together.

Lasso Regularization (L1 norm)

Lasso regression is also known as Lasso Regularization or L1 Regularization. Lasso stands for Least Absolute Shrinkage and Selection Operator. Lasso regression is good to use if there is a large number of features as it shrinks the less important features' coefficients to a very small number—almost zero.

Ridge Regression (L2 norm)

Ridge regression is also known as Ridge Regularization or L2 Regularization. This technique works very well to avoid overfitting, and the coefficients get smaller as the degree grows, but without getting as small as they do in Lasso regression.

Training and Testing ML Models

Confusion Matrix

A confusion matrix is a table used to evaluate the performance of a classification model. It compares predicted outcomes with actual outcomes, showing the counts of true positives, true negatives, false positives, and false negatives. This helps us understand where the model is making mistakes and how well it's distinguishing between different classes.

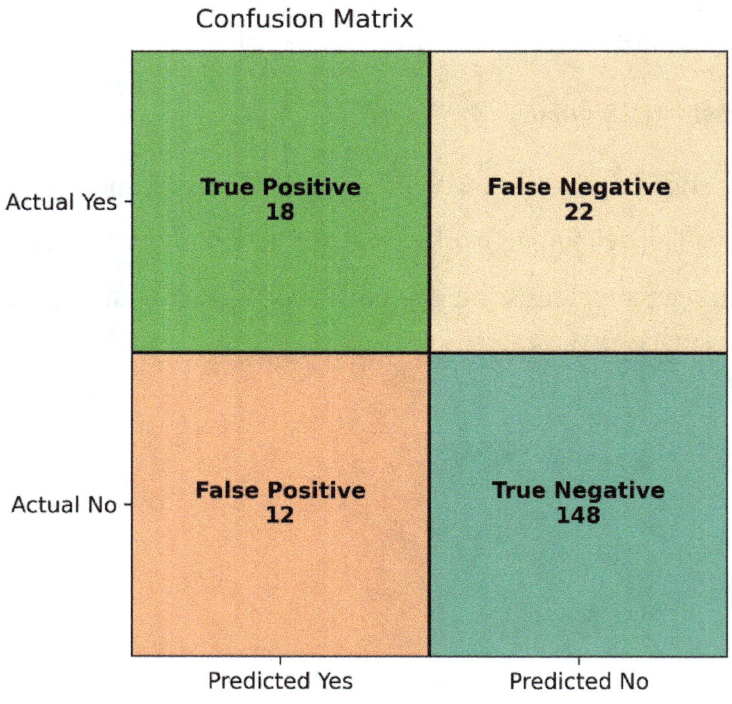

Figure 10-3: Confusion Matrix

- **True Positives (TP)** represent the number of instances where a model correctly predicted the positive class. Essentially, TP indicates the model accurately identified cases that truly belong to the positive class.
- **True Negatives (TN)** represent the number of negative examples that were correctly classified as negative by a model. Essentially, it's the count of instances where the model predicted "no" and the actual outcome was also "no "
- **False Positive (FP),** also known as a Type I error, it means concluding that something is true when it is actually false. This is also referred to as a "false alarm "
- **False Negative (FN)**, also known as a Type II error, occurs when a test fails to detect a condition that is actually present. In simpler terms, it's when a test result wrongly indicates that something is not the case when it actually is. For example, a pregnancy test might show negative results even though a woman is pregnant.

Accuracy: How often is my model correct?

Accuracy is the most common way to evaluate a classification model. It represents the percentage of times that a model is correct and is the ratio between the number of correctly predicted data points and the total number of data points.

$$Accuracy = \frac{\text{Correct Predictions}}{\text{All Predictions}}$$

$$Accuracy = \frac{TP + TN}{TP + TN + FP + FN}$$

For example, if you evaluate a model on a test dataset of 1,000 samples and the model predicted the correct label of the samples 875 times, the model has an accuracy of $875 / 1000 = 0.875$, or 87.5%. The higher the accuracy, the better. You can achieve a perfect accuracy of 1.0 when every prediction the model makes is correct.

Why Accuracy is not sufficient

Accuracy is a very useful metric, but it does not paint the whole picture of the model. While it calculates the ratio between correct and total predictions, it can fail in certain cases, especially when the positive and negative labels are unbalanced.

For instance, consider a Coronavirus dataset where 10% of patients have Covid and 90% do not. When the dataset is imbalanced, or where one kind of mistake (False Negative or False Positive) is more costly than the other, it is better to optimize for one of the other metrics instead. For heavily imbalanced datasets where one class appears only 1% of the time, a model that predicts negative 100% of the time would score 99% on accuracy despite being useless. In such cases, precision and recall metrics are more important for evaluation.

Identifying Spam and Ham Emails

Imagine that the actual balance of spam and non-spam emails looks like this: out of 60 emails, only 3 (or 5%) are truly spam. It is easy to get high accuracy in this case. To do that, you simply need to predict that nothing will happen and label every email as non-spam. The model predicting the majority class all the time will mostly be right, leading to very high accuracy.

In this specific example, the accuracy is 95%. Even if the model missed every spam email, it was still right in 57 cases out of 60. However, this accuracy is now meaningless. The model does not serve the primary goal and does not help identify the target event.

Precision

Precision is a metric that measures how often a machine learning model correctly predicts the positive class.

$$Precision = \frac{TP}{TP + FP}$$

You can measure precision on a scale of 0 to 1 or as a percentage. The higher the precision, the better. You can achieve a perfect precision of 1.0 when the model is always right when predicting the target class; it never flags anything in error.

Recall

Recall is a metric that measures how often a machine learning model correctly identifies positive instances from all the actual positive samples in the dataset.

$$Recall = \frac{TP}{TP + FN}$$

You can measure recall on a scale of 0 to 1 or as a percentage. The higher the recall, the better. You can achieve a perfect recall of 1.0 when the model can find all instances of the target class in the dataset. Recall can also be called sensitivity or true positive rate.

Specificity

Specificity refers to a model's ability to correctly identify negative instances, which means correctly classifying those that are truly negative. It is a measure of how well the model avoids false positives.

Specificity is also known as the true negative rate (TNR), which is the proportion of actual negatives correctly predicted.

$$Specificity = \frac{TN}{TN + FP}$$

High specificity is crucial when the cost of a false positive is significant, such as in medical diagnostics, fraud detection, or spam filtering, where misclassifying a negative instance as positive can have serious consequences.

F1 Score

The F1 score in machine learning is a metric used to evaluate the performance of a classification model, particularly when dealing with imbalanced datasets. It provides a balance between precision and recall, telling us about the model's ability to correctly identify both positive and negative cases.

$$F1 \text{ Score} = 2 \times \frac{Precision \times Recall}{Precision + Recall}$$

It is also called the Harmonic mean. The F1 score is widely used in various applications, including fraud detection, medical diagnosis, and text classification.

What is a ROC curve?

The ROC curve stands for the Receiver Operating Characteristic curve. It is a graphical representation of the performance of a binary classifier at different classification thresholds.

The curve plots the possible True Positive rates (TPR) against the False Positive rates (FPR).

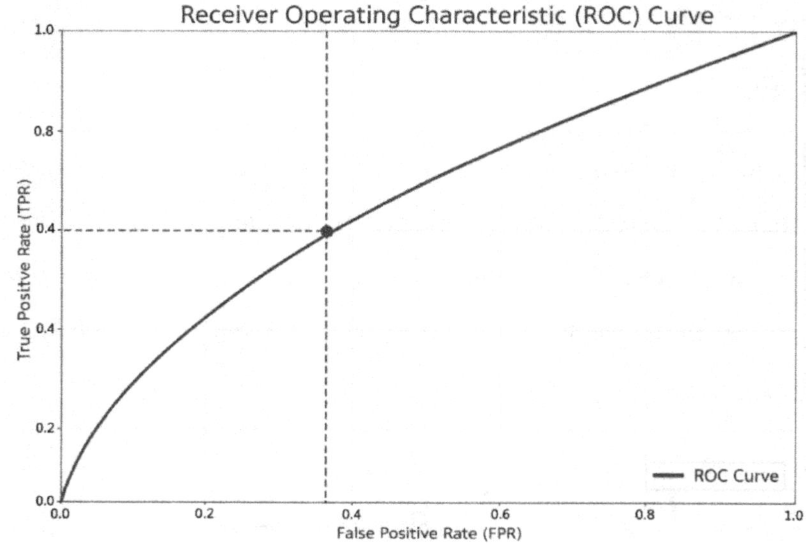

Figure 10-4: ROC Curve

What is a ROC AUC score?

ROC AUC stands for Receiver Operating Characteristic Area Under the Curve. The ROC AUC score is a single number that summarizes the classifier's performance across all possible classification thresholds. To get the score, you must measure the area under the ROC curve.

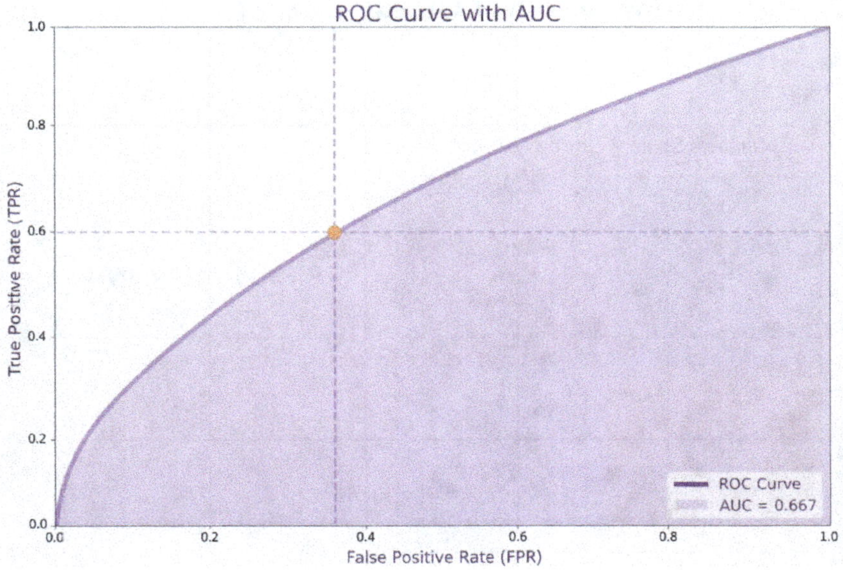

Figure 10-5: ROC Curve with AUC

ROC AUC Score

The ROC AUC score shows how well the classifier distinguishes between positive and negative classes. It can take values from 0 to 1. A higher ROC AUC indicates better performance. A perfect model would have an AUC of 1, while a random model would have an AUC of 0.5.

How does the ROC curve work?

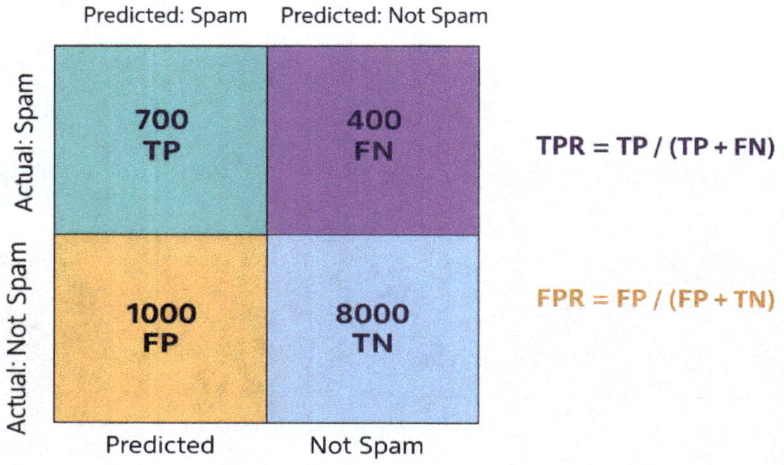

Figure 10-6: TPR and FPR

TPR (True Positive Rate or Recall) The TPR shows the share of detected true positives. For example, it represents the share of emails correctly labeled as spam out of all spam emails in the dataset.

$$\text{Recall} = \frac{\text{True Positives}}{\text{True Positives} + \text{False Negatives}}$$

Figure 10-7: Recall

$$TPR = \frac{700}{700 + 400} = 0.64$$

In this case, the model successfully detected 64% of all spam emails.

FPR (False Positive Rate) The FPR shows the share of objects falsely assigned a positive class out of all objects of the negative class. For example, it is the proportion of legitimate emails falsely labeled as spam.

$$\text{FPR} = \frac{\text{False Positives}}{\text{False Positives + True Negatives}}$$

Figure 10-8: False Positive Rate

$$FPR = \frac{1000}{1000 + 8000} = 0.11$$

The model falsely flagged 11% of legitimate emails as spam. To create the ROC curve, you plot the FPR values against TPR values at different decision thresholds.

Classification Threshold

What do "different" TPR and FPR values mean? Did we not just calculate them once and for all? In fact, we calculated the values for a given confusion matrix at a given decision threshold. But for a probabilistic classification model, these TPR and FPR values are not set in stone.

You can vary the decision threshold that defines how to convert the model predictions into labels. This, in turn, can change the number of errors the model makes. A probabilistic classification model returns a number from 0 to 1 for each object. For example, for each email, it predicts how likely that email is to be spam. For a given email, it can be 0.1, 0.55, 0.99, or any other number.

You then have to decide at which probability you convert this prediction to a label. For instance, you can label all emails with a predicted probability of over 0.5 as spam. Or, you can only apply this decision when the score is 0.8 or higher. This choice is what sets the classification threshold. As you change the threshold, you will usually get new combinations of errors of different types and new confusion matrices.

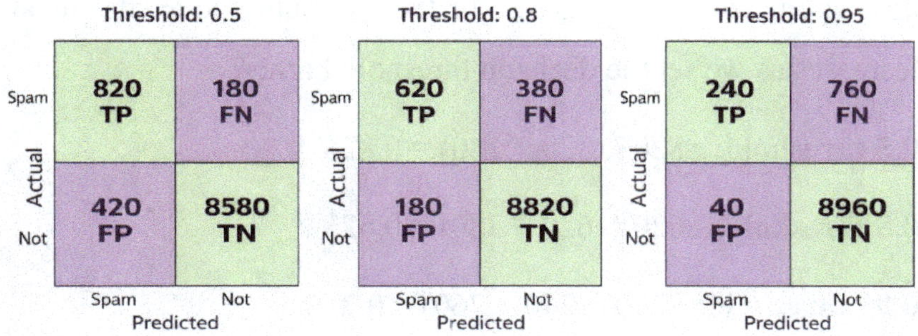

Figure 10-9: Effects of changing Threshold

Setting a Higher Threshold

When you set the threshold higher, you make the model "more conservative." It assigns the True label when it is "more confident." But therefore, you typically have lower recall: you detect fewer examples of the target class overall.

Setting a Lower Threshold

When you set the threshold lower, you make the model "less strict." It assigns the True label more often, even when "less confident." Consequently, you increase recall: you will detect more examples of the target class. However, this may also lead to lower precision, as the model may make more False Positive predictions.

TPR and FPR change in the same direction. The higher the recall (TPR), the higher the rate of false positive errors (FPR). The lower the recall, the fewer false alarms the model gives. In the example above, the recall (TPR) decreases as we set the decision threshold higher:

- **0.5 threshold:** $820 / (820 + 180) = 0.82$
- **0.8 threshold:** $620 / (620 + 380) = 0.62$
- **0.95 threshold:** $240 / (240 + 760) = 0.24$

The FPR also goes down:

- **0.5 threshold:** $420 / (420 + 8580) = 0.046$
- **0.8 threshold:** $180 / (180 + 8820) = 0.02$
- **0.95 threshold:** $40 / (40 + 8960) = 0.004$

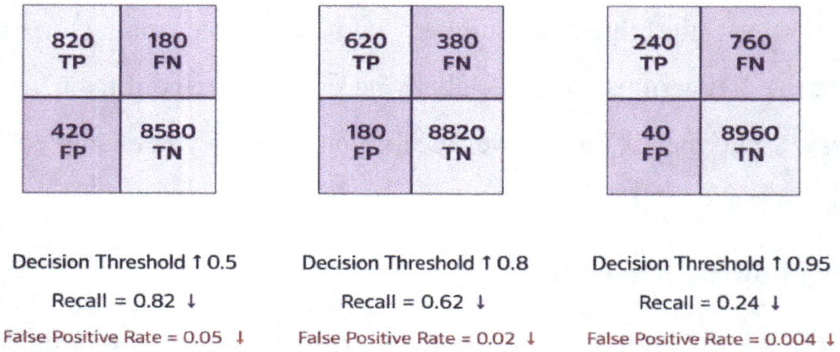

Figure 10-10: Effects of Threshold values

Plotting the ROC curve

The ROC curve illustrates this trade-off between the TPR and FPR. Unless your model is near-perfect, you have to balance the two.

As you try to increase the TPR (i.e., correctly identify more positive cases), the FPR may also increase (i.e., you get more false alarms).

For example, the more spam you want to detect, the more legitimate emails you falsely flag as suspicious.

The ROC curve is a visual representation of this choice. Each point on the curve corresponds to a combination of TPR and FPR values at a specific decision threshold.

To create the curve, you should plot the FPR values as the x-axis and the TPR values as the y-axis.

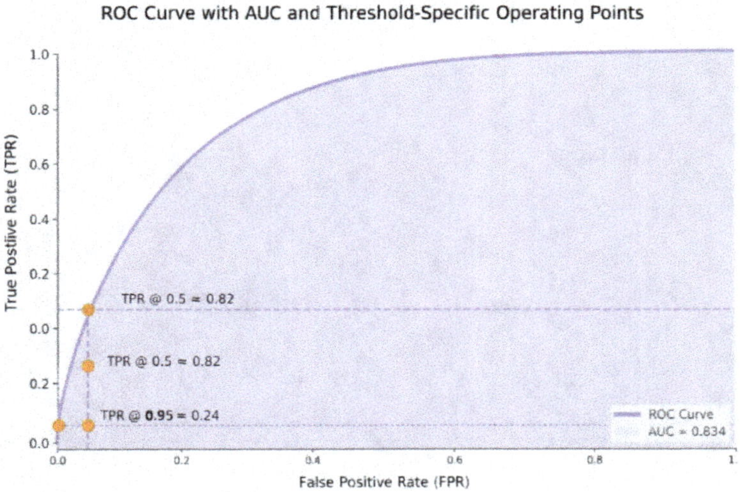

Figure 10-11: ROC with AUC and Threshold Specific points

Most values are "crowded" to the left.

The left side of the curve corresponds to the more "confident" thresholds: a higher threshold leads to lower recall and fewer false positive errors. The extreme point is when both recall and FPR are 0. In this case, there are no correct detections but also no false ones.

The right side of the curve represents the "less strict" scenarios when the threshold is low. Both recall and False Positive rates are higher, ultimately reaching 100%. If you put the threshold at 0, the model will always predict a positive class: both recall and the FPR will be 1.

When you increase the threshold, you move left on the curve. If you decrease the threshold, you move to the right.

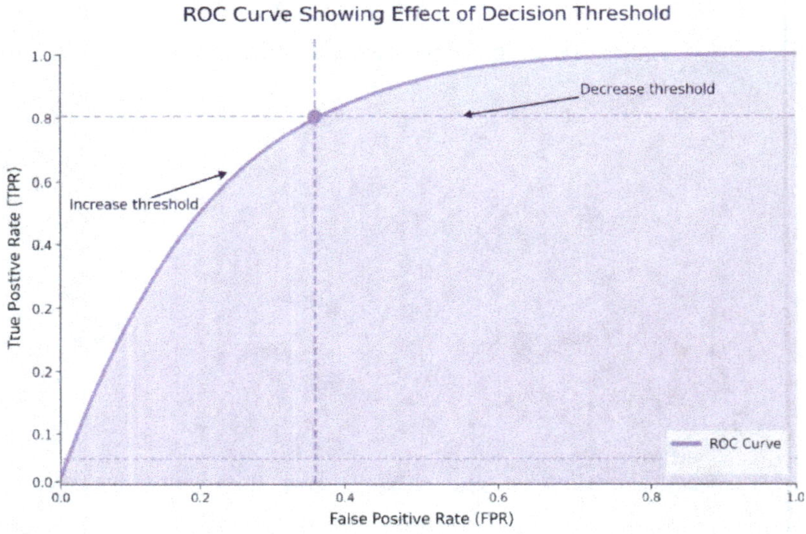

Figure 10-12 : ROC showing effects of Decision Threshold

Perfect Scenario

- If our model is correct in all the predictions, all the time, it means that the TPR is always 1.0, and FPR is 0. It finds all the cases and never gives false alarms.
- Here is how the ROC curve would look.

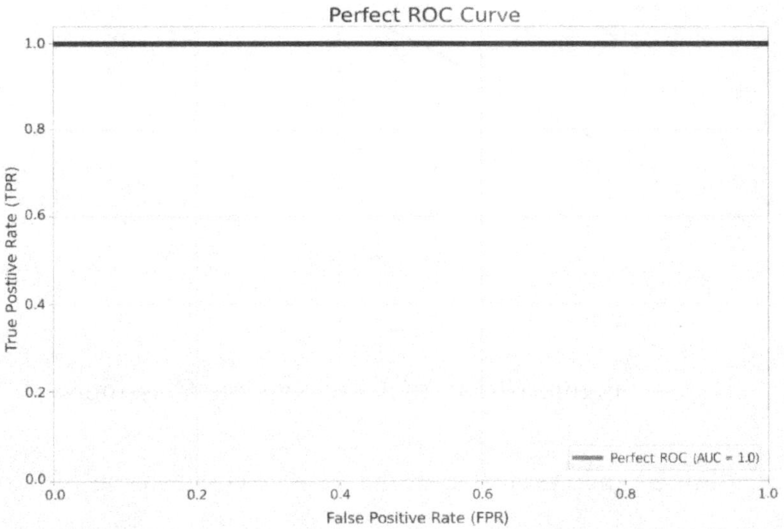

Figure 10-13 : Perfect ROC Curve

Worst-Case Scenario

- If our model is random. In other words, it cannot distinguish between the two classes, and its predictions are no better than chance.

- A genuinely random model will predict the positive and negative classes with equal probability.

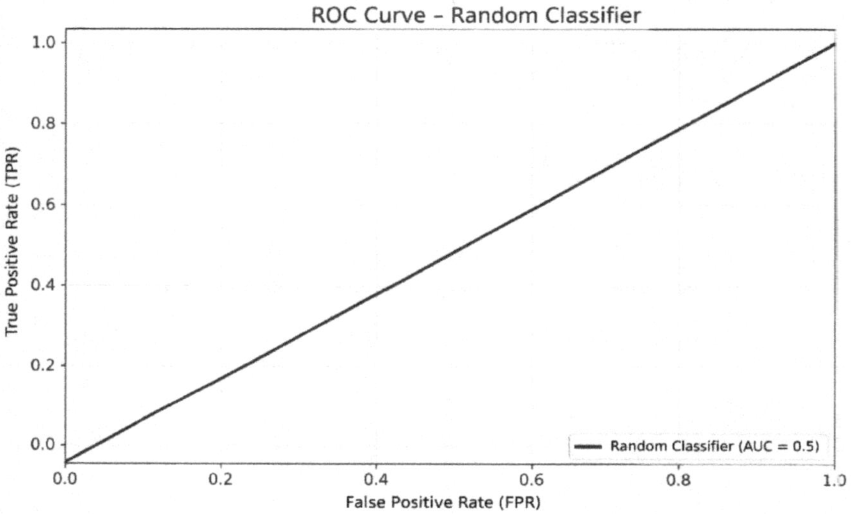

Figure 10-14: ROC for Random Classifier

- For a random classifier, the TPR is equal to the FPR because it makes the same number of true and false positive predictions for any threshold value. As the classification threshold changes, the TPR goes up or down in the same proportion as the FPR.
- Most real-world models will fall somewhere between the two extremes. The better the model can distinguish between positive and negative classes, the closer the curve is to the top left corner of the graph.

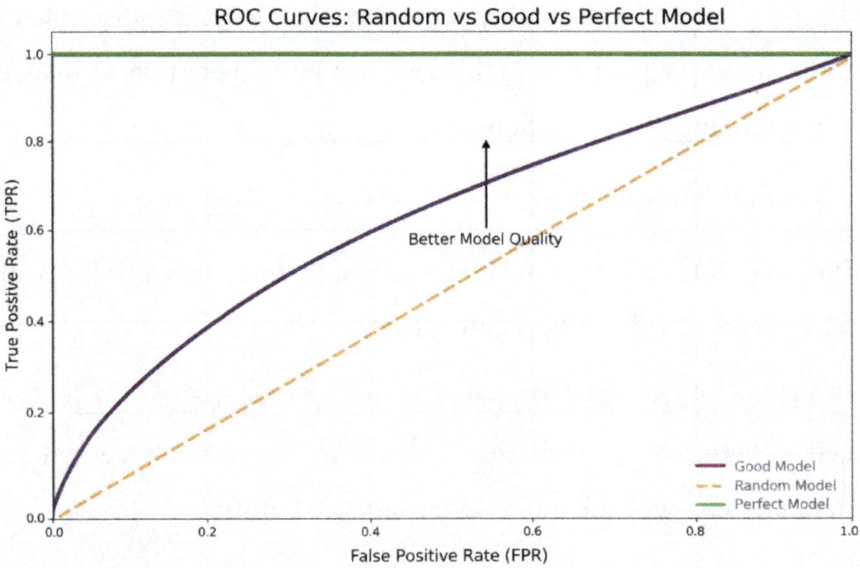

Figure 10-15 : ROC for Random vs Good vs Perfect Model

Summary

In this chapter, we have explored essential evaluation metrics and techniques for understanding and optimizing machine learning models, focusing on their behavior as the classification threshold is adjusted. These metrics provide crucial insights into model performance, especially in terms of false positives, false negatives, and model generalization.

1. Overfitting vs. Underfitting

Overfitting occurs when a model becomes too complex and memorizes the training data, leading to high performance on training data but poor generalization on new, unseen data.

Underfitting, on the other hand, happens when the model is too simple to capture the underlying patterns in the data, resulting in poor performance both on the training and validation datasets.

2. Performance Metrics

True Positive Rate (TPR), also known as Recall, measures the ability of the model to correctly identify positive cases.

False Positive Rate (FPR) measures the proportion of negatives incorrectly classified as positives. These two metrics are central to understanding how well the model discriminates between classes.

Precision quantifies the accuracy of positive predictions, while **Recall** quantifies the model's ability to find all positive cases. The **F1 Score** combines both Precision and Recall into a single metric that balances the two.

3. Threshold Selection and ROC Curve

By adjusting the classification threshold, we can control the trade-off between Precision and Recall. Lowering the threshold increases the number of positives predicted, boosting recall but potentially lowering precision due to more false positives. Increasing the threshold has the opposite effect.

The **Receiver Operating Characteristic (ROC)** curve plots the True Positive Rate (TPR) against the False Positive Rate (FPR) for various thresholds, providing a visualization of the model's performance across all possible thresholds.

Area Under the ROC Curve (AUC) summarizes the overall performance of the classifier, with higher AUC indicating better model performance. A perfect classifier has an AUC of 1, while random guessing corresponds to an AUC of 0.5.

4. Choosing the Optimal Threshold

The threshold plays a critical role in determining model output and can significantly influence performance. It's important to select an appropriate threshold depending on the application and the cost of false positives versus false negatives. For example, in medical diagnosis, recall is often prioritized to minimize false negatives, even at the cost of reducing precision.

5. Evaluating Model Performance

ROC curves and AUC are useful for comparing models and selecting the best performing one, particularly when the dataset is imbalanced.

Precision-Recall curves offer an alternative when dealing with highly imbalanced datasets, as they emphasize the performance with respect to the minority class.

When model performance is not acceptable, techniques like regularization, cross-validation, and simplifying the model can help reduce overfitting or underfitting.

6. Practical Application

The chapter includes practical exercises to help reinforce the concepts of evaluating performance metrics, calculating confusion matrix values, analyzing the ROC curve, and tuning the classification threshold to optimize for different tasks.

In real-world applications, model performance often involves a balancing act between minimizing false negatives and false positives, depending on the specific costs and risks of each type of error.

By understanding and carefully adjusting thresholds, using the ROC curve, and interpreting key evaluation metrics like Precision, Recall, and AUC, you will be better equipped to assess your model's performance and make informed decisions about its deployment.

This chapter lays the foundation for a deeper understanding and effective application of performance metrics in machine learning model evaluation, especially when working with classification problems.

Exercises

1. Conceptual Questions

- **Explain the difference between Underfitting and Overfitting.**
  - What symptoms would you observe in training error vs. validation error?
- **A model achieves:**
  - 99% training accuracy
  - 65% validation accuracy
  - What issue is the model likely experiencing? Explain why.
- **List three techniques used to reduce Overfitting.**

2. Decision Metrics

- **Describe situations where Precision is more important than Recall, and vice versa.**

2. Confusion Matrix Calculations

Consider the following confusion matrix from a binary classifier:

	Predicted Positive	**Predicted Negative**
Actual Positive	70	30
Actual Negative	20	80

Table 10-1

Questions

1. Compute:
    - **True Positive Rate**
    - **False Positive Rate**
    - **Precision**
    - **Recall**
2. Interpret the results. Is the model better at detecting positives or avoiding false alarms?

3. Metric Comparison

Two models produce the following metrics:

Model	**Precision**	**Recall**
A	0.90	0.50
B	0.65	0.85

Table 10-2

Questions:

1. Which model is better for **fraud detection**? Explain.
2. Which model is better for **email spam filtering**?
3. Compute the **F1 score** for both models.

4. Threshold Selection

A classifier outputs probabilities for the positive class:

Instance	True Label	Predicted Probability
1	1	0.92
2	1	0.81
3	1	0.63
4	0	0.55
5	0	0.40
6	0	0.25

Table 10-3

Tasks

1. Using threshold **0.5**, compute:
    - Confusion matrix
    - **Precision**
    - **Recall**
2. Using threshold **0.7**, recompute the metrics.
3. Explain how changing the threshold affects:
    - **True Positive Rate**
    - **False Positive Rate**

5. ROC Curve Interpretation

A classifier produces the following points on a **Receiver Operating Characteristic**:

Threshold	TPR	FPR
0.9	0.30	0.05
0.7	0.55	0.10
0.5	0.75	0.25
0.3	0.90	0.50

Table 10-4

Questions:

1. Plot the ROC curve.
2. Which threshold gives the best trade-off?
3. Explain how **Area Under the ROC Curve** summarizes model performance.

6. Model Diagnosis

A model has:

- Training accuracy: **95%**
- Validation accuracy: **93%**

Another model has:

- Training accuracy: **95%**
- Validation accuracy: **60%**

Questions:

1. Which model generalizes better?
2. Which one likely suffers from **overfitting**?
3. Suggest improvements.

7. Advanced Exercise (Realistic Scenario)

A medical screening test predicts whether patients have a disease.

Confusion matrix:

	Predicted Disease	Predicted Healthy
Actual Disease	180	20
Actual Healthy	120	680

Table 10-5

Questions:

1. Compute:
    - Precision
    - Recall
    - **TPR**
    - **FPR**
2. Would you increase or decrease the threshold for medical screening? Explain.
3. Discuss the trade-off between **false positives** and **false negatives** in healthcare.

References

1. Tom Mitchell, *Machine Learning*, McGraw-Hill, 1997.
2. Christopher M. Bishop, *Pattern Recognition and Machine Learning*, Springer, 2006.
3. Trevor Hastie, Robert Tibshirani, and Jerome Friedman, *The Elements of Statistical Learning: Data Mining, Inference, and Prediction*, Springer, 2009.
4. Kevin P. Murphy, *Machine Learning: A Probabilistic Perspective*, MIT Press, 2012.
5. Tom Fawcett, "An Introduction to ROC Analysis," *Pattern Recognition Letters*, vol. 27, no. 8, pp. 861–874, 2006. (OUCI)
6. Andrew P. Bradley, "The Use of the Area Under the ROC Curve in the Evaluation of Machine Learning Algorithms," *Pattern Recognition*, vol. 30, no. 7, pp. 1145–1159, 1997. (ScienceDirect)
7. Tilmann Gneiting and Peter Vogel, "Receiver Operating Characteristic (ROC) Curves: Equivalences, Beta Model, and Minimum Distance Estimation," *Machine Learning*, vol. 111, pp. 2147–2159, 2022. (Springer Nature Link)
8. David J. Hand, "Measuring Classifier Performance: A Coherent Alternative to the Area Under the ROC Curve," *Machine Learning*, vol. 77, no. 1, pp. 103–123, 2009. (Springer Nature Link)

9. Kevin Woods and Kevin W. Bowyer, "Generating ROC Curves for Artificial Neural Networks," *IEEE Transactions on Medical Imaging*, vol. 16, no. 3, pp. 329–337, 1997. (PubMed)

10. Tom Fawcett. **"An Introduction to ROC Analysis."** *Pattern Recognition Letters*, 27(8), 861–874, 2006.

11. Chapter 11: Naïve Bayes Classifier

Learning Objectives

After reading this chapter, you will be able to:

1. Apply Bayes' theorem to compute conditional probabilities.
2. Explain the independence assumption in Naive Bayes classification.
3. Perform step-by-step probability calculations for classification tasks.
4. Implement Naive Bayes models using Scikit-learn.
5. Apply Naive Bayes to real-world problems such as text classification.

Introduction

The Naive Bayes algorithm is a classification technique derived from Bayes' Theorem. The term *naive* means simple. It is called naive because it assumes that all input features are independent of one another, an assumption that is often unrealistic in real-world data.

Naive Bayes classifiers are simple probabilistic models that apply Bayes' theorem to compute class probabilities. Although the independence assumption is rarely fully true in practice, the algorithm performs surprisingly well in many real-world applications due to its simplicity, computational efficiency, and strong predictive performance.

The classifier assumes that the effect of a particular feature on the class outcome is independent of other features. For example, when evaluating whether a loan applicant is eligible, factors such as income, previous loan history, transaction behavior, age, and location may actually be interrelated. However, Naive Bayes treats each of these features as independent. This simplifying assumption reduces computational complexity, which is why the model is described as "naive."

Bayes' Theorem

Bayes' Theorem describes how to calculate the conditional probability of an event based on the occurrence of another related event. It states that:

$$P(A|B) = \frac{P(B|A) \times P(A)}{P(B)}$$

Where:

- P(A | B) is the probability that event A occurs given that event B has occurred.
  For example, if we know an email contains the word "offer" (B), this tells us how likely it is that the email is spam (A).
- P(B | A) is the probability of observing event B given that A is true.

If we know an email is spam (A), this indicates how likely it is to contain the word "offer" (B).

- P(A) is the prior probability of A.
  This represents how likely an email is to be spam before considering any specific features.
- P(B) is the prior probability of B.
  This refers to how likely it is to observe the feature "offer" in any email, regardless of whether it is spam or not.

Together, these probabilities allow us to update our belief about an event as new evidence becomes available.

Conditional Probability

Conditional probability is the likelihood of an event occurring, given that another event has already occurred. In probability this is denoted as A given B, expressed as P (A | B), indicating the probability of event A when event B has already occurred.

Example:

We flip two coins. What is the probability that both are heads, given that at least one of them is heads?

We are given that there is at least one head. So there are three possibilities HH, HT, TH. Only one outcome has both coins as heads: HH.

So our answer is = 1/3

$$P(B/A) = \frac{P(B \cap A)}{P(A)}$$

Conditional probability is defined as the likelihood of an event or outcome occurring, based on the occurrence of a previous event or outcome.

Independent vs Mutually exclusive events:

If P(A/B) is P(A) or P(B/A) is P(B) then A & B are known as independent events.

If P(A/B) = P(B/A) =0, then A & B are known as mutually exclusive event

Conditional probability is defined as the likelihood of an event or outcome occurring, based on the occurrence of a previous event or outcome.

Independent vs Mutually exclusive events:

if P(a/b) is P(a) or P(b/a) is P(b) then A & B known as independent event.

if P(a/b) = P(b/a) =0 then A & B known as mutually exclusive event

Independent vs Mutually Exclusive events

$$\textbf{posterior} = \frac{\textbf{prior} \times \textbf{likelihood}}{\textbf{evidence}}$$

Applications

1) Naive Bayes considered as benchmark (base line) model specially for **text classification**
2) **Spam Filtering**: The use of algorithms to identify and block unsolicited emails or messages.
3) **Sentiment Analysis**: The use of natural language processing to determine the sentiment expressed in a piece of text.
4) **Medical Diagnosis:** Helps in predicting the likelihood of a disease based on symptoms.
5) **Credit Scoring:** Evaluates creditworthiness of individuals for loan approval.
6) **Weather Prediction**: Classifies weather conditions based on various factors.

Types of Naïve Bayes Classifier

1. Multinomial Naive Bayes:

   This variant is primarily used for text and document classification tasks, such as determining whether a document belongs to categories like sports, politics, or technology. The features used by this model are typically the frequency or count of words present in the document.

2. Bernoulli Naive Bayes:

   This model is similar to Multinomial Naive Bayes; however, the predictors are binary (Boolean) variables. Instead of word counts, it considers whether a particular word appears or does not appear in the document—represented as Yes/No (1/0).

3. Gaussian Naive Bayes:

   This variant is used when the predictors are continuous-valued features rather than discrete ones. It assumes that the feature values follow a Gaussian (normal) distribution within each class.

$$f(x) = \frac{1}{\sqrt{2\pi}} e^{-\frac{x^2}{2}}$$

Gaussian Distribution

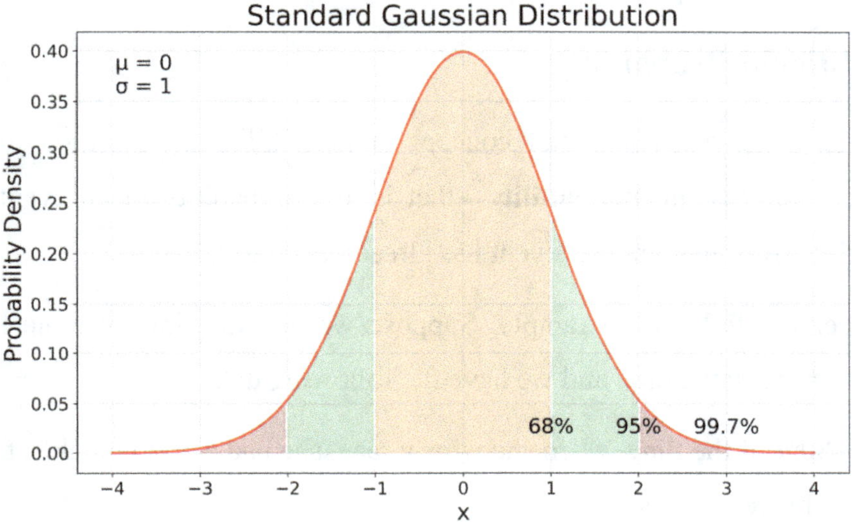

Figure 11-1: Gaussian Distribution

The Gaussian distribution, often called the normal distribution or "bell curve," is a continuous probability distribution in which most values cluster around a central average. It is symmetric and effectively models many real-world phenomena.

Key Parameters

The shape of a Gaussian curve is fully determined by two parameters:

Mean (μ): This is the central peak of the distribution. For a Gaussian distribution, the mean, median, and mode are all the same.

Standard Deviation (σ): This indicates how spread out the data is. A smaller standard deviation results in a tall, narrow curve, whereas a larger standard deviation produces a wider, flatter curve.

Conditional Probability

Bayes' rule is a fundamental concept in probability theory used to compute **conditional probability**—that is, the probability of an event occurring given that another event has already occurred.

Consider the following example. Suppose we are advising an athlete about her pre-game diet, and we have the following data:

- 80% of the time, when she **wins** a race, she had a good breakfast. This represents
  $P(\text{Breakfast} \mid \text{Win}) = 0.8.$
- 60% of the time, she eats a good breakfast. This is
  $P(\text{Breakfast}) = 0.6.$
- She wins 20% of her races overall. This gives
  $P(\text{Win}) = 0.2.$

Using Bayes' rule, we can calculate the probability that she wins **given** that she had a good breakfast:

$$\boldsymbol{P(\text{Win} \mid \text{Breakfast}) = \frac{P(\text{Breakfast} \mid \text{Win}) \times P(\text{Win})}{P(\text{Breakfast})} = \frac{0.8 \times 0.2}{0.6} = 0.26}$$

This means that the probability she wins the race given that she had a good breakfast is **26%**.

In practical terms, this suggests that a nutritious breakfast may contribute positively to her performance—perhaps those extra carbohydrates provide sustained energy throughout the competition.

How Naïve Bayes Algorithm works?

Our objective is to predict whether a player will **Play** or **Not Play** based on the prevailing weather conditions. To achieve this, we will train a dataset using weather attributes as input features and **'Play'** as the target variable.

Weather	Play
Sunny	No
Overcast	Yes
Rainy	Yes
Sunny	Yes
Overcast	No
Rainy	No
Sunny	Yes
Rainy	Yes
Overcast	No
Rainy	Yes

Figure 11-2

Naïve Bayes Algorithm

Example 1

Problem: Players will play if weather is sunny. Is this statement correct?

$$P(\text{Yes} \mid \text{Sunny}) = \frac{P(\text{Sunny} \mid \text{Yes}) \times P(\text{Yes})}{P(\text{Sunny})}$$

Weather	Play
Sunny	No
Overcast	Yes
Rainy	Yes
Sunny	Yes
Sunny	Yes
Overcast	Yes
Rainy	No
Rainy	No
Sunny	Yes
Rainy	Yes
Sunny	No
Overcast	Yes
Overcast	Yes
Rainy	No

Frequency Table

Weather	No	Yes
Overcast	0	4
Rainy	3	2
Sunny	2	3
Grand Total	5	9

Likelihood Table

Weather	No	Yes	P(Yes | Weather)
Overcast	0/14	4/14	0.29
Rainy	3/14	2/14	0.36
Sunny	2/14	3/14	0.36
All	5/14	9/14	

Figure 11-3

Problem: Players will play if weather is sunny. Is this statement correct?

$$P(\text{Yes} \mid \text{Sunny}) = \frac{P(\text{Sunny} \mid \text{Yes}) \times P(\text{Yes})}{P(\text{Sunny})}$$

Here we have:

$$P(\text{Sunny} \mid \text{Yes}) = \frac{3}{9} = 0.33$$

$$P(\text{Sunny}) = \frac{5}{14} = 0.36$$

$$P(\text{Yes}) = \frac{9}{14} = 0.64$$

Now,

$$P(\text{Yes} \mid \text{Sunny}) = \frac{0.33 \times 0.64}{0.36} = 0.60 \text{ (high probability)}$$

Weather	Play
Sunny	No
Overcast	Yes
Rainy	Yes
Sunny	Yes
Sunny	Yes
Overcast	Yes
Rainy	No
Sunny	Yes

Frequency Table		
Weather	No	Yes
Overcast	0	4
Rainy	3	2
Sunny	2	3
Grand Total	5	9

Likelihood Table			
Weather	No	Yes	P(Yes I Weather)
Overcast	0/14	4/14	0.29
Rainy	3/14	2/14	0.36
Sunny	2/14	3/14	0.36
All	5/14	9/14	

Figure 11-4

Example 2

For Outlook = Rainy, Temp = Mild, Humidity = Normal,

Windy = True, YES or No?

Outlook	Temp	Humidity	Windy	Play Golf
Rainy	Hot	High	False	No
Rainy	Hot	High	True	No
Overcast	Hot	High	False	Yes
Sunny	Mild	High	False	Yes
Sunny	Cool	Normal	False	Yes
Sunny	Cool	Normal	False	Yes
Sunny	Cool	Normal	True	No
Rainy	Mild	High	False	No
Rainy	Cool	Normal	False	Yes
Overcast	Mild	Normal	True	Yes
Sunny	Mild	High	True	No

Problem2: Rainy Mild Normal True ???

Figure 11-5

Here, first let us prepare frequency tables.

Frequency Tables

		Play Golf	
		Yes	No
Outlook	Sunny	3 9/9	2 2/9
	Overcast	4 4/9	0 0/5
	Rainy	2 2/9	3 3/5

		Play Golf	
		Yes	No
Temp.	Hot	2 2/9	2 2/5
	Mild	4 4/9	2 2/5
	Cool	3 3/9	1 1/5

		Play Golf	
		Yes	No
Humidity	High	3 9/9	4 4/9
	Normal	6 6/9	1 1/5

		Play Golf	
		Yes	No
Windy	False	6 9/9	2 2/5
	True	3 3/9	3 3/5

Figure 11-6

		Play Golf	
		Yes	No
Outlook	Sunny	3.3/9	2 2/5
	Overcast	4 4/9	0 0/5
	Rainy	2.2/9	3 3/5

		Play Golf	
		Yes	No
Temp.	Hot	2.2/9	2 2/9
	Mild	4.6/9	2 2/5
	Cool	3.9/9	1 1/5

		Play Golf	
		Yes	No
Humidity	High	3.9/9	4 4/9
	Normal	6.6/9	1 1/5

		Play Golf	
		Yes	No
Windy	False	6.6/9	2 3/5
	True	3.3/9	2 3/5

Figure 11-7

Problem2: For Outlook = Rainy, Temp = Mild, Humidity = Normal, Windy = True, YES or No?

Likelihood of Yes

= P(Outlook = Rainy | Yes) × P(Temp = Mild | Yes) × P(Humidity = Normal | Yes) × P(Windy = True | Yes) × P(Yes)

$$= \left(\frac{2}{9}\right)\times\left(\frac{4}{9}\right)\times\left(\frac{6}{9}\right)\times\left(\frac{6}{9}\right)\times\left(\frac{3}{9}\right)\times\left(\frac{9}{14}\right) = \mathbf{0.141}$$

Likelihood of No

= P(Outlook = Rainy | No) × P(Temp = Mild | No) × P(Humidity = Normal | No) × P(Windy = True | No) × P(No)

$$= \left(\frac{3}{5}\right)\times\left(\frac{2}{5}\right)\times\left(\frac{1}{5}\right)\times\left(\frac{3}{5}\right)\times\left(\frac{3}{14}\right)\times\left(\frac{5}{14}\right) = \mathbf{0.0103}$$

= **0.0103**

		Play Golf	
		Yes	No
Outlook	Sunny	3 3/9	2 2/5
	Overcast	4 4/9	0 0/5
	Rainy	2 2/9	3 3/5

		Play Golf	
		Yes	No
Temp.	Hot	2 2/9	2 2/5
	Mild	4 4/9	2 2/5
	Cool	3 3/9	1 1/5

		Play Golf	
		Yes	No
Humidity	High	3 3/9	4 4/9
	Normal	6 6/9	1 1/5

		Play Golf	
		Yes	No
Windy	False	6 6/9	2 2/5
	True	3 3/9	3 3/5

Problem2: For Outlook = Rainy, Temp = Mild, Humidity = Normal, Windy = True, YES or No?

Likelihood of yes = **0.141**
Likelihood of No = **0.0103**

After Normalizaion,
Yes = 0.141 / / (0.1411 + 0.0103) = **0.58**
No = 0.0103 / (0.1411 + 0.0103) = **0.42**

Figure 11-8

Problem2: For Outlook = Rainy, Temp = Mild, Humidity = Normal, Windy = True, YES or No?

YES

		Play Golf	
		Yes	No
Outlook.	Sunny	3 3/9	2 2/9
	Overcast	4 4/9	0 0/5
	Rainy	2 2/9	3 3/5

		Play Golf	
		Yes	No
Temp.	Hot	2 2/9	2 2/5
	Mild	4 4/9	2 2/5
	Cool	3 3/9	1 3/5

		Play Golf	
		Yes	No
Humidity	High	3 3/9	4 4/9
	Normal	6 6/9	1 1/5

		Play Golf	
		Yes	No
Windy	False	6 9/9	2 2/5
	True	3 3/9	3 3/5

Figure 11-9

Hands-On Real-World Classification Project

Problem Statement - Build a Breast Cancer Detection classifier using Gaussian Naive Bayes. You will use the Wisconsin Diagnostic Breast Cancer (WDBC) dataset (available through scikit-learn's load_breast_cancer() function). Your goal is to predict whether a tumor is malignant or benign using 30 numeric features.

Instructions

Fill in the blanks (____) in the code snippets. Run each step in your Jupyter notebook. After each step, answer the short questions to confirm understanding.

Step 1 — Import Libraries

Explanation: Import NumPy/Pandas for data handling and scikit-learn utilities for loading data, splitting, scaling, modeling, and evaluation.

```
import numpy as np
import pandas as pd

from sklearn.datasets import load_breast_cancer
from sklearn.model_selection import train_test_split
from sklearn.preprocessing import StandardScaler
from sklearn.naive_bayes import GaussianNB
from sklearn.metrics import accuracy_score, confusion_matrix, classification_report
```

Step 2 — Load the Dataset

Explanation: load_breast_cancer() returns a Bunch object containing features (data), labels (target), feature names, and class names.

```
data = ____

X = ____   # features
y = ____   # target labels

print("X shape:", X.shape)
print("y shape:", y.shape)
```

Checkpoint: What are the number of samples and features?

Answer: samples = _________ , features = _________

Step 3 — Create a DataFrame (Optional but Helpful)

Explanation: A DataFrame makes it easier to inspect feature names, summary stats, and class distribution.

```
feature_names = ____
df = pd.DataFrame(____, columns=feature_names)

# 0 = malignant, 1 = benign in this dataset
df["target"] = ____

df.head()
```

Checkpoint: What does target=0 represent? _________ What does target=1 represent? _________

Step 4 — Basic Data Checks

Explanation: Check class balance to ensure both classes are represented; this matters for evaluation.

```
print(df["target"].value_counts())  # class distribution
print(df.describe().T.head(8))      # quick stats (first 8 features)
```

Question: Is the dataset balanced? (Yes/No) ________ Briefly explain: ________________________________

Step 5 — Train/Test Split

Explanation: Split the data so we train on one portion and evaluate on unseen data. Use stratify=y to preserve class ratio.

```
X_train, X_test, y_train, y_test = train_test_split(
    ____, ____, test_size=____, random_state=____, stratify=____
)

print("Train size:", X_train.shape[0])
print("Test size :", X_test.shape[0])
```

Fill: test_size = ______ random_state = _______ stratify = _______

Step 6 — Standardize Features

Explanation: GaussianNB assumes each feature is normally distributed within each class. Scaling is not strictly required for GaussianNB, but it often helps numerical stability and fair contribution of features.

```
scaler = StandardScaler()

X_train_scaled = scaler.fit_transform(____)  # fit on train
X_test_scaled = scaler.transform(____)       # transform test
```

Question: Why do we fit the scaler only on the training data? ________________________________

Step 7 — Train Gaussian Naive Bayes

Explanation: Train GaussianNB using the scaled training data.

```
model = GaussianNB(____)

model.fit(____, ____)
```

Fill: model parameters (if any) = _____ Fit inputs = (_____ , _____)

Step 8 — Evaluate the Model

Explanation: Evaluate accuracy and inspect errors using confusion matrix and classification report (precision/recall/F1).

```
y_pred = model.predict(____)

acc = accuracy_score(____, ____)
print("Accuracy:", round(acc, 4))

cm = confusion_matrix(____, ____)
print("Confusion Matrix:\n", cm)

print(classification_report(____, ____, target_names=data.target_names))
```

Checkpoint: Write your accuracy here: ________

Question: Which class is more important to catch correctly in medical screening? Why? ______________________________

Step 9 — Predict One Sample

Explanation: Predict class label and probability for a single example. This helps interpret model output.

```
sample = X_test_scaled[0].reshape(1, -1)

pred_class = model.predict(____)[0]
pred_prob = model.predict_proba(____)[0]

print("Predicted class:", data.target_names[pred_class])
print("Probabilities [malignant, benign]:", np.round(pred_prob, 4))
```

Checkpoint: Predicted class = ______ Probabilities = ___________

Mini Exercises

1) Change test_size to 0.30 and re-run Steps 5–8. New accuracy: ________

2) Skip scaling (use X_train and X_test directly) and re-run Steps 7–8. Accuracy without scaling: ________

3) Explain one limitation of the Naive Bayes independence assumption for this dataset: ________________________________

Summary

In this chapter, we explored the **Naive Bayes classifier**, a probabilistic algorithm based on **Bayes' Theorem**. The model is called *naive* because it assumes that all features are conditionally independent given the class label. Although this assumption is often unrealistic, it simplifies computation and makes the algorithm highly efficient.

We discussed how Naive Bayes computes posterior probabilities using prior probability and likelihood, and then selects the class with the highest probability. The three main variants—**Multinomial**, **Bernoulli**, and **Gaussian Naive Bayes**—were introduced for handling count-based, binary, and continuous features respectively.

Despite its simplicity, Naive Bayes performs well in real-world applications such as text classification, spam detection, and decision-making problems, making it a widely used and practical classification technique.

Exercises

Section A: Conceptual Questions

1. Define Bayes' Theorem. Explain each term in the formula.
2. Why is the Naive Bayes classifier called "naive"?

3. What is meant by conditional independence? Why is this assumption important in Naive Bayes?
4. Differentiate between:
    - Multinomial Naive Bayes
    - Bernoulli Naive Bayes
    - Gaussian Naive Bayes
5. In which situations would Gaussian Naive Bayes be preferred over Multinomial Naive Bayes?
6. Even though the independence assumption is often unrealistic, Naive Bayes performs well in practice. Why?

Section B: Mathematical Problems

Exercise 1 Basic Bayes Theorem Application

A company finds that:

- 30% of emails are spam.
- 70% of spam emails contain the word “discount.”
- 20% of non-spam emails contain the word “discount.”

Find:

a) $P(\text{discount})$

b) $P(\text{Spam} \mid \text{discount})$

Exercise 2 Weather Classification Problem

Given the dataset:

Weather	Play
Sunny	No
Sunny	No
Overcast	Yes
Rainy	Yes
Rainy	Yes
Sunny	Yes

Table 11-1

Using Naive Bayes, compute:

a) $P(\text{Yes})$

b) $P(\text{Sunny} \mid \text{Yes})$

c) $P(\text{Sunny} \mid \text{No})$

d) Predict whether a player will play if Weather = Sunny.

Exercise 3 Continuous Feature Problem (Gaussian NB)

Suppose exam scores follow a normal distribution:

Class A:

- Mean = 70
- Standard deviation = 5

Class B:

- Mean = 60
- Standard deviation = 4

Prior probabilities:

- $P(A) = 0.6$
- $P(B) = 0.4$

A student scores 65.

Using Gaussian Naive Bayes:

a) Compute likelihood under both classes.

b) Compute posterior probabilities.

c) Predict the class.

References

1. C. M. Bishop, *Pattern Recognition and Machine Learning*. New York, NY, USA: Springer, 2006.
2. T. M. Mitchell, *Machine Learning*. New York, NY, USA: McGraw-Hill, 1997.
3. K. P. Murphy, *Machine Learning: A Probabilistic Perspective*. Cambridge, MA, USA: MIT Press, 2012.
4. J. Han, M. Kamber, and J. Pei, *Data Mining: Concepts and Techniques*, 3rd ed. Burlington, MA, USA: Morgan Kaufmann, 2011.
5. D. D. Lewis, "Naive (Bayes) at forty: The independence assumption in information retrieval," in *Proc. Eur. Conf. Mach. Learn. (ECML)*, 1998.
6. H. Zhang, "The optimality of Naive Bayes," in *Proc. 17th Int. Florida Artif. Intell. Res. Soc. Conf. (FLAIRS)*, 2004.
   A. McCallum and K. Nigam, "A comparison of event models for Naive Bayes text classification," in *Proc. AAAI-98 Workshop on Learning for Text Categorization*, 1998.
7. J. D. M. Rennie, L. Shih, J. Teevan, and D. R. Karger, "Tackling the poor assumptions of Naive Bayes text classifiers," in *Proc. 20th Int. Conf. Mach. Learn. (ICML)*, 2003.
8. W. H. Wolberg, O. L. Mangasarian, N. Street, and W. Street, "Breast Cancer Wisconsin (Diagnostic) (WDBC)," UCI Machine Learning Repository, 1993. doi: 10.24432/C5DW2B.

9. scikit-learn, "sklearn.datasets.load_breast_cancer," Documentation.
10. scikit-learn, "sklearn.naive_bayes.GaussianNB," Documentation.
11. scikit-learn, "sklearn.model_selection.train_test_split," Documentation.
12. scikit-learn, "sklearn.preprocessing.StandardScaler," Documentation.

12. Chapter 12: Decision Trees

Learning Objectives

After reading this chapter, you will be able to:

1. Explain how decision trees model decision-making processes.
2. Calculate entropy, information gain, and Gini index for splitting.
3. Construct and interpret decision tree models.
4. Control overfitting using pruning techniques.
5. Implement decision trees using Scikit-learn for classification tasks.

Introduction

Decision Tree classification algorithm is a tree-based model that consists of internal nodes, branches, and leaves. The internal nodes represent the features or attributes of the data, the branches represent the decisions or rules, and the leaves represent the outcomes or predictions.

Decision tree algorithm is used to classify or predict outcomes based on a set of rules.

It works by splitting the data into subsets based on the values of the input features.

The algorithm recursively splits the data until it reaches a point where the data in each subset belongs to the same class or has the same value for the target variable.

The resulting tree is a set of decision rules that can be used to make predictions or classify new data.

Decision Tree algorithm works by selecting the best feature to split the data at each node.

The best feature is the one that provides the most information gain or the most reduction in entropy.

Information gain is a measure of the amount of information gained by splitting the data at a particular feature,

Entropy is a measure of randomness or disorder in the data.

The algorithm uses these measures to determine the best feature to split the data at each node.

Types of Decision Trees

Classification trees: They are designed to predict categorical outcomes, which means they classify data into different classes.

They can determine whether an email is "spam" or "not spam" based on various features of the email.

Regression trees: These are used when the target variable is continuous.

It predicts numerical values rather than categories. For example, a regression tree can estimate the price of a house based on its size, location, and other features.

ID3:

Ross Quinlan is credited within the development of ID3, which is shorthand for “Iterative Dichotomiser 3.” This algorithm leverages entropy and information gain as metrics to evaluate candidate splits.

C4.5:

This algorithm is considered a later iteration of ID3, which was also developed by Quinlan. It can use information gain or gain ratios to evaluate split points within the decision trees.

CART:

The term, CART, is an abbreviation for “classification and regression trees” and was introduced by Leo Breiman. This algorithm typically utilizes Gini impurity to identify the ideal attribute to split on. Gini impurity measures how often a randomly chosen attribute is misclassified. When evaluating using Gini impurity, a lower value is more ideal.

Age	**income**	**student**	**credit_rating**	**buys_computer**
<=20	high	No	Fair	no
<=20	high	No	excellent	no
20…30	high	No	Fair	Yes
>30	medium	Fair	no	yes
>30	Low	Yes	Fair	Yes
>30	low	Yes	Excellent	yes
20..30	Medium	No	Fair	no
<=20	Medium	Yes	excellent	no
>30	Medium	Yes	Fair	Yes
20..30	Medium	No	Excellent	Yes
<=20	high	Yes	Fair	yes
>30	Medium	Yes	excellent	yes
20..30	high	Yes	excellent	yes
>30	medium	No	excellent	no

Table 12-1

Output: A Decision Tree for "*buys_computer*"

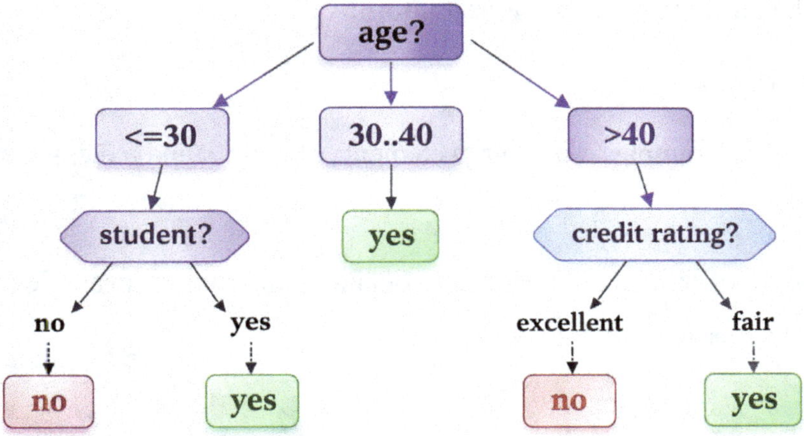

Figure 12-1: Decision Tree for "Buys computer"

Attribute Selection Measure

1) Information gain (ID3/C4.5)

All attributes are assumed to be categorical

Can be modified for continuous-valued attributes

2) Gini index (CART)

All attributes are assumed continuous valued

Assume there exist several possible split values for each attribute

May need other tools, such as clustering, to get the possible split values

Can be modified for categorical attributes

Information Gain (ID3/C4.5)

Select the attribute with the highest information gain

Assume there are two classes, *P* and *N*

Let the set of examples *S* contain *p* elements of class *P* and *n* elements of class *N*

The amount of information needed to decide if an arbitrary example in *S* belongs to *P* or *N* is defined as

$$I(p,n) = -\frac{p}{p+n}\log_2\frac{p}{p+n} - \frac{n}{p+n}\log_2\frac{n}{p+n}$$

Entropy

$$E = -\sum_{i=1}^{n} p_i \, log_2(p_i)$$

Where the pi is the probability of randomly selecting an example in class i.

Entropy values can fall between 0 and 1.

If all samples in data set, S, belong to one class, then entropy will equal zero.

If half of the samples are classified as one class and the other half are in another class, entropy will be at its highest at 1.

To select the best feature to split on and find the optimal decision tree, the attribute with the smallest amount of entropy should be used.

Information Gain

Information gain represents the difference in entropy before and after a split on a given attribute. The attribute with the highest information gain produces the best split because it classifies the training data most effectively according to its target classification.

Information gain is usually represented with the following formula:

$$\text{Information Gain}(S, a) = Entropy(S) - \sum_{v \in values(a)} \frac{|S_v|}{|S|} Entropy(S_v)$$

A represents a specific attribute or class label, and

Entropy(S) is the entropy of dataset, S

|Sv|/|S| represents the proportion of the values in Sv to the number of values in dataset, S.

Information Gain in Decision Tree Induction

Assume that using attribute A a set *S* will be partitioned into sets $\{S_1, S_2, \ldots, S_v\}$

If S_i contains p_i examples of P and n_i examples of N, the entropy, or the expected information needed to classify objects in all subtrees S_i is

The encoding information that would be gained by branching on A

$$E(A) = \sum_{i=1}^{v} \frac{p_i + n_i}{p + n} I(p_i, n_i)$$

$$Gain(A) = I(p, n) - E(A)$$

Attribute Selection by Information Gain Computation

Class P: buys_computer = "yes"

Class N: buys_computer = "no"

I(p, n) = I(9, 5) =0.940

Compute the entropy for *age*:

age	p_i	n_i	$I(p_i, n_i)$
<=30	2	3	0.971
30...40	4	0	0
>40	3	2	0.971

Table 12-2

$$E(age) = \frac{5}{14} I(2,3) + \frac{4}{14} I(4,0) + \frac{5}{14} I(3,2) = 0.971$$

Hence

$$Gain(age) = I(p,n) - E(age)$$

Similarly,

$Gain(income) = 0.029$
$Gain(student) = 0.151$
$Gain(credit\_rating) = 0.048$

Extracting Classification Rules from Trees

1) Represent the knowledge in the form of IF-THEN rules
2) One rule is created for each path from the root to a leaf
3) Each attribute-value pair along a path forms a conjunction
4) The leaf node holds the class prediction
5) Rules are easier for humans to understand

Example

```
IF age <= 20 AND student = no THEN buys_computer = no
IF age <= 20 AND student = yes THEN buys_computer = yes
IF age = 21 to 30 THEN buys_computer = yes
IF age > 30 AND credit_rating = excellent THEN buys_computer = yes
IF age <= 20 AND credit_rating = fair THEN buys_computer = no
```

Enhancements to Basic Decision Tree Induction

Basic decision tree induction can be improved in several ways to increase accuracy and flexibility.

One enhancement is allowing continuous valued attributes. This involves dynamically defining new discrete valued attributes that partition continuous attribute values into a set of meaningful intervals.

Another improvement is handling missing attribute values. This can be done by assigning the most common value of the attribute or by assigning probabilities to each of the possible values.

Attribute construction is also an important enhancement. New attributes can be created based on existing ones that are sparsely represented. This helps reduce fragmentation, repetition, and replication within the decision tree.

Decision Tree Implementation Example

This example illustrates how to implement a Decision Tree classifier in Python.

In this example, social network advertisements data is used. The dataset contains information about users such as gender, age, and estimated salary. Based on these features, each user is classified according to whether they purchase insurance or not.

Step 1 - Import Libraries

Pandas is used for data manipulation, NumPy is used for mathematical calculations, and Matplotlib and Seaborn are used for data visualization. Sklearn libraries are used to perform machine learning operations.

Step 2 - Import Data

Download the dataset from Kaggle here [11] and upload it to your notebook and read it into the pandas dataframe.

Dataset

User ID	Gender	Age	EstimatedSalary	Purchased
15624510	Male	19	19000	0
15810944	Male	35	20000	0
15668575	Female	26	43000	0
15603246	Female	27	57000	0
15804002	Male	19	76000	0

Table 12-3

Step 3 - Data Analysis / Preprocessing

1) **Exploratory Data Analysis (EDA)** is a process of analyzing and summarizing the main characteristics of a dataset, with the goal of gaining insight into the underlying structure, relationships, and patterns within the data. EDA helps to identify important features, anomalies, and trends in the data that can inform further analysis and modeling.
2) EDA typically involves several key steps, including:
3) **Data cleaning and preparation** involve removing missing or

incorrect values, transforming variables, and handling outliers.

4) **Data visualization** is the process of creating graphs, charts, and other visual representations of the data to help identify patterns, relationships, and anomalies.

5) **Statistical analysis** involves applying mathematical and statistical methods to the data to identify important features and relationships.

6) Preprocessing aims to prepare the data in a way that will enable effective analysis and modeling and remove any biases or errors that may affect the results.

7) Get Required Data

8) Drop not required columns. – userid

9) Describe data

10) Get statistical description of data using Pandas describe() function. It shows us the count, mean, standard deviation, and range of data.

11) Distribution of data

12) Check data distribution.

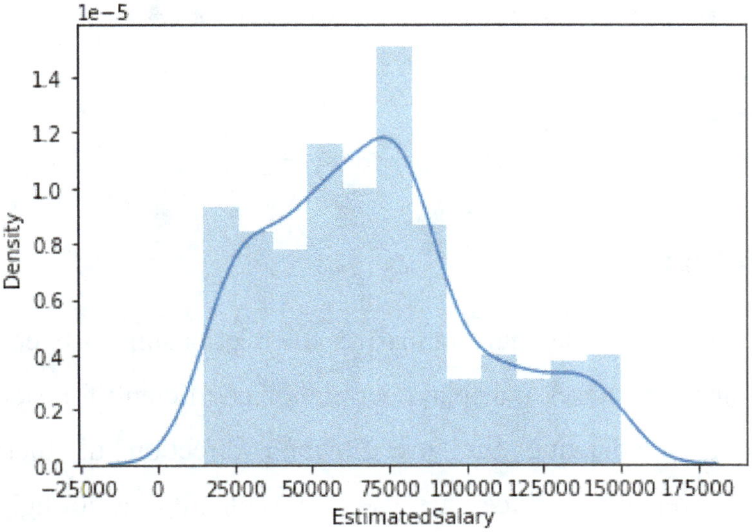

Figure 12-2

Label Encoding

Label encoding is a preprocessing technique in machine learning and data analysis where categorical data is converted into numerical values so it can be used in mathematical operations and machine learning models.

In label encoding, each unique category is assigned a unique integer value, typically starting from zero. This allows categorical data to be treated as numerical data.

```
from sklearn.preprocessing import LabelEncoder

le = LabelEncoder()
df_net["Gender"] = le.fit_transform(df_net["Gender"])
```

Correlation Matrix

A correlation matrix is a table that summarizes the relationships between multiple variables in a dataset. It displays correlation coefficients for each pair of variables, indicating the strength and direction of their relationships. Correlation matrices are useful for identifying strongly related variables and selecting features for further analysis.

The correlation coefficient ranges from negative one to positive one.

A value of negative one indicates a strong negative relationship between two variables.

A value of zero indicates no relationship between two variables.

A value of one indicates a strong positive relationship between two variables.

```
import seaborn as sns
import matplotlib.pyplot as plt

correlation_matrix = df_net.corr()

sns.heatmap(correlation_matrix)

plt.show()
```

	Age	EstimatedSalary	Purchased
Age	1.000000	0.155238	0.622454
EstimatedSalary	0.155238	1.000000	0.362083
Purchased	0.622454	0.362083	1.000000

Table 12-4

Figure 12-3: Heatmap

Drop insignificant data

From the correlation matrix, we see that Gender is not correlated with the other attributes, so it can be dropped from the dataset.

```
# Drop Gender column
df_net.drop(columns=["Gender"], inplace=True)
```

	Age	EstimatedSalary	Purchased
0	19	19000	0
1	35	20000	0
2	26	43000	0
3	27	57000	0
4	19	76000	0

Table 12-5

Step 4 - Split Data

Splitting data into independent and dependent variables involves separating the input features from the target variable. Independent variables are used to predict the value of the dependent variable.

The data is then split into a training set and a test set. The training set is used to fit the model, while the test set is used to evaluate its performance.

Independent and Dependent Variables

In this dataset, Age and EstimatedSalary are the independent variables assigned to X, while Purchased is the dependent variable assigned to y.

```
# Split data into dependent and independent variables
X = df_net.iloc[:, :-1].values
y = df_net.iloc[:, -1].values
```

Train and Test Split

The dataset is divided into two parts, with most of the data used for training and a smaller portion used for testing.

The training set helps the model learn optimal parameters. The test set evaluates how well the model performs on unseen data. This is important because training and testing on the same data can cause the model to overfit and perform poorly on new data.

Here, the data is split into 75 percent for training and 25 percent for testing.

```
from sklearn.model_selection import train_test_split

X_train, X_test, y_train, y_test = train_test_split(
    X, y, test_size=0.25, random_state=True
)
```

Step 5 - Feature Scaling

Feature scaling transforms numeric variables so they share a common scale, as many machine learning algorithms are sensitive to differences in feature magnitudes.

There are two common methods of feature scaling: normalization and standardization.

Normalization scales values between 0 and 1 by subtracting the minimum value and dividing by the range.

Standardization transforms values so they have a mean of zero and a standard deviation of one by subtracting the mean and dividing by the standard deviation.

Feature scaling is usually performed before training a model because it can improve performance, reduce training time, and prevent the algorithm from being biased toward features with larger values.

```
from sklearn.preprocessing import StandardScaler

sc = StandardScaler()
X_train = sc.fit_transform(X_train)
X_test = sc.transform(X_test)
```

Step 6 - Train Model

Training a machine learning model involves using the training dataset to estimate the model parameters. The learning algorithm iteratively updates these parameters by minimizing a loss function, which measures the difference between predicted and actual values.

The Decision Tree classifier is trained by passing X_train and y_train into the fit method.

```
from sklearn.tree import DecisionTreeClassifier

classifier = DecisionTreeClassifier(criterion="entropy", random_state=0)
classifier.fit(X_train, y_train)
```

Step 7 - Predict Results and Score Model

Once the model is trained, it can be used to make predictions on new data. Predictions are made by traversing the tree from the root node to a leaf node based on feature values.

The model's accuracy is evaluated using the test set that was held out during training.

```
import numpy as np

y_pred = classifier.predict(X_test)
print(
    np.concatenate(
        (y_pred.reshape(len(y_pred), 1), y_test.reshape(len(y_test), 1)), axis=1
    )
)
```

Classification report

A classification report is a summary of the performance of a classification model. It provides several metrics for evaluating the performance of the model on a classification task, including precision, recall, f1-score, and support.

The classification report also provides a weighted average of the individual class scores, which takes into account the imbalance in the distribution of classes in the dataset.

```
from sklearn.metrics import classification_report

print(f"Classification Report:\n{classification_report(y_test, y_pred)}")
```

```
Classification Report
              precision    recall  f1-score   support

           0       0.87      0.83      0.85        58
           1       0.78      0.83      0.80        42

    accuracy                           0.83       100
   macro avg       0.83      0.83      0.83       100
weighted avg       0.83      0.83      0.83       100
```

Figure 12-4: Classification Report

F1 score

F1-score is the harmonic mean of precision and recall. It provides a single score that balances precision and recall. Support is the number of instances of each class in the evaluation dataset.

```
from sklearn.metrics import f1_score

print(f"F1 Score: {f1_score(y_test, y_pred)}")
```

Confusion Matrix

A confusion matrix evaluates the performance of a classification model by comparing actual class labels with predicted class labels.

True Positives are correctly predicted positive instances.

False Positives are incorrectly predicted positive instances.

True Negatives are correctly predicted negative instances.

False Negatives are incorrectly predicted negative instances.

It provides a clear understanding of model performance and highlights areas for improvement.

```
from sklearn.metrics import confusion_matrix
import seaborn as sns
import matplotlib.pyplot as plt

cf_matrix = confusion_matrix(y_test, y_pred)
sns.heatmap(cf_matrix, annot=True, fmt="d", cmap="Blues", cbar=False)
plt.show()
```

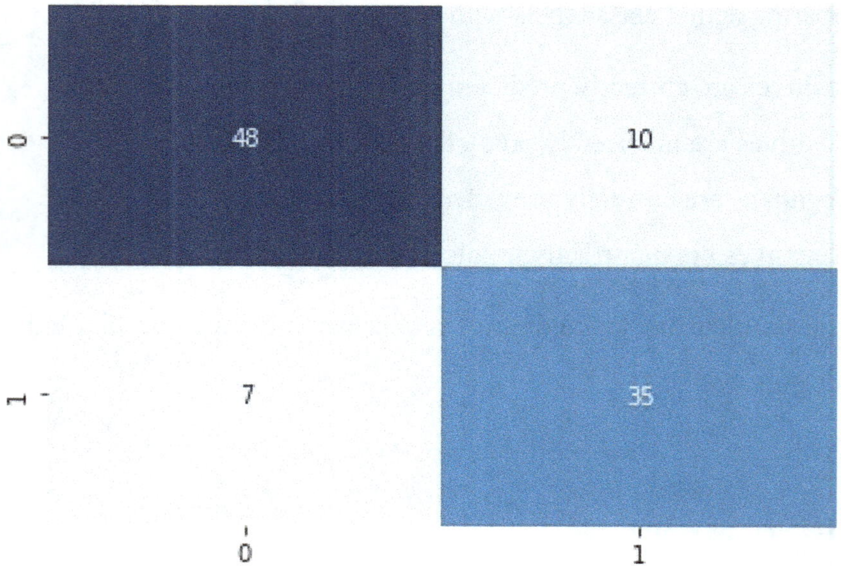

Figure 12-5

Example

Let's see with an example of an Age of 45 and a Salary of 97000 and check if the user is likely to purchase the insurance or not.

```
# Predict purchase with Age 45 and Salary 97000
print(classifier.predict(sc.transform([[45, 97000]])))
```

Predicted value [1] means the user is going to purchase the insurance.

Controlling Overfitting Using Pruning Techniques

In decision tree models, one of the most common challenges is **overfitting**. A decision tree can grow very deep and complex, perfectly fitting the training data. While this may look ideal initially, such a model often fails to generalize to unseen data.

To address this issue, we use a technique called **pruning**, which simplifies the tree by removing unnecessary branches. Pruning helps in improving model generalization, reducing complexity, and making the model more interpretable.

What is Overfitting in Decision Trees?

Overfitting occurs when the decision tree:

- Captures noise instead of true patterns
- Creates overly specific decision rules
- Performs extremely well on training data but poorly on test data

A fully grown tree often has:

- Many levels (depth)
- Small leaf nodes (few samples)
- Complex branching

Such trees are **not robust** for real-world predictions.

What is Pruning?

Pruning is the process of **removing branches of a decision tree that do not contribute significantly to predictive performance**.

The goal is to:

- Reduce model complexity
- Improve generalization
- Avoid memorization of training data

Types of Pruning

There are two main types of pruning techniques:

1. Pre-Pruning

Pre-pruning stops the tree from growing beyond a certain point during training.

Common Pre-Pruning Conditions:

- Maximum depth of the tree (max_depth)
- Minimum samples required to split (min_samples_split)
- Minimum samples required at leaf nodes (min_samples_leaf)
- Minimum impurity decrease

Example

If max_depth = 3, the tree will stop growing after 3 levels, even if further splits are possible.

Advantages

- Faster training
- Prevents overly complex trees early

Limitation

- May stop too early → **underfitting risk**

2. Post-Pruning (Cost Complexity Pruning)

Post-pruning allows the tree to grow fully and then removes unnecessary branches.

The most commonly used method is:

Cost Complexity Pruning (CCP)

Cost Complexity Pruning Concept

In this approach, we balance:

- Tree complexity (number of nodes)
- Model error

The objective is to minimize:

- Prediction error + penalty for complexity

A parameter called **alpha (α)** controls pruning:

- Small α → complex tree
- Large α → simpler tree

How Pruning Works

- Evaluate each subtree
- Check if removing it improves validation performance
- If yes → prune the branch

This results in a **simpler and more generalizable tree**

A simpler tree that generalizes well is better than a complex tree that memorizes data.

Hands-On Implementation (Scikit-learn)

Expected Learning Outcome

After completing this notebook, students will be able to:

- Implement Decision Tree for classification
- Evaluate model performance
- Understand overfitting and pruning
- Apply ML to real-world financial problems

Step 1: Train Full Tree

```
from sklearn.tree import DecisionTreeClassifier

model = DecisionTreeClassifier(random_state=42)
model.fit(X_train, y_train)
```

Step 2: Apply Pre-Pruning

```
model = DecisionTreeClassifier(
    max_depth=4,
    min_samples_split=10,
    min_samples_leaf=5,
    random_state=42
)

model.fit(X_train, y_train)
```

Step 3: Apply Post-Pruning (Cost Complexity)

```
path = model.cost_complexity_pruning_path(X_train, y_train)
alphas = path.ccp_alphas

models = []
for alpha in alphas:
    clf = DecisionTreeClassifier(ccp_alpha=alpha)
    clf.fit(X_train, y_train)
    models.append(clf)
```

Step 4: Select Best Model

```
from sklearn.metrics import accuracy_score

for clf in models:
    y_pred = clf.predict(X_test)
    print(accuracy_score(y_test, y_pred))
```

Effect of Pruning

Model Type	Training Accuracy	Test Accuracy	Complexity
No Pruning	High	Low	Very High
Pre-Pruned	Moderate	High	Moderate
Post-Pruned	Balanced	Highest	Optimal

Table 12-6

When to Use Pruning

- When model shows **high variance**
- When training accuracy >> testing accuracy
- When tree becomes too deep and complex
- When interpretability is required

Pruning vs No Pruning

- Without pruning → very deep tree (overfit)
- With pruning → simpler tree (generalized)

Real-World Insight

- In **healthcare**, pruning helps avoid overly specific rules that may not generalize across patients
- In **finance**, it prevents decisions based on noise in historical data
- In **business analytics**, it improves model interpretability

Hands on Project for Decision Tree

Problem - Design and develop a Machine learning model that can help in Loan repayment Prediction using Decision Tree algorithm

Dataset - Loan Repayment dataset

The Loan Repayment dataset is made up of 1000 rows and six columns. Each row represents information about a particular person that relates to loan repayment. This dataset is perfect for classification algorithms such as the decision tree. The six columns are the following.

Initial payment.

Last payment.

Credit score.

House number.

Sum.

Result.

Step 1: Import Required Libraries

```
# Import required libraries

import _______ as np
import _______ as pd

from sklearn.model_selection import _______
from sklearn.tree import _______
from sklearn.metrics import _______, _______, _______
```

Step 2: Load the Dataset

```
# Load dataset

data = pd.read_csv("_______.csv")

# Display first 5 rows
data._______()
```

Step 3: Explore the Dataset

```
# Check dataset shape
print(data._______)

# Check data types
print(data._______())

# Check missing values
print(data._______())
```

Step 4: Define Features and Target

```
# Define input features (X) and target variable (y)

X = data.drop("_______", axis=1)
y = data["_______"]
```

Step 5: Split the Dataset

```
# Split into training and testing data

X_train, X_test, y_train, y_test = train_test_split(
    X, y,
    test_size=_______,
    random_state=_______
)
```

Step 6: Build Decision Tree Model

```
# Create Decision Tree model

model = DecisionTreeClassifier(
    max_depth=_______,
    random_state=_______
)

# Train the model
model._______(X_train, y_train)
```

Step 7: Make Predictions

```
# Predict on test data

y_pred = model._______(X_test)
```

Step 8: Evaluate the Model

```
# Accuracy
accuracy = ________(y_test, y_pred)
print("Accuracy:", accuracy)

# Confusion Matrix
cm = ________(y_test, y_pred)
print("Confusion Matrix:\n", cm)

# Classification Report
report = ________(y_test, y_pred)
print("Classification Report:\n", report)
```

Step 9: Interpret Results

```
# Print feature importance

importance = model.________
print("Feature Importance:", importance)
```

Step 10: Try Pruning (Control Overfitting)

```
# Apply pruning using max_depth

model_pruned = DecisionTreeClassifier(
    max_depth=________
)

model_pruned.fit(X_train, y_train)

y_pred_pruned = model_pruned.predict(X_test)

print("Pruned Accuracy:", ________(y_test, y_pred_pruned))
```

Summary

In this chapter, we explored **Decision Trees**, one of the most intuitive and widely used supervised learning algorithms for both **classification and regression tasks**. Decision trees mimic human decision-making by breaking down a problem into a series of simple, interpretable rules.

We began by understanding how a decision tree is structured using **nodes, branches, and leaf nodes**, where each split represents a decision based on feature values. The model recursively partitions the dataset to create increasingly homogeneous subsets.

A key concept introduced was **Entropy**, which measures the level of impurity or uncertainty in the data. Lower entropy indicates more homogeneous data. To determine the best feature for splitting the data, we studied **Information Gain**, which quantifies the reduction in entropy after a split. Features with higher information gain are preferred as they create more informative partitions.

We then implemented decision tree models using **Scikit-learn**, learning how to train, test, and evaluate model performance using real-world datasets. This hands-on approach demonstrated how decision trees can be effectively applied to solve practical classification problems.

An important challenge discussed was **overfitting**, where the model becomes too complex and captures noise from the training data. To address this, we explored **pruning techniques**, including:

- **Pre-pruning**, which restricts tree growth during training
- **Post-pruning (Cost Complexity Pruning)**, which simplifies the fully grown tree

These techniques help improve **model generalization**, reduce complexity, and enhance interpretability.

Overall, this chapter provided both **theoretical understanding and practical implementation skills**, enabling learners to build, evaluate, and optimize decision tree models for real-world applications such as finance, healthcare, and business analytics.

Exercises

1. What is a Decision Tree? Explain how it mimics human decision-making.
2. Differentiate between:
   - Root node
   - Internal node
   - Leaf node
3. What is **Entropy**? Why is it important in decision tree construction?
4. Explain **Information Gain** and how it helps in selecting the best feature.
5. What is the difference between **classification trees** and

regression trees?

6. Define **overfitting** in decision trees with an example.
7. What is **pruning** and why is it necessary?
8. Differentiate between **pre-pruning** and **post-pruning**.

Q1: Entropy Calculation

A dataset has 10 samples:

- 6 belong to Class A
- 4 belong to Class B

Calculate the **entropy**.

Q2: Information Gain

A dataset is split using a feature into two subsets:

- Subset 1: 4 A, 1 B
- Subset 2: 2 A, 3 B

Calculate:

1. Entropy of each subset
2. Weighted entropy after split
3. Information Gain

References

1. L. Breiman, J. H. Friedman, R. A. Olshen, and C. J. Stone, *Classification and Regression Trees*. Belmont, CA, USA: Wadsworth, 1984.
2. J. R. Quinlan, "Induction of Decision Trees," *Machine Learning*, vol. 1, no. 1, pp. 81–106, 1986.
3. J. R. Quinlan, *C4.5: Programs for Machine Learning*. San Mateo, CA, USA: Morgan Kaufmann, 1993.
4. T. M. Mitchell, *Machine Learning*. New York, NY, USA: McGraw-Hill, 1997.
5. T. Hastie, R. Tibshirani, and J. Friedman, *The Elements of Statistical Learning*, 2nd ed. New York, NY, USA: Springer, 2009.
6. S. Kotsiantis, "Decision Trees: A Recent Overview," *Artificial Intelligence Review*, vol. 39, no. 4, pp. 261–283, 2013.
7. L. Rokach and O. Maimon, "Top-Down Induction of Decision Trees Classifiers—A Survey," *IEEE Transactions on Systems, Man, and Cybernetics, Part C*, vol. 35, no. 4, pp. 476–487, Nov. 2005.
8. P. Domingos, "A Unified Bias-Variance Decomposition for Zero-One and Squared Loss," in *Proc. AAAI*, 2000, pp. 564–569.
9. A. Liaw and M. Wiener, "Classification and Regression by randomForest," *R News*, vol. 2, no. 3, pp. 18–22, 2002.
10. F. Pedregosa et al., "Scikit-learn: Machine Learning in Python," *Journal of Machine Learning Research*, vol. 12, pp. 2825–2830, 2011.

11. Kaggle dataset https://www.kaggle.com/datasets/rakeshrau/social-network-ads

13. Chapter 13: Neural Networks

Learning Objectives

After reading this chapter, you will be able to:

1. Describe the structure and components of artificial neural networks.
2. Perform forward propagation and understand activation functions.
3. Explain backpropagation and weight updates.
4. Train neural networks using TensorFlow/Keras.
5. Apply neural networks to real-world prediction and classification problems.

Neural Networks

Neural networks are a type of machine learning algorithm inspired by the structure and function of the human brain. Neural networks are sometimes called artificial neural networks (ANNs)

They are used to recognize patterns and make decisions and are the foundation of deep learning algorithms.

Neural networks consist of interconnected nodes or neurons that process data and learn from it.

A neural network makes decisions in a manner similar to the human brain, by using processes that mimic the way biological neurons work together to identify phenomena, weigh options and arrive at conclusions

Biological Neuron

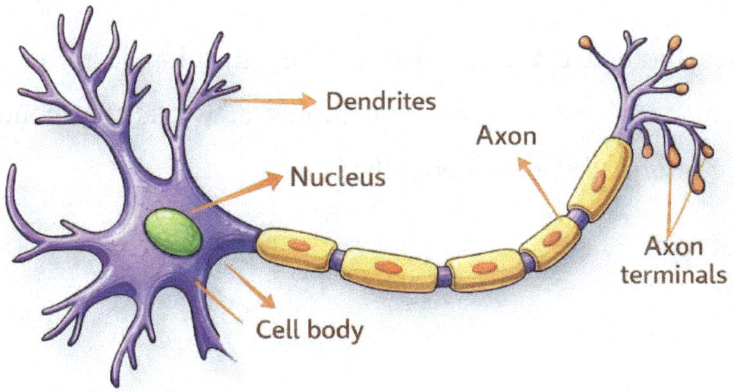

Figure 13-1: Bilogical Neuron

A **biological neuron** is a specialized nerve cell that processes and transmits information in the nervous system using electrical and chemical signals. It is the fundamental unit of the brain, spinal cord, and peripheral nerves.

A neuron consists of several key parts. **Dendrites** receive incoming signals from other neurons or sensory receptors. These signals are integrated in the **cell body (soma)**, which contains the nucleus and controls the cell's metabolic activities. If the combined signal is strong enough, an electrical impulse called an **action potential** is generated and travels along the **axon**. The axon may be covered with a myelin sheath, which increases the speed of signal transmission. At the end of the axon, **axon terminals** transmit the signal to the next neuron or target cell across a synapse using chemical neurotransmitters.

In essence, biological neurons enable communication, learning, memory, and decision-making by forming complex networks that continuously exchange information throughout the body.

Perceptron

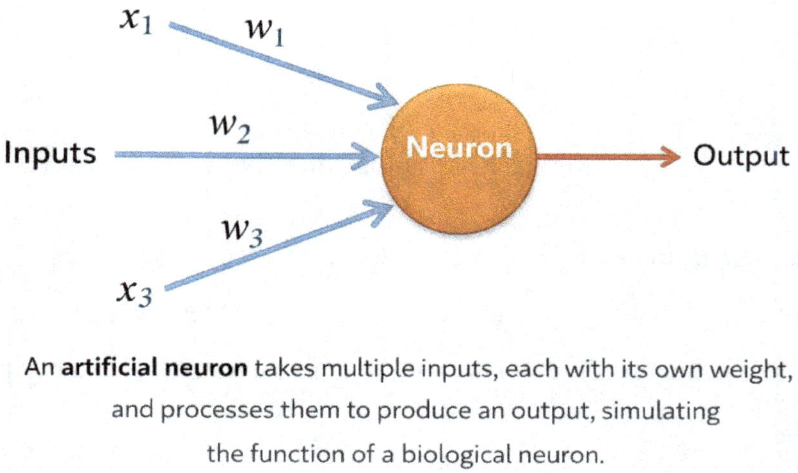

Figure 13-2: Perceptron

A perceptron is the fundamental building block of artificial neural networks, representing a simplified model of a biological neuron.

It takes multiple binary inputs, applies weights to them, sums the weighted inputs, and then passes the sum through an activation function to produce a single binary output.

Perceptron is used for binary classification tasks, deciding whether an input belongs to one class or another.

Model of Artificial Neural Network

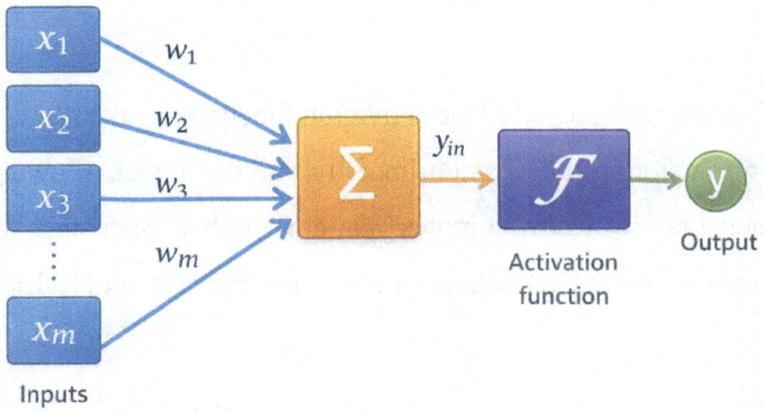

Figure 13-3: Model of Artificial Neural Network

The diagram illustrates the working of a single artificial neuron, which is the fundamental computational unit of a neural network.

On the left side, the neuron receives multiple input features $x_1, x_2, x_3, \dots, x_m$. Each input is associated with a weight $w_1, w_2, w_3, \dots, w_m$. These weights represent the relative importance of each input in contributing to the final output. Inputs that are more relevant to the task are assigned higher weights during training.

All weighted inputs are combined in the summation unit (Σ). This unit computes a weighted sum of the inputs, producing an intermediate value called the net input y_{in}. Mathematically, this can be expressed as:

$$y_{in} = \sum_{i=1}^{m} w_i x_i$$

The net input is then passed to the activation function, denoted by F. The activation function introduces non-linearity into the model, allowing the neural network to learn complex patterns rather than just linear relationships. Common activation functions include sigmoid, ReLU, and tanh.

Finally, the activation function produces the output $y$of the neuron. This output may either serve as the final prediction (in the case of a single-layer model) or be forwarded as input to neurons in the next layer of the network.

In summary, the artificial neuron mimics the behavior of a biological neuron by receiving inputs, weighting them, combining them, applying a decision function, and generating an output.

Neural Network

A **basic neural network** is composed of three primary components: the **input layer**, the **hidden layer(s)**, and the **output layer**.

The **input layer** consists of input nodes that receive raw data from the external environment. This data represents the features provided to the model for learning. The input nodes do not perform any computation; they simply pass the received information to the next layer in the network.

The **hidden layer** is where the actual processing and computation take place. It is made up of artificial neurons that apply mathematical operations to the incoming data. A neural network may contain one or more hidden layers, depending on the complexity of the problem. The simplest form of a neural network includes a single hidden layer.

The **output layer** generates the final result of the network after all internal computations are completed. It may consist of one or multiple neurons. In binary classification tasks, the output layer typically contains a single neuron, whereas in multi-class classification problems, it usually contains multiple neurons—one for each class.

Overall, a neural network is structured as a series of interconnected layers of artificial neurons. Each neuron is linked to neurons in adjacent layers through weighted connections and includes a threshold (or bias) value. When the computed output of a neuron exceeds its threshold, the neuron is activated and passes its output to the next layer. If the threshold is not reached, the neuron remains inactive and does not transmit any signal forward.

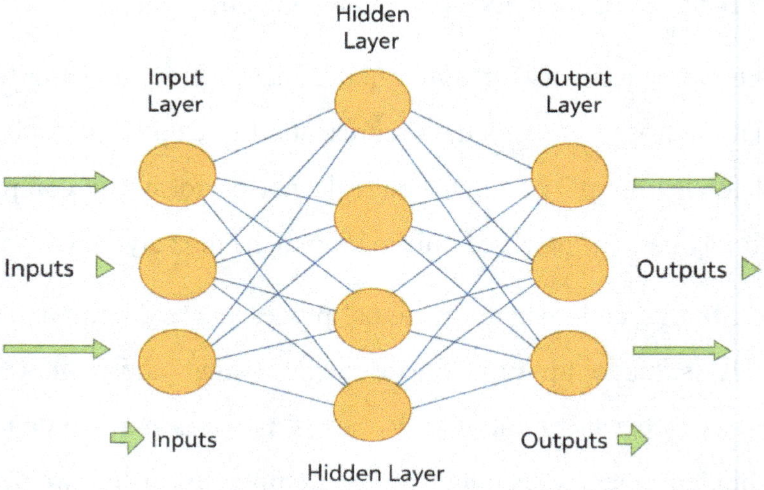

Figure 13-4

The diagram represents a **simple feed-forward artificial neural network** consisting of three main layers: the **input layer**, **hidden layer**, and **output layer**.

The **input arrows** on the left indicate the flow of raw input features into the network. Each input node passes its value to neurons in the hidden layer through weighted connections. These weights determine how strongly each input influences the computation.

The **hidden layer** performs the core processing of the network. Neurons in this layer combine the incoming signals, apply activation functions, and extract meaningful patterns or representations from the input data.

The **output layer** produces the final results of the network. The **output arrows** on the right show the direction in which the processed information leaves the network as predictions or decisions. Depending on the task, the output may represent class labels, probabilities, or numerical values.

Overall, the diagram illustrates how data flows forward through the network—from inputs, through hidden computations, to final outputs—forming the basis of learning and prediction in neural networks.

Multilayer Perceptron

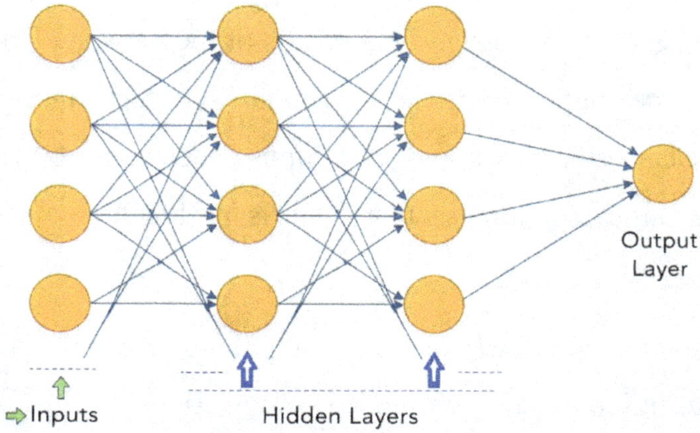

Figure 13-5: Multilayer Perceptron

A **Multilayer Perceptron (MLP)**, also referred to as an **Artificial Neural Network (ANN)**, is composed of multiple perceptrons organized into more than one layer, forming a **multi-layer neural architecture**.

This Artificial Neural Network consists of **four interconnected layers**:

- An **input layer** containing **six input nodes**, which receive the input features.
- **Hidden Layer 1**, consisting of **four hidden nodes (perceptrons)** that perform intermediate computations.
- **Hidden Layer 2**, also consisting of **four hidden nodes**, enabling

the network to learn more complex patterns.

- An **output layer** with **a single output node**, which produces the final prediction or decision of the network.

By stacking multiple hidden layers, the multilayer ANN can model nonlinear relationships and extract hierarchical representations from the input data.

Types of Neural Networks

Neural networks can be classified into several common categories based on their structure and learning mechanisms. Each type is designed to solve specific classes of problems efficiently.

The most widely used neural network types include:

- **Feedforward Neural Networks**
- **Multilayer Feedforward Networks (ANN / MLP)**
- **Convolutional Neural Networks (CNNs)**
- **Backpropagation-Based Neural Networks**

Feedforward Neural Networks

A **feedforward neural network** is the simplest form of artificial neural network. In this architecture, information flows strictly in one direction—from the input layer to the output layer—without forming cycles or feedback loops during inference.

Each neuron in a layer is typically connected to every neuron in the subsequent layer. During training, the network uses feedback in the form of error signals to adjust its weights and improve prediction accuracy over time.

Single-Layer Feedforward Network

A **single-layer feedforward network** consists of only one weighted layer. In this structure:

- The **input layer** is directly connected to the **output layer**
- There are **no hidden layers**
- The network can model only **linearly separable problems**

Because of its simplicity, this type of network has limited representational power.

Multilayer Feedforward Network (ANN / MLP)

A **multilayer feedforward network**, commonly known as an **Artificial Neural Network (ANN)** or **Multilayer Perceptron (MLP)**, contains more than one weighted layer.

These networks include one or more **hidden layers** positioned between the input and output layers. The presence of hidden layers enables the network to learn complex, nonlinear relationships in the data, making multilayer networks suitable for real-world problems such as classification, regression, and pattern recognition.

Convolutional Neural Networks (CNNs)

Convolutional Neural Networks (CNNs) are a specialized class of feedforward neural networks designed to process structured grid-like data such as images, audio signals, and text sequences. They are especially effective in computer vision tasks due to their ability to automatically learn spatial features.

CNNs use **convolution operations** in their hidden layers to extract meaningful patterns such as edges, textures, and shapes. These operations act as feature detectors, enabling the network to focus on important local structures in the input data. CNNs are also commonly referred to as **ConvNets**.

Typical Architecture of a CNN

A CNN is generally composed of the following layers:

- **Input Layer** – Accepts raw input data (e.g., image pixels)
- **Convolutional Layers** – Apply filters to extract features
- **Activation Functions** – Introduce non-linearity
- **Pooling Layers** – Reduce spatial dimensions and computational cost
- **Fully Connected Layers** – Perform high-level reasoning and classification
- **Output Layer** – Produces the final prediction

Applications of CNNs

CNNs are widely used in many real-world applications, including:

1. **Image Classification** – Assigning labels to images (e.g., cat vs. dog)
2. **Object Detection** – Identifying and localizing objects within images
3. **Semantic Segmentation** – Pixel-level image labeling
4. **Video Analysis** – Object tracking and activity recognition
5. **Natural Language Processing** – Text classification and sentiment analysis
6. **Autonomous Systems** – Lane detection, obstacle detection, and traffic sign recognition

Backpropagation Algorithm

The **backpropagation algorithm** is the core learning mechanism used to train artificial neural networks. It enables the network to learn by minimizing prediction errors through iterative weight updates.

Conceptually, information flows forward from the input layer to the output layer along multiple paths. After producing an output, the network compares the predicted result with the actual target value to compute an error.

The learning process follows these steps:

1. Each neuron generates an output based on current weights
2. The error between predicted and actual output is calculated
3. Errors are propagated backward through the network
4. Weights that contribute to correct predictions are strengthened
5. Weights leading to incorrect predictions are reduced
6. The process repeats for each training example

Through repeated iterations, the network gradually converges toward an optimal set of weights.

Activation Functions

What Is an Activation Function?

An **activation function** is a mathematical function applied to a neuron's output to determine whether it should be activated. Activation functions introduce non-linearity into the network, allowing it to model complex relationships.

Activation functions directly influence:

- Model accuracy
- Learning speed
- Computational efficiency

Common Types of Activation Functions

1. Linear

2. Sigmoid
3. Hyperbolic Tangent (tanh)
4. ReLU (Rectified Linear Unit)
5. Softmax

Linear Activation Function

$$f(x) = x$$

The **linear activation function** outputs the input value without modification. It is primarily used in **regression problems** where the output is a continuous numeric value.

However, using linear activation in hidden layers does not introduce non-linearity, which limits the learning capability of deep networks.

Sigmoid Function

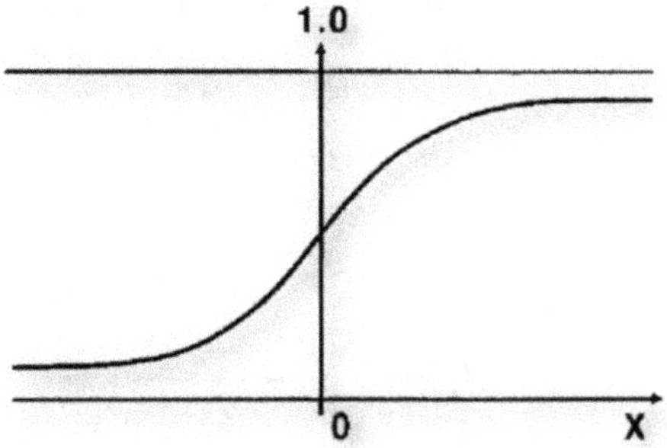

$$f(x) = \frac{1}{1 + e^{-(x)}}$$

Figure 13-6 : Sigmoid Function

The **sigmoid function** maps real-valued inputs to a range between 0 and 1. It is commonly used in **binary classification problems**, where the output represents a probability.

One limitation of sigmoid is the **vanishing gradient problem**, which can slow down learning in deep networks.

Step Function

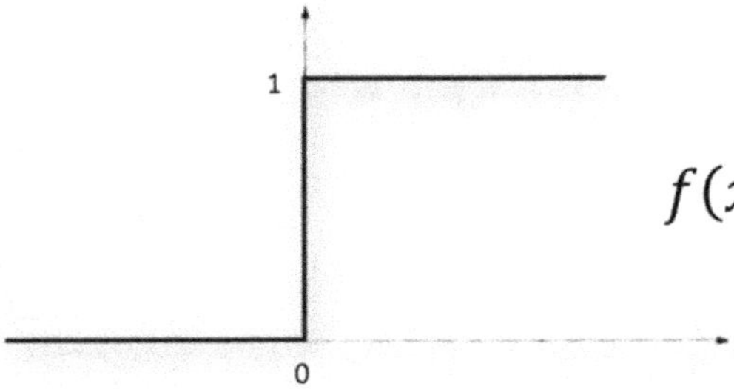

$$f(x) = \begin{cases} 0 \ if \ x < 0 \\ 1 \ if \ x \geq 0 \end{cases}$$

Figure 13-7: Step Function

The **step function** produces a binary output based on a fixed threshold. While simple, it is not differentiable and therefore unsuitable for gradient-based learning methods.

Hyperbolic Tangent (tanh)

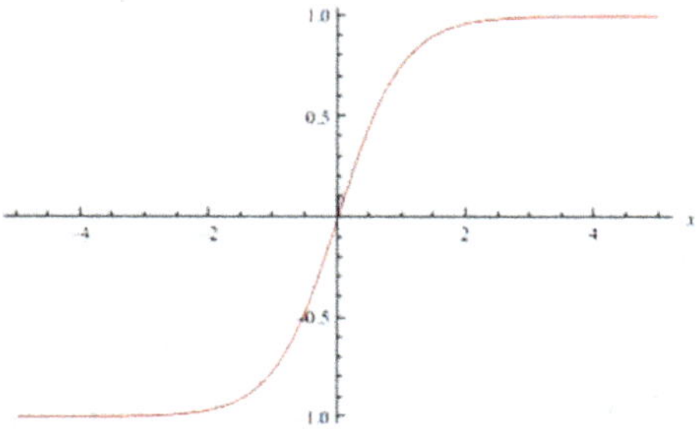

$$\cosh x = \frac{e^x + e^{-x}}{2}$$

$$\sinh x = \frac{e^x - e^{-x}}{2}$$

$$\tanh x = \frac{e^x - e^{-x}}{e^x + e^{-x}}$$

Figure 13-8: Hyperbolic Tangent

The **tanh function** maps inputs to a range between −1 and 1. Because it is zero-centered, it often converges faster than sigmoid during training. However, tanh can still suffer from vanishing gradients in deep networks.

ReLU (Rectified Linear Unit)

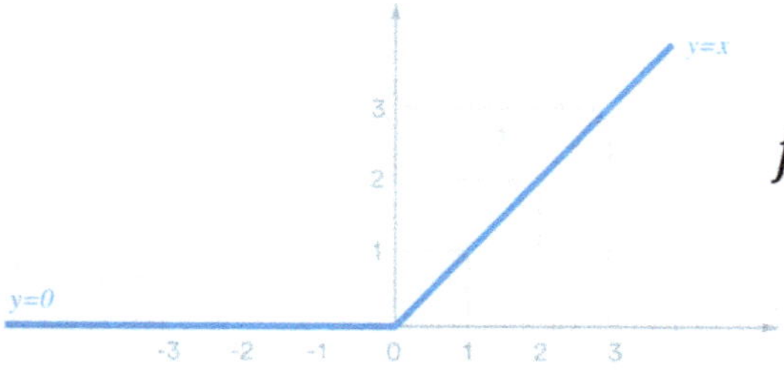

$$f(x) = \max(0, x)$$

Figure 13-9: ReLU Function

The **ReLU function** outputs the input directly if it is positive; otherwise, it outputs zero. ReLU is computationally efficient and helps alleviate the vanishing gradient problem, making it the most commonly used activation function in hidden layers.

Cost Function

$$C = \frac{\sum (y - a)^2}{n}$$

y = actual values

a = predicted values

A **cost function** (or loss function) measures the difference between the actual output and the predicted output of the model. It quantifies the error that the learning algorithm seeks to minimize during training.

Softmax Function

The **softmax function** converts a vector of real-valued scores into a probability distribution where the sum of all probabilities equals 1. It is typically used in the **output layer of multi-class classification models** to determine the most likely class.

Applications of Neural Networks

Handwriting Recognition

Digitizing handwritten documents and automating mail sorting.

Facial Recognition

Used in security systems, social media tagging, and personalized advertising.

Medical Image Analysis

Detecting anomalies in medical images such as X rays and MRI scans. This helps with disease diagnosis and treatment planning.

TensorFlow and Keras

TensorFlow is an open-source framework developed in late 2015 by Google for building machine learning and deep learning models. TensorFlow is free and open source.

TensorFlow is an end-to-end open-source machine learning platform with a focus on deep neural networks. Deep learning is a subtype of machine learning that analyses massive amounts of unstructured data.

Install TensorFlow

TensorFlow is a library for machine learning and artificial intelligence. It can be installed with following command in Jupyter notebook.

!pip install tensorflow

What is Keras?

Keras is an API built on Python that reduces the cognitive load associated with programming models through human readability and simple, consistent structures.

Keras is often described as a wrapper for TensorFlow and is intended for rapid experimentation.

Example Notebook

Let's study an example Jupyter Notebook that shows the implementation of a neural network using TensorFlow and Keras.

TensorFlow provides:

- Efficient numerical computation using **tensors**
- Automatic differentiation for training neural networks
- High-level APIs (tf.keras) for rapid model development
- Support for CPUs, GPUs, and TPUs
- Easy deployment to cloud, mobile, and edge devices

At its core, TensorFlow allows us to define **computational graphs** where data flows through layers, gets transformed, and produces predictions.

Hands-On Example: Neural Network Using a Real Dataset

Real-World Scenario: Breast Cancer Detection Using Machine Learning

Breast cancer is one of the most common cancers affecting women worldwide. Early detection plays a critical role in improving survival rates and enabling effective treatment. However, analyzing medical test results and identifying cancerous tumors can sometimes be complex and time-consuming for healthcare professionals. Machine learning can assist doctors by providing **decision-support tools that analyze medical data and predict whether a tumor is malignant or benign**.

Consider a scenario in which a patient visits a hospital after noticing an abnormal lump in the breast. The doctor performs a **Fine Needle Aspiration (FNA) biopsy**, which extracts a small sample of cells from the breast tissue. These cells are then examined under a microscope and digitized into medical images.

From these images, several measurable characteristics of the cell nuclei are extracted, such as:

- Size of the cell nucleus (radius and area)
- Texture of the cell surface
- Shape irregularity and concavity
- Symmetry of the cell structure

These numerical measurements form a **dataset of features** representing the biological properties of the tumor cells.

A machine learning model can be trained using historical medical data where the diagnosis is already known (benign or malignant). The model learns patterns that distinguish cancerous tumors from non-cancerous ones. Once trained, the model can analyze the features extracted from a new patient's biopsy and make a prediction.

For example, suppose the model observes that malignant tumors often have:

- Larger cell nuclei
- Irregular shapes
- Higher concavity values
- Greater variation in texture

Based on these patterns, the machine learning algorithm calculates the probability that the tumor is malignant.

The prediction is then provided to the doctor as a **decision support recommendation**:

Patient ID	Radius	Texture	Concavity	Prediction
P1023	17.9	22.3	0.15	Malignant

Table 13-1

The physician uses this information along with clinical expertise, imaging results, and other tests to make the final diagnosis.

It is important to note that machine learning models **do not replace medical professionals**. Instead, they assist healthcare providers by:

- Quickly analyzing large volumes of medical data
- Identifying patterns that may not be obvious to the human eye

- Supporting early detection of potential cancer cases

Early detection enabled by machine learning systems can help doctors recommend timely treatment, which significantly improves patient outcomes.

Thus, machine learning has become an important tool in **medical diagnostics**, particularly in tasks such as breast cancer detection, where accurate and early classification of tumors can save lives.

Problem Statement

We will build a **binary classification neural network** using the **Breast Cancer Wisconsin dataset**, a widely used real-world dataset in machine learning research.

Goal: Predict whether a tumor is **benign (0)** or **malignant (1)** based on medical features.

Dataset

The **Breast Cancer Wisconsin Dataset** is based on **real medical measurements**, but it is **anonymized and preprocessed** for research and educational use.

Key Facts About the Dataset

1. Real Clinical Data

- The dataset originates from the **University of Wisconsin Hospitals**.

- It was created by **Dr. William H. Wolberg** and colleagues.
- The measurements were obtained from **Fine Needle Aspirate (FNA)** images of breast masses.

2. Features Derived from Medical Images

Each record contains numeric features extracted from cell nuclei in biopsy images, such as:

- Radius
- Texture
- Perimeter
- Area
- Smoothness
- Compactness
- Concavity
- Symmetry
- Fractal dimension

These values were computed from microscopic images of breast tissue.

3. Classification Labels

The dataset labels each tumor as:

- **Benign (B)** – non-cancerous
- **Malignant (M)** – cancerous

This makes it a **binary classification problem**, which is why it is commonly used in machine learning textbooks and tutorials.

4. Privacy Protection

- Patient identifiers were **removed**.
- Only **numeric features and diagnosis labels** remain.
- Therefore, it is safe for **education, research, and ML experimentation**.

It is available from the **UCI Machine Learning Repository** and also directly through **Scikit-learn** via sklearn.datasets.load_breast_cancer().

5. Environment Setup

```
import tensorflow as tf
import numpy as np
import pandas as pd
from sklearn.datasets import load_breast_cancer
from sklearn.model_selection import train_test_split
from sklearn.preprocessing import StandardScaler
from sklearn.metrics import accuracy_score, confusion_matrix
```

Explanation

- tensorflow: Core deep learning framework
- numpy: Numerical operations
- pandas: Data handling
- sklearn: Dataset loading, preprocessing, and evaluation

6. Loading and Exploring the Dataset

```
data = load_breast_cancer()

X = data.data
y = data.target

print("Feature shape:", X.shape)
print("Target shape:", y.shape)
```

Explanation

- The dataset contains **569 samples** and **30 numeric features**
- Each row represents a patient
- Target variable:
    - 0 → benign
    - 1 → malignant

Understanding data shape is critical before model building.

7. Data Preprocessing

```
X_train, X_test, y_train, y_test = train_test_split(
    X, y, test_size=0.2, random_state=42
)

scaler = StandardScaler()
X_train = scaler.fit_transform(X_train)
X_test = scaler.transform(X_test)
```

Why Scaling Matters

Neural networks are sensitive to feature scale:

- Faster convergence
- Stable gradient updates
- Better overall performance

8. Building the Neural Network Model

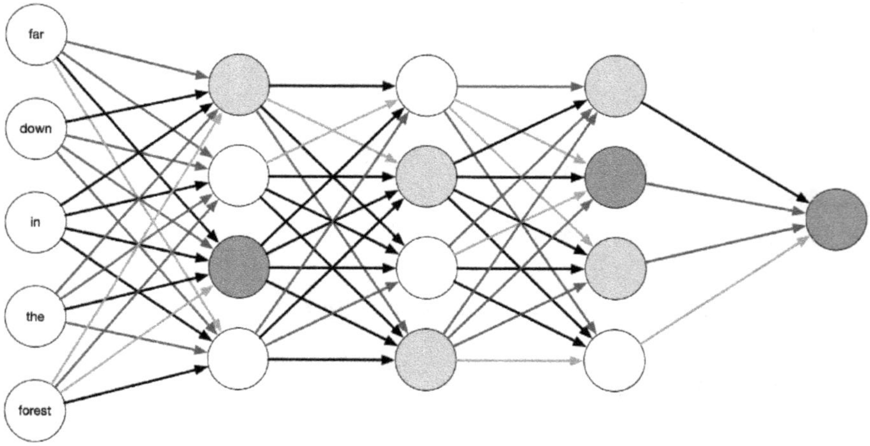

Figure 13-10

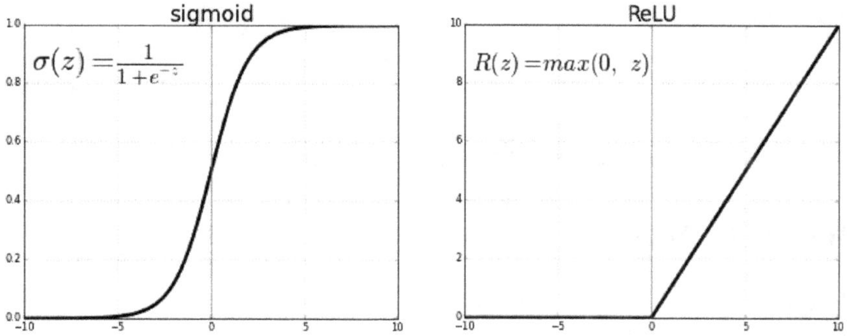

Figure 13-11

```
model = tf.keras.Sequential([
    tf.keras.layers.Dense(128, activation="relu", input_shape=(X_train.shape[1],)),
    tf.keras.layers.Dense(64, activation="relu"),
    tf.keras.layers.Dense(1, activation="sigmoid")
])
```

Explanation

Layer 1 (Input + Hidden)

- 128 neurons
- ReLU activation helps learn non-linear patterns
- Input shape matches feature count (30)

Layer 2 (Hidden)

- Reduces dimensionality
- Learns higher-level abstractions

Output Layer

- Single neuron
- Sigmoid outputs probability between 0 and 1

9. Compiling the Model

```
model.compile(
    optimizer="adam",
    loss="binary_crossentropy",
    metrics=["accuracy"]
)
```

Explanation

- **Adam optimizer**: Adaptive learning rate, widely used
- **Binary cross-entropy**: Correct loss for binary classification
- **Accuracy**: Intuitive performance metric

10. Training the Neural Network

```
history = model.fit(
    X_train,
    y_train,
    epochs=50,
    batch_size=32,
    validation_split=0.2
)
```

Key Training Concepts

- **Epoch**: One full pass through training data
- **Batch size**: Samples processed before weight update
- **Validation split**: Helps detect overfitting

During training:

- Loss should decrease
- Accuracy should increase

11. Model Evaluation

```
loss, accuracy = model.evaluate(X_test, y_test)
print("Test Accuracy:", accuracy)
```

```
y_pred = model.predict(X_test)
y_pred = (y_pred > 0.5).astype(int)

print("Confusion Matrix:")
print(confusion_matrix(y_test, y_pred))
```

Interpretation

- High accuracy indicates good generalization
- Confusion matrix shows:
    - True positives
    - False positives

- False negatives

12. Saving and Loading the Model

```
model.save("breast_cancer_nn_model")

loaded_model = tf.keras.models.load_model("breast_cancer_nn_model")
```

Why This Matters

- Enables deployment
- Avoids retraining
- Essential for production systems

13. Common Mistakes and Best Practices

Not scaling input data

Too many layers → overfitting

Wrong loss function

Use validation data

Start simple, then scale

Hands on Implementation Project for Neural Networks

Problem Statement –

Design and develop a machine learning model using an Artificial Neural Network (ANN) to predict customer churn. A simple neural network architecture will be used to analyze customer data and identify patterns that indicate whether a customer is likely to leave a service.

Customer churn prediction refers to the process of identifying customers who are likely to **stop using a product, service, or subscription in the near future**. By analyzing historical customer behavior, businesses can forecast potential churn and recognize customers who are at risk of discontinuing the service.

Predicting churn is an important component of business strategy, particularly for **subscription-based businesses**, because retaining existing customers is typically **more cost-effective than acquiring new ones**. By detecting churn risk early, organizations can implement targeted retention strategies such as personalized offers, improved customer support, or service enhancements to maintain long-term customer relationships.

Dataset – Churn dataset

The data set includes information about:

- Customers who left within the last month – the column is called Churn
- Services that each customer has signed up for – phone, multiple lines, internet, online security, online backup, device protection, tech support, and streaming TV and movies
- Customer account information – how long they've been a customer, contract, payment method, paperless billing, monthly

charges, and total charges

- Demographic info about customers – gender, age range, and if they have partners and dependents

2. Import Required Libraries

In this step, we import all the required libraries for data handling, preprocessing, visualization, model building, and evaluation.

```
import _____ as np
import _____ as pd
import matplotlib.pyplot as plt
import seaborn as sns

from sklearn.model_selection import __________
from sklearn.preprocessing import __________, __________
from sklearn.compose import __________
from sklearn.pipeline import __________
from sklearn.metrics import __________, __________, __________, __________

import tensorflow as tf
from tensorflow import keras
from tensorflow.keras import Sequential
from tensorflow.keras.layers import _______, _______
```

3. Load the Dataset

Now we load the customer churn dataset into a Pandas DataFrame and inspect the first few rows.

```
df = pd.read_csv("_______________")
df.head()
```

```
df.shape
```

```
df.info()
```

4. Understand the Data

Let us check the column names and understand the target variable.

Code Cell

```
df.columns
```

```
df["__________"].value_counts()
```

```
sns.countplot(x="__________", data=df)
plt.title("Customer Churn Distribution")
plt.show()
```

5. Data Preprocessing

5.1 Drop Unnecessary Columns

Some columns, such as customer ID, may not help in prediction. We remove such columns.

```
df = df.drop(["____________"], axis=1)
df.head()
```

5.2 Check Missing Values

```
df.isnull().sum()
```

If missing values are present, handle them appropriately.

```
df = df.dropna()
```

5.3 Separate Features and Target

```
X = df.drop("__________", axis=1)
y = df["__________"]
```

5.4 Convert Target Variable to Numeric

ANN requires numeric values. Convert the churn column into 0 and 1.

```
y = y.map({"No": __, "Yes": __})
y.head()
```

5.5 Identify Numerical and Categorical Columns

```
cat_cols = X.select_dtypes(include=["object"]).columns
num_cols = X.select_dtypes(exclude=["object"]).columns

print("Categorical columns:", cat_cols)
print("Numerical columns:", num_cols)
```

5.6 Create Preprocessing Pipeline

Categorical columns are encoded and numerical columns are scaled.

```
preprocessor = ColumnTransformer([
    ("num", ___________, num_cols),
    ("cat", ___________(handle_unknown="ignore"), cat_cols)
])
```

6. Split the Dataset

We divide the data into training and testing sets.

```
X_train, X_test, y_train, y_test = train_test_split(
    X, y,
    test_size=____,
    random_state=____,
    stratify=____
)
```

7. Apply Preprocessing

```
X_train_processed = preprocessor.fit_transform(X_train)
X_test_processed = preprocessor.transform(X_test)
```

```
X_train_processed.shape, X_test_processed.shape
```

8. Build the ANN Model

We now create a simple ANN with:

- Input layer
- One hidden dense layer
- Dropout layer
- Output layer with sigmoid activation

Code Cell

```
model = Sequential([
    Dense(____, activation="_______", input_shape=(X_train_processed.shape[1],)),
    Dropout(____),
    Dense(____, activation="_______")
])
```

9. Compile the Model

Compile the model using:

- optimizer = Adam
- loss = binary crossentropy
- metric = accuracy

Code Cell

```
model.compile(
    optimizer="________",
    loss="______________",
    metrics=["________"]
)
```

10. Train the Model

Code Cell

```
history = model.fit(
    X_train_processed,
    y_train,
    epochs=____,
    batch_size=____,
    validation_split=____,
    verbose=1
)
```

11. Plot Training Performance

We now visualize accuracy and loss during training.

Code Cell

```
plt.plot(history.history["accuracy"], label="Training Accuracy")
plt.plot(history.history["val_accuracy"], label="Validation Accuracy")
plt.title("Model Accuracy")
plt.xlabel("Epoch")
plt.ylabel("Accuracy")
plt.legend()
plt.show()
```

```
plt.plot(history.history["loss"], label="Training Loss")
plt.plot(history.history["val_loss"], label="Validation Loss")
plt.title("Model Loss")
plt.xlabel("Epoch")
plt.ylabel("Loss")
plt.legend()
plt.show()
```

12. Make Predictions

Code Cell

```
y_pred_prob = model.predict(X_test_processed)
y_pred_prob[:5]
```

Convert predicted probabilities into class labels using threshold 0.5.

Code Cell

```
y_pred = (y_pred_prob > ____).astype(int)
y_pred[:5]
```

13. Evaluate the Model

Code Cell

```
print("Accuracy:", accuracy_score(y_test, y_pred))
print("Precision:", precision_score(y_test, y_pred))
print("Recall:", recall_score(y_test, y_pred))
print("F1-score:", f1_score(y_test, y_pred))
```

Code Cell

```
cm = confusion_matrix(y_test, y_pred)
cm
```

```
sns.heatmap(cm, annot=True, fmt="d", cmap="Purples")
plt.title("Confusion Matrix")
plt.xlabel("Predicted")
plt.ylabel("Actual")
plt.show()
```

```
print(classification_report(y_test, y_pred))
```

14. Interpret the Results

Fill in the blanks below:

- The ANN model achieved an accuracy of ______________.
- Precision tells us ____________________________________.
- Recall tells us ______________________________________.
- F1-score is useful because ____________________________.

- If recall is low, it means ______________________________.
- If precision is low, it means __________________________.

Conclusion

Complete the conclusion:

In this notebook, we built a ________________________ model for ________________________ prediction.

First, we loaded and preprocessed the dataset by handling categorical and numerical features. Then we trained a ________________________ neural network using Keras. Finally, we evaluated the model using ________________________, ________________________, and ________________________.

Customer churn prediction is useful because it helps businesses ____.

Summary

In this chapter, you explored the fundamental concepts and practical implementation of **TensorFlow** and **Neural Networks**, which are among the most powerful tools used in modern machine learning and deep learning applications.

• **Learned TensorFlow Fundamentals**

You were introduced to the TensorFlow framework, one of the most widely used open-source libraries for building machine learning and deep learning models. The chapter explained how TensorFlow works, how tensors represent multidimensional data, and how the framework efficiently performs numerical computations required for training neural networks.

• **Understood Neural Network Internals**

You studied the internal structure of neural networks, including neurons, layers, weights, biases, and activation functions. The chapter explained how information flows through input layers, hidden layers, and output layers, and how neural networks learn patterns from data using forward propagation and backpropagation.

• **Built a Real Neural Network Using Medical Data**

Through a hands-on implementation, you constructed a neural network model using a real-world medical dataset. You learned how to preprocess data, split it into training and testing sets, define the architecture of the neural network, train the model using TensorFlow/Keras, and evaluate its performance.

• **Interpreted Model Results**

You analyzed the results produced by the neural network model. This included evaluating model accuracy, understanding prediction outputs, and interpreting performance metrics to determine how well the model learned patterns in the dataset.

• **Saved and Reused Trained Models**

Finally, you learned how to save trained models so they can be reused later without retraining. This capability is essential for deploying machine learning models in real-world applications such as healthcare systems, recommendation engines, and predictive analytics platforms.

Overall, this chapter provided both the **theoretical understanding and practical skills needed to build and use neural networks with TensorFlow**, preparing you for more advanced deep learning applications.

Exercises

1. Why is feature scaling important for neural networks?
2. What happens if sigmoid is replaced with ReLU in the output layer?
3. Modify the model to use three hidden layers
4. Change batch size and observe training behavior
5. Add Dropout layers and compare accuracy
6. Explain why Adam converges faster than SGD
7. How does overfitting appear in training vs validation curves?
8. When would you choose softmax over sigmoid?

References

1. Y. LeCun, Y. Bengio, and G. Hinton, "Deep Learning," *Nature*, 2015.
2. M. Abadi et al., "TensorFlow: A System for Large-Scale Machine Learning," in *USENIX / Google Research*, 2016.
3. Goodfellow, Y. Bengio, and A. Courville, *Deep Learning*. Cambridge, MA, USA: MIT Press, 2016.
4. IEEE Xplore, "Neural Networks and Deep Learning Applications."
5. ACM Digital Library, "Machine Learning Systems and Frameworks."
6. Géron, *Hands-On Machine Learning with Scikit-Learn, Keras, and TensorFlow*. Sebastopol, CA, USA: O'Reilly Media.
7. W. H. Wolberg, W. N. Street, and O. L. Mangasarian, "Breast Cancer Wisconsin (Diagnostic) Dataset," UCI Machine Learning Repository, University of California, Irvine, CA, USA. [Online]. Available: https://archive.ics.uci.edu/ml/datasets/Breast+Cancer+Wisconsin+(Diagnostic)
8. Blastchar, "Telco Customer Churn Dataset," Kaggle. [Online]. Available: https://www.kaggle.com/datasets/blastchar/telco-customer-churn
9. IBM, "Telco Customer Churn," IBM Documentation.

14. Chapter 14: K-Nearest Neighbors (KNN)

Learning Objectives

After reading this chapter, you will be able to:

1. Explain the working principle of the KNN algorithm.
2. Compute distances using common distance metrics.
3. Select appropriate value of K for optimal performance.
4. Apply feature scaling for improving KNN results.
5. Implement KNN using Scikit-learn for classification and regression tasks.

Introduction

K-Nearest Neighbors (KNN) is one of the simplest and most intuitive machine learning algorithms used for **classification and regression problems**. Unlike many other algorithms, KNN does not build an explicit model during training. Instead, it stores the entire training dataset and makes predictions based on the similarity between data points.

The basic idea behind KNN is straightforward:
Similar data points tend to belong to the same category.

When a new data instance needs to be classified, the algorithm identifies the **K closest data points in the training dataset** and assigns the most common class among those neighbors.

KNN is widely used because it is:

- Simple to understand and implement
- Effective for small to medium sized datasets
- Useful for pattern recognition problems
- A strong baseline model for classification tasks

However, KNN can become computationally expensive when working with very large datasets because it requires calculating distances between the new point and all training samples.

Understanding KNN

To understand the concept of the **K-Nearest Neighbors (KNN)** algorithm, consider a simple example involving physical attributes such as **height** and **weight**.

Imagine a dataset where each point represents a person plotted in a two-dimensional space. The **horizontal axis represents weight**, and the **vertical axis represents height**. In this dataset, individuals belong to one of two categories:

- **Athletes**
- **Non-Athletes**

These categories are represented using different markers on the graph.

When a **new person** is added to the dataset, their class label is initially unknown. The KNN algorithm determines the class of this new individual by examining the **closest existing data points** in the dataset.

The underlying idea is that **people with similar physical characteristics tend to belong to similar categories**. Therefore, if the majority of nearby individuals are athletes, the new person is likely to be classified as an **Athlete**.

Conceptual Illustration

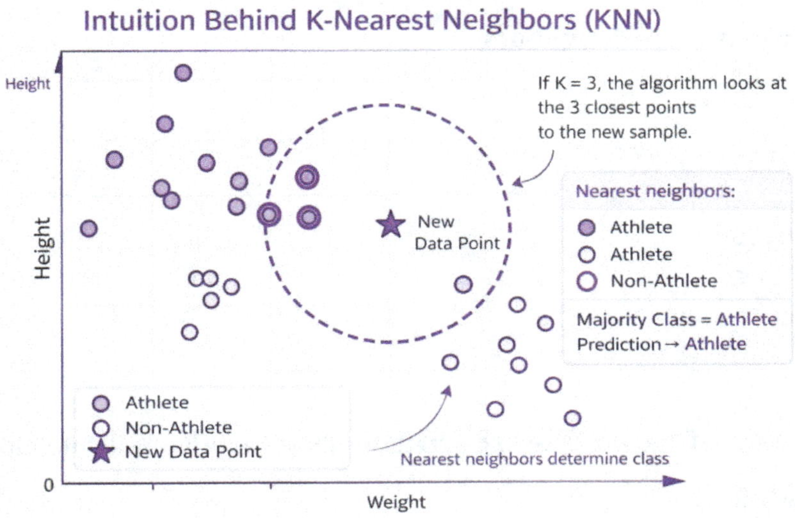

Figure 14-1: K Nearest Neighbors

In this diagram:

1. • represents Athletes

2. ○ represents Non-Athletes
3. ★ represents the new person whose class we want to predict

How KNN Makes the Decision

The algorithm calculates the **distance between the new point and all existing points** in the dataset. After computing these distances, it selects the **K closest data points**, called the **nearest neighbors**.

For example, if **K = 3**, the algorithm considers the **three closest individuals** to the new person.

Example of Nearest Neighbors

```
Nearest neighbors:

• Athlete
• Athlete
o Non-Athlete
```

Since **two out of the three nearest neighbors are Athletes**, the majority class is **Athlete**.

```
Majority Class = Athlete
Predicted Class → Athlete
```

Key Idea

The KNN algorithm follows a very intuitive principle:

Objects that are close to each other in the feature space are likely to belong to the same category.

Thus, the class of a new observation is determined by the **majority vote of its nearest neighbors**.

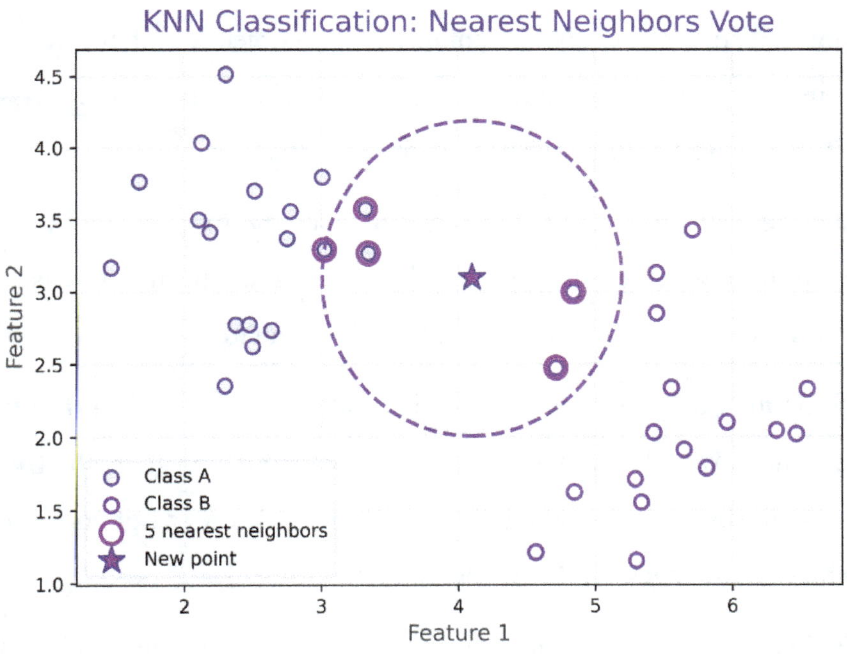

Figure 14-2: KNN Nearest Neighbors Vote

KNN Classification – Nearest Neighbors Vote

The diagram illustrates how the **K-Nearest Neighbors (KNN) classification algorithm** works when predicting the class of a new data point.

The horizontal axis represents **Feature 1**, while the vertical axis represents **Feature 2**. Each point on the graph corresponds to an observation in the training dataset. The observations belong to two different classes: **Class A** and **Class B**, represented by different markers in the plot.

At the center of the diagram, the **star-shaped marker** represents a **new data point** whose class label is unknown. The objective of the KNN algorithm is to determine whether this new point should belong to **Class A or Class B** based on the classes of nearby points.

To make the prediction, the algorithm calculates the **distance between the new point and all existing data points** in the dataset. In most cases, the **Euclidean distance** metric is used for this calculation.

After computing the distances, the algorithm identifies the **K closest data points**. In this example, **K = 5**, meaning the algorithm considers the **five nearest neighbors** surrounding the new point. These neighbors are highlighted with **larger circles** in the diagram.

The **dashed circle** around the star represents the neighborhood that contains the five closest data points. Once these neighbors are identified, the algorithm performs a **majority voting process**. The class that appears most frequently among the five nearest neighbors becomes the predicted class for the new data point.

For example:

- If most of the five nearest neighbors belong to **Class A**, the new point will be classified as **Class A**.
- If the majority belong to **Class B**, the new point will be classified as **Class B**.

This voting process is why the algorithm is referred to as **"Nearest Neighbors Vote."**

This diagram also demonstrates an important property of KNN: **classification decisions are based entirely on the local structure of the data**. Instead of learning a global mathematical model, KNN relies on the similarity between observations in the feature space.

Overall, the figure visually explains the key steps of the KNN algorithm:

1. Plot the training data in feature space.
2. Introduce a new data point whose class is unknown.
3. Measure the distance between the new point and all training points.
4. Select the **K nearest neighbors**.
5. Use **majority voting** among these neighbors to determine the predicted class.

This approach makes KNN one of the simplest and most intuitive machine learning algorithms used for **classification and pattern**

recognition tasks.

How KNN works?

The KNN algorithm works using **distance measurements** between data points.

The most commonly used distance metric is **Euclidean Distance**.

Euclidean Distance Formula

$$d(x, y) = \sqrt{(x_1 - y_1)^2 + (x_2 - y_2)^2 + ... + (x_n - y_n)^2}$$

Where

- (x) = new data point
- (y) = training data point
- (n) = number of features

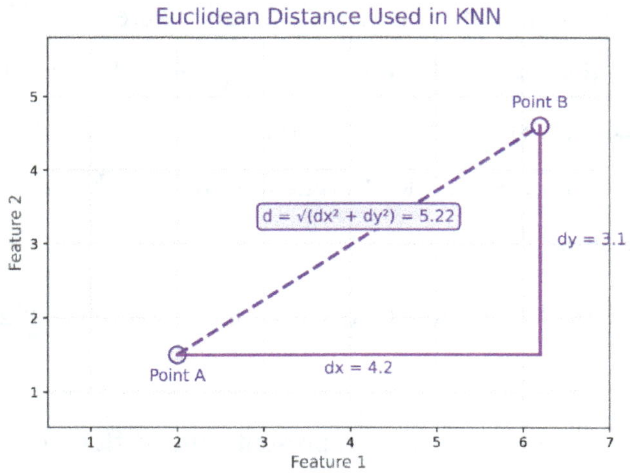

Figure 14-3: Euclidean Distance used in KNN

Euclidean Distance Used in KNN

The diagram illustrates how **Euclidean distance** is used in the **K-Nearest Neighbors (KNN)** algorithm to measure the similarity between data points.

In the figure, the horizontal axis represents **Feature 1**, and the vertical axis represents **Feature 2**. Each point in this two-dimensional space represents an observation described by two numerical features.

Two specific points are shown:

- **Point A** with coordinates approximately *(2.0, 1.5)*
- **Point B** with coordinates approximately *(6.2, 4.6)*

To determine how similar these two observations are, the KNN algorithm calculates the **distance between the two points**. The most commonly used distance measure for continuous variables is the **Euclidean distance**, which represents the straight-line distance between two points in the feature space.

In the diagram, the distance is illustrated using a **right-triangle geometry**:

- The horizontal segment represents the difference in the first feature, labeled **dx = 4.2**.
- The vertical segment represents the difference in the second feature, labeled **dy = 3.1**.
- The **dashed diagonal line** connecting Point A and Point B represents the actual Euclidean distance between the two points.

The Euclidean distance is calculated using the formula:

$$d = \sqrt{dx^2 + dy^2}$$

Substituting the values from the diagram:

$$d = \sqrt{(4.2)^2 + (3.1)^2}$$

$$d = \sqrt{17.64 + 9.61}$$

$$d = \sqrt{27.25}$$

$$d \approx 5.22$$

Thus, the distance between **Point A and Point B is approximately 5.22 units**.

This distance calculation is fundamental to the **KNN algorithm**, because it allows the model to determine which data points are **closest to a new observation**. When a new data point is introduced, the algorithm computes the Euclidean distance between the new point and all existing points in the dataset. The **K closest points (nearest neighbors)** are then selected, and their class labels are used to determine the predicted class for the new observation.

Therefore, Euclidean distance plays a crucial role in KNN by providing a mathematical way to measure **similarity between observations in the feature space**.

KNN Algorithm

The working steps of KNN are:

1. Choose the value of **K**
2. Compute distance between the new data point and all training data

points

3. Sort the distances in ascending order
4. Select the **K nearest neighbors**
5. Determine the majority class among neighbors
6. Assign that class to the new data point

6. Example: Student Performance Classification

Suppose we classify students as **Pass or Fail** based on:

- Study Hours
- Attendance Percentage

Training Dataset

Study Hours	Attendance	Result
2	60	Fail
3	65	Fail
5	70	Pass
7	80	Pass
8	90	Pass

Table 14-1

Now a new student has:

Study Hours = 6

Attendance = 75

We calculate the distance to each point.

Distance Table

Student	Distance	Result
1	3.61	Fail
2	2.83	Fail
3	1.41	Pass
4	2.23	Pass
5	3.61	Pass

Table 14-2

If **K = 3**, nearest neighbors are:

Distance	**Result**
1.41	Pass
2.23	Pass
2.83	Fail

Table 14-3

Majority class = **Pass**

Prediction → **Pass**

7. Choosing the Value of K

Choosing the Correct Value of K in K-Nearest Neighbors

Selecting an appropriate value for **K**, the number of nearest neighbors considered by the algorithm, is one of the most important decisions when using the **K-Nearest Neighbors (KNN)** algorithm. The value of **K** directly influences how the model makes predictions and how well it generalizes to new data.

If the value of **K** is too small or too large, the model may perform poorly. Therefore, it is essential to carefully choose a value that balances model flexibility and stability.

Effect of a Small Value of K

When **K is small** (for example, K = 1 or K = 3), the algorithm considers only a few nearby data points when making a prediction.

This can make the model **very sensitive to noise** in the dataset. If one of the nearby data points happens to be mislabeled or an outlier, it can strongly influence the prediction. As a result, the decision boundary becomes highly irregular and may fluctuate significantly.

Characteristics of **small K values**:

- Very sensitive to individual data points
- Strong influence of noise and outliers
- Highly flexible decision boundary
- **High variance**

High variance means that the model may perform very well on the training data but may not generalize well to new unseen data.

Effect of a Large Value of K

When **K is large**, the algorithm considers many neighbors before deciding the class label. Instead of relying on a few points, it looks at a broader neighborhood of data.

This generally produces a **smoother decision boundary**, making the model less sensitive to individual noisy observations.

However, using a very large value of **K** can also create problems. If the neighborhood becomes too large, points from different classes may dominate the voting process. In particular, the model may **favor the majority class** in the dataset and ignore smaller groups.

Characteristics of **large K values**:

- More stable predictions
- Less sensitivity to noise
- **Smoother decision boundaries**
- May ignore important local patterns
- **May misclassify minority classes**

This situation is common in datasets where the class distribution is imbalanced.

Bias–Variance Tradeoff

The choice of **K** also reflects the **bias–variance tradeoff** in machine learning.

- **Small K → Low bias but high variance**
- **Large K → Higher bias but lower variance**

A good model aims to balance these two effects so that it performs well on both training data and unseen test data.

Typical Practice for Choosing K

A commonly used heuristic is:

$$K = \sqrt{N}$$

where **N** represents the total number of samples in the training dataset.

For example:

- If the dataset has **100 samples**, a reasonable starting value might be

$$K = \sqrt{100} = 10$$

This rule provides a useful starting point, but it may not always produce the best result for every dataset.

Using Cross-Validation to Select K

A more reliable approach for selecting **K** is **cross-validation**.

In this method:

1. Several values of **K** are tested (for example K = 1, 3, 5, 7, 9, 11).
2. The model is trained and evaluated for each value.
3. The value of **K** that produces the **best validation accuracy** is selected.

Cross-validation allows us to systematically determine which value of **K** leads to the most accurate and robust model.

Choosing the right value of **K** is essential for achieving good performance with the KNN algorithm. Small values of **K** make the model sensitive to noise and produce high variance, while large values of **K** create smoother decision boundaries but may overlook important local patterns and misclassify minority classes. In practice, the value of **K** can be initially estimated using the rule $K = \sqrt{N},$ but it is often better to determine the optimal value through **cross-validation**.

Applications of KNN

Applications of K-Nearest Neighbors (KNN)

The **K-Nearest Neighbors (KNN)** algorithm is widely used in many real-world domains because of its simplicity and effectiveness in identifying patterns based on similarity. Since KNN classifies a new data point by examining the characteristics of nearby observations, it works particularly well in problems where **similar items tend to belong to the same category**. Below are some common applications of KNN across different fields.

1. Image Recognition

One of the most common uses of KNN is in **image recognition and computer vision**. In these tasks, images are represented using numerical features such as pixel values, color intensities, or extracted visual features. When a new image is provided, the KNN algorithm compares it with existing images in the dataset and identifies the most similar ones.

Based on the classes of these similar images, the algorithm determines the category of the new image.

Example:

- **Handwritten Digit Recognition**

In handwritten digit recognition systems, such as those using the **MNIST dataset**, each image of a handwritten digit is converted into a set of pixel values. When a new handwritten digit image is input into the system, the KNN algorithm compares it with thousands of stored images and finds the closest matches. The digit label that appears most frequently among the nearest neighbors becomes the predicted digit.

2. Recommendation Systems

KNN is widely used in **recommendation systems**, where the goal is to suggest items to users based on similarity with other users or items.

In this scenario, the algorithm identifies users who have similar preferences and recommends items that those similar users have liked or purchased.

Example:

- **Movie Recommendation**

In a movie recommendation system, users rate different movies. If two users have rated several movies similarly, they are considered **neighbors**. When a new recommendation is needed for a user, the system identifies the most similar users and recommends movies that those users have enjoyed.

This approach is commonly used in platforms such as **streaming services, online retail websites, and music recommendation systems**.

3. Medical Diagnosis

KNN can also be applied in **healthcare and medical diagnosis** to classify patients based on their medical data.

In medical datasets, each patient record may include features such as age, blood pressure, cholesterol level, glucose level, or other clinical measurements. When a new patient's data is entered, the KNN algorithm compares the patient with other patients in the dataset.

The diagnosis can then be predicted based on the outcomes of similar patients.

Example:

- **Disease Prediction**

KNN can help identify whether a patient is likely to have a certain disease based on the medical records of patients with similar symptoms or medical measurements. For instance, it may be used in predicting conditions such as **heart disease, diabetes, or cancer risk**.

4. Credit Risk Analysis

Financial institutions often need to determine whether a customer is likely to **repay a loan or default**. KNN can assist in making such predictions by comparing the financial profile of a new customer with those of previous customers.

Customer attributes may include:

- Income level
- Credit history
- Employment status
- Existing debts
- Payment history

By identifying customers with similar financial characteristics, the algorithm can estimate the likelihood that the new customer will default on a loan.

This helps banks and financial organizations **assess credit risk and make informed lending decisions**.

5. Document Classification

KNN is also used in **text mining and natural language processing (NLP)** tasks such as document classification.

Documents can be represented numerically using techniques like **term frequency (TF) or TF-IDF**, which convert text into vectors of numerical values. The KNN algorithm then compares these vectors to determine document similarity.

Example:

• **Topic Classification**

If a new document is submitted to a system, the algorithm finds the most similar documents in the dataset and assigns the new document to the category that appears most frequently among those neighbors. For example, documents may be classified into topics such as **sports, technology, politics, or entertainment**.

KNN is a versatile algorithm that can be applied in a wide range of domains where classification based on similarity is required. Its ability to work without building an explicit model makes it particularly useful for **pattern recognition, recommendation systems, medical diagnosis, financial risk assessment, and text classification tasks**. Despite its simplicity, KNN continues to be an important algorithm in many practical machine learning applications.

Advantages of K-Nearest Neighbors (KNN)

The **K-Nearest Neighbors (KNN)** algorithm is widely appreciated for its simplicity and effectiveness in many machine learning applications. Because it relies on measuring similarity between data points rather than building a complex mathematical model, it is often used as a baseline algorithm in classification and regression problems.

1. Simple Algorithm

One of the biggest advantages of KNN is that it is **very simple and intuitive to understand**. The core idea is straightforward: classify a new data point based on the majority class of its nearest neighbors. This makes the algorithm easy to explain, visualize, and apply, especially for beginners learning machine learning concepts.

2. No Training Phase

Unlike many machine learning algorithms that require an explicit training process to build a predictive model, KNN is known as a **lazy learning algorithm**. It does not learn a model during the training phase. Instead, it simply stores the training dataset. When a new data point needs to be classified, the algorithm performs calculations at that time by comparing the new point with existing data points.

Because of this characteristic, the **training phase is very fast**, although the prediction phase can take longer.

3. Works Well with Non-Linear Decision Boundaries

KNN is capable of handling **complex and non-linear decision boundaries**. Many algorithms assume a specific mathematical relationship between input variables and output classes, but KNN does not make such assumptions. It determines class labels based entirely on local neighborhood information. This flexibility allows the algorithm to adapt to irregular patterns in the data.

4. Easy to Implement

The implementation of KNN is relatively straightforward and requires only a few steps:

1. Choose the value of **K**
2. Compute distances between points

3. Identify the nearest neighbors
4. Perform majority voting

Because of its simplicity, KNN is widely available in many machine learning libraries such as **Scikit-learn**, making it easy to apply in real-world applications.

Limitations of K-Nearest Neighbors (KNN)

Despite its simplicity and usefulness, the KNN algorithm also has several limitations that must be considered when applying it to real-world problems.

1. Computationally Expensive for Large Datasets

Since KNN stores the entire training dataset and compares each new data point with all existing points, the prediction process can become **computationally expensive** when the dataset is very large. For every prediction, the algorithm must calculate distances to many data points, which increases processing time and memory usage.

As a result, KNN may not scale efficiently for **very large datasets** unless special optimization techniques are used.

2. Sensitive to Irrelevant Features

KNN relies heavily on distance calculations. If the dataset contains **irrelevant or noisy features**, these features can distort the distance measurements and negatively affect the model's accuracy. Therefore, feature selection or dimensionality reduction techniques are often required before applying KNN.

3. Requires Feature Scaling

Because KNN uses distance metrics such as **Euclidean distance**, features with larger numerical ranges can dominate the distance calculation. For example, if one feature ranges from 0 to 1000 while another ranges from 0 to 1, the larger-scale feature will have a much greater influence on the distance.

To prevent this problem, it is important to apply **feature scaling techniques** such as:

- Standardization (StandardScaler)
- Normalization (Min-Max scaling)

These methods ensure that all features contribute equally to the distance calculation.

4. Performance Decreases in High-Dimensional Data

KNN performs best when the number of features is relatively small. When the number of dimensions increases significantly, the algorithm suffers from a phenomenon known as the **curse of dimensionality**. In high-dimensional spaces, distances between points become less meaningful because many data points appear to be equally distant from each other.

As a result, identifying meaningful nearest neighbors becomes difficult, and the performance of the KNN model may degrade.

While KNN is a simple and flexible algorithm that works well for many classification and regression tasks, it is important to understand both its strengths and limitations. The algorithm is easy to implement and can handle complex decision boundaries, but it can become computationally expensive for large datasets and may struggle with irrelevant features and high-dimensional data. Careful preprocessing, feature scaling, and dimensionality reduction can help improve the effectiveness of KNN in practical applications.

Hands-On Exercise Notebook: (KNN) Software Defect Prediction

This worksheet guides you through implementing a K-Nearest Neighbors (KNN) machine learning model to predict whether a software module is likely to contain defects. The exercise uses the NASA KC1 software metrics dataset. Students will complete the missing parts of the code and observe how the model is trained and evaluated.

Real-World Scenario

You are part of a software quality engineering team. Every week many code modules are modified. Testing every module equally can be inefficient. A machine learning model can help predict which modules are most likely to contain defects so that testing and code review efforts can focus on the most risky modules.

Dataset

We use the NASA KC1 dataset which contains software metrics for different code modules. The dataset includes attributes such as complexity, number of operators, and other code metrics. A column named 'defects' indicates how many defects were observed in the module.

Machine Learning Goal

Our goal is to build a KNN classification model that predicts whether a module is defective. We convert the 'defects' column into a binary label:

Defective = 1 if defects > 0

Defective = 0 if defects = 0

Step 1: Import Libraries

Explanation:
We import the libraries required for data processing, visualization, and machine learning.

Fill in the blanks in the code below.

Code:

```
import numpy as np
import pandas as pd
import matplotlib.pyplot as plt

from sklearn.model_selection import train_test_split
from sklearn.preprocessing import StandardScaler
from sklearn.neighbors import KNeighborsClassifier
from sklearn.pipeline import make_pipeline
from sklearn.metrics import accuracy_score, confusion_matrix, classification_report
```

Step 2: Load the Dataset

Explanation:

The dataset is stored online as a CSV file. We load it using pandas.

```
url = "DATASET_URL"
df = pd._______(url)

print("Shape:", df.shape)
df.head()
```

Step 3: Explore the Dataset

Explanation:

Understanding the dataset structure is important before building a model.

We check column types and missing values.

```
df.____()

print("Missing values:")
print(df.____().sum())
```

Step 4: Create Target Variable

Explanation:

We convert the 'defects' column into a binary classification variable.

```
df["defective"] = (df["______"] > 0).astype(int)

print(df[["defects","defective"]].head())
```

Step 5: Prepare Features and Labels

Explanation:

Machine learning models require two components:

• Feature matrix (X)

• Target variable (y)

```
X = df.drop(columns=["______","______"])
y = df["______"]
```

Step 6: Split Training and Testing Data

Explanation:

We split the dataset so that the model learns from one part and is tested on unseen data.

```
X_train, X_test, y_train, y_test = _______(
 X, y, test_size=__, random_state=__, stratify=__
)
```

Step 7: Train the KNN Model

Explanation:

KNN relies on distance between data points. Because features may have different scales,
we apply StandardScaler before training.

```
k = __

model = _______(
 _______(),
 _______(n_neighbors=k)
)

model.fit(______, ______)
```

Step 8: Evaluate the Model

Explanation:

After training, we test the model on unseen data and measure accuracy.

```
y_pred = model._______(X_test)

acc = _______(y_test, y_pred)
print("Accuracy:", acc)

print(confusion_matrix(y_test, y_pred))
print(classification_report(y_test, y_pred))
```

Step 9: Tune the Value of K

Explanation:

Different values of K can produce different results. We try multiple values and select the best.

```
ks = list(range(1, __, __))
scores = []

for k in ks:
 m = make_pipeline(_______(), _______(n_neighbors=k))
 m.fit(______, ______)
 pred = m._______(X_test)
 scores.append(_______(y_test, pred))
```

Step 10: Visualize Accuracy vs K

Explanation:

We plot model accuracy for different values of K to identify the optimal number of neighbors.

```
plt.figure(figsize=(8,5))
plt.plot(ks, scores, marker="o", linewidth=__, color="______")
plt.title("Accuracy vs K")
plt.xlabel("K")
plt.ylabel("Accuracy")
plt.show()
```

Questions

1. Why is feature scaling important for KNN?
2. How does the value of K affect the decision boundary?
3. Why might recall be important in software defect prediction?
4. What would happen if the dataset is highly imbalanced?

Summary

In this chapter, we studied the **K-Nearest Neighbors algorithm**, one of the simplest machine learning techniques used for classification and regression tasks. The algorithm predicts the class of a new data point based on the majority class among its nearest neighbors. We explored the theoretical foundation of the algorithm, including the use of distance metrics such as Euclidean distance, and learned how the choice of K affects model performance.

We also implemented KNN using **Python and Scikit-Learn** and observed how the algorithm can be applied to real datasets. Despite its simplicity, KNN is a powerful baseline model and an important algorithm to understand when learning machine learning fundamentals.

Exercises

Exercise 1

What is the main idea behind KNN classification?

Exercise 2

Why is feature scaling important when using KNN?

Exercise 3

Calculate Euclidean distance between two points:

A (3,4)

B (7,1)

Exercise 4

If K=5 and the nearest neighbors belong to classes

A, A, B, A, B

What will be the predicted class?

Exercise 5

Write Python code to implement KNN with **K = 5**.

Exercise 6 (Hands-On)

Modify the notebook to:

- Change K value
- Observe accuracy changes

References

1. Cover, T., & Hart, P. (1967). *Nearest Neighbor Pattern Classification*. IEEE Transactions on Information Theory, 13(1), 21–27.
2. Hastie, T., Tibshirani, R., & Friedman, J. (2009). *The Elements of Statistical Learning*. Springer.
3. Bishop, C. M. (2006). *Pattern Recognition and Machine Learning*. Springer.
4. Pedregosa, F., et al. (2011). *Scikit-learn: Machine Learning in Python*. Journal of Machine Learning Research, 12, 2825–2830.
5. Fisher, R. A. (1936). *The Use of Multiple Measurements in Taxonomic Problems*. Annals of Eugenics, 7(2), 179–188.

15. Chapter 15: Support Vector Machines (SVM)

Learning Objectives

After reading this chapter, you will be able to:

1. Explain the concept of maximum margin classification.
2. Define hyperplanes and identify support vectors.
3. Differentiate between linear and non-linear SVM.
4. Apply kernel functions such as linear and RBF.
5. Implement SVM using Scikit-learn for classification problems.

Introduction

A Support Vector Machine (SVM) is a supervised machine learning algorithm used for classification and regression problems. It is mainly used to separate data into different classes by finding an optimal boundary between them.

The main idea behind SVM is to draw a decision boundary called a hyperplane that best separates the data points belonging to different classes.

Key Idea of SVM

SVM does not simply draw any separating line.
Instead, it finds a hyperplane that maximizes the margin between two classes.

- Hyperplane → Decision boundary that separates classes
- Margin → Distance between the boundary and the closest data points
- Support Vectors → The data points closest to the boundary

These support vectors determine the position of the hyperplane.

Simple Example

Suppose we want to classify emails as Spam or Not Spam.

Features might include:

- Number of links in the email
- Number of suspicious words

SVM will try to find a line (or hyperplane) that separates spam emails from non-spam emails with the largest possible margin.

Mathematical Representation

The hyperplane equation used in SVM is:

$$w \cdot x + b = 0$$

Where

- w = weight vector
- x = feature vector
- b = bias

Classification rule:

$$w \cdot x + b > 0 \rightarrow Class\ 1$$
$$w \cdot x + b < 0 \rightarrow Class\ 0$$

When Data is Not Linearly Separable

Sometimes data cannot be separated using a straight line.

In such cases SVM uses a technique called the Kernel Trick, which transforms the data into a higher dimensional space where separation becomes possible.

Common kernels include:

- Linear Kernel
- Polynomial Kernel
- Radial Basis Function (RBF) Kernel
- Sigmoid Kernel

Advantages of SVM

- Works well in high dimensional data

- Effective for small and medium datasets
- Can handle non-linear classification using kernels
- Robust against overfitting

Limitations of SVM

- Computationally expensive for large datasets
- Requires careful kernel selection
- Less interpretable than some models

Support Vector Machines (SVM) are powerful supervised learning algorithms used for **classification and regression tasks**. The main idea behind SVM is to find an optimal boundary that separates data points belonging to different classes.

Unlike many traditional algorithms that simply try to separate classes, SVM focuses on finding a **decision boundary with the maximum margin**, which improves the model's ability to generalize to unseen data.

The boundary that separates classes is called a **hyperplane**. The data points closest to this hyperplane are called **support vectors**, and they play a critical role in determining the position of the decision boundary.

SVM is widely used in applications such as:

- Image recognition
- Text classification
- Bioinformatics

• Financial forecasting

• Fraud detection

One of the key strengths of SVM is its ability to work effectively in **high-dimensional spaces** and its ability to handle **non-linear data using kernel functions**.

Basic Concepts of SVM

Hyperplane

A hyperplane is a boundary that separates data points belonging to different classes.

For a 2-dimensional dataset:

Hyperplane → line

For a 3-dimensional dataset:

Hyperplane → plane

For higher dimensions:

Hyperplane → n-dimensional boundary

Support Vectors

Support vectors are the **data points closest to the decision boundary**.

These points determine:

• position of the hyperplane

• margin size

• classification boundary

Removing support vectors changes the decision boundary.

Margin

Margin is the distance between the hyperplane and the nearest data points from each class.

Goal of SVM:

Maximize the margin.

A larger margin generally leads to **better generalization performance**.

3. Maximum Margin Classifier

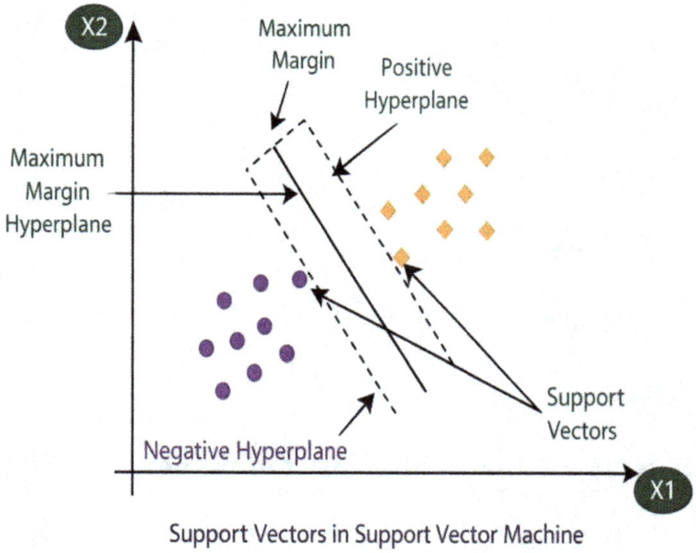

Figure 15-1: Support Vectors in SVM

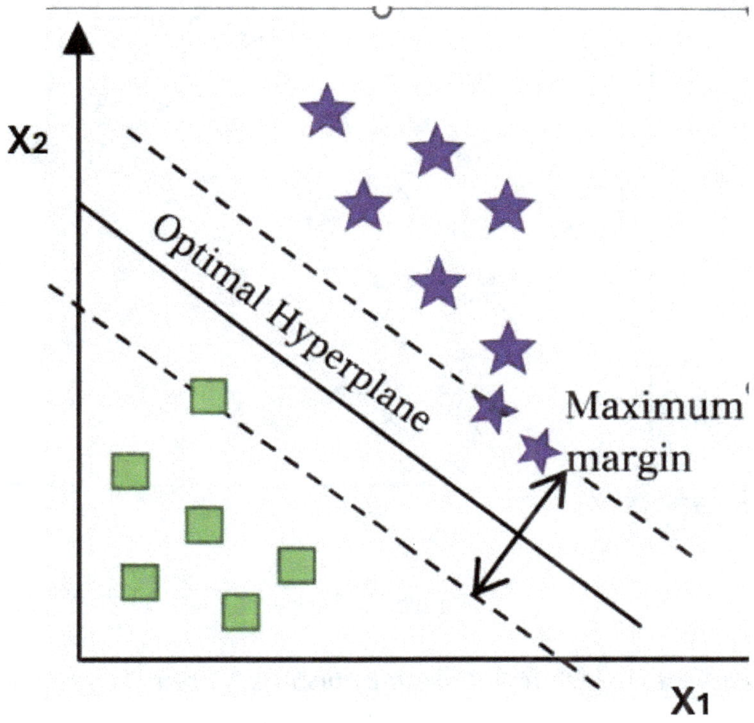

Figure 15-2: Maximum Margin in SVM

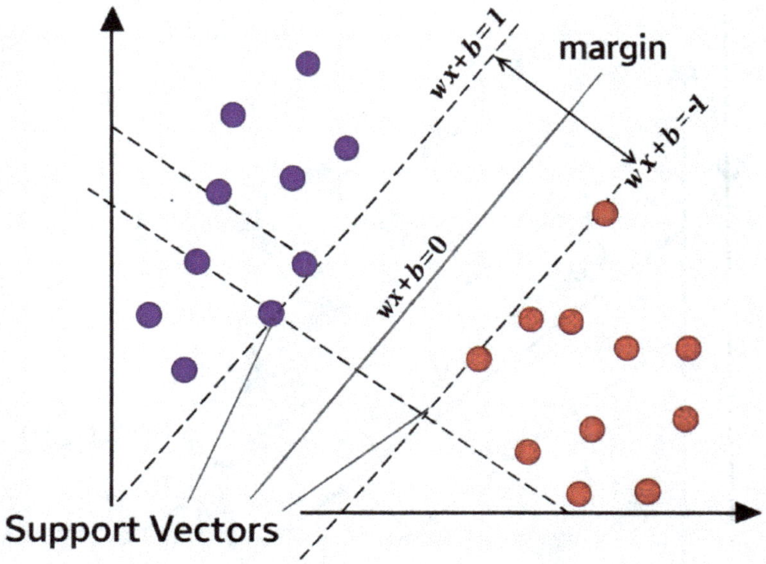

Figure 15-3

Support Vector Machine Decision Boundary, Margin, and Support Vectors

Consider a dataset with two classes:

Class A → red circles

Class B → purple circles

There can be many possible separating lines.

However, SVM selects the **line that maximizes the margin** between the two classes.

Mathematically the hyperplane is defined as:

$$w \cdot x + b = 0$$

Where

w → weight vector

x → input feature vector

b → bias

For classification:

$$w \cdot x + b \geq 1$$

for one class

$$w \cdot x + b \leq -1$$

for the other class

Support Vector Machine Decision Boundary and Margin

The above diagram illustrates the working principle of a **Support Vector Machine (SVM)** for a binary classification problem.

The horizontal axis represents **feature (X_1)** and the vertical axis represents **feature (X_2)**. Each point in the plot represents a training data sample belonging to one of two classes.

- **Purple dots** represent data points from one class.
- **Red dots** represent data points from the other class.

The goal of SVM is to find a decision boundary that separates these two classes.

Decision Boundary (Hyperplane)

The solid line shown in the diagram represents the **optimal separating hyperplane**. This line is the decision boundary that separates the two classes of data.

Mathematically, the decision boundary is defined as:

$$wx + b = 0$$

where

- (w) is the weight vector
- (x) is the input feature vector
- (b) is the bias term

Any point that lies on this line satisfies the equation

$$wx + b = 0.$$

Margin

The two dashed lines represent the **margin boundaries**. These are parallel lines on both sides of the decision boundary.

They are defined by the equations:

Upper margin:

$$wx + b = 1$$

Lower margin:

$$wx + b = -1$$

The distance between these two dashed lines is called the **margin**.

SVM selects the hyperplane that **maximizes this margin**, because a larger margin generally improves the model's ability to classify unseen data correctly.

Support Vectors

The data points that lie **closest to the margin boundaries** are called **support vectors**.

These points are extremely important because:

- They determine the position of the decision boundary.
- If these points move, the hyperplane will also move.

In the diagram, the points lying exactly on the dashed margin lines are the **support vectors**.

Interestingly, SVM uses **only these support vectors** to construct the classifier, while the other data points do not directly influence the final decision boundary.

Key Idea Illustrated in the Diagram

This figure demonstrates the central idea of SVM:

1. Separate two classes using a hyperplane.
2. Maximize the distance (margin) between the closest data points of the two classes.
3. Use only the support vectors to determine the optimal boundary.

Because of this **maximum margin principle**, SVM models often provide strong performance and good generalization ability.

4. Hard Margin vs Soft Margin

Hard Margin SVM

Used when data is **perfectly separable**.

Conditions:

No misclassification allowed.

Limitations:

Sensitive to noise.

Soft Margin SVM

Allows **some misclassification**.

Introduces parameter **C**.

C controls the trade-off between

- maximizing margin
- minimizing classification error

Small C → wider margin but more errors

Large C → smaller margin but fewer errors

5. Kernel Trick

The **Kernel Trick** is a powerful technique used in machine learning (especially in Support Vector Machines) to handle **non-linearly separable data**.

In many real-world problems, data cannot be separated using a straight line (or hyperplane) in its original space. The kernel trick solves this by **transforming the data into a higher-dimensional feature space**, where it becomes **linearly separable**.

Why Do We Need the Kernel Trick?

- In the original (input) space:
    - Data may be mixed and not separable
    - Decision boundaries are complex (curved)
- In the transformed (feature) space:
    - Data becomes separable using a **simple linear plane**
    - Model becomes easier to train and interpret

How It Works

1. Start with data in **input space** (2D or low dimension)
2. Apply a transformation function **φ (phi)**
3. Map data into **higher-dimensional feature space**
4. Find a **linear decision boundary (hyperplane)**
5. Map results back to original space → gives **non-linear boundary**

Mathematical Insight

Instead of computing:

$$\phi(x) \cdot \phi(x')$$

We use a **kernel function**:

$$K(x, x') = \phi(x) \cdot \phi(x')$$

This avoids explicitly computing high-dimensional transformations.

Common Kernel Functions

1. **Linear Kernel**
   - Used when data is already linearly separable
2. **Polynomial Kernel**
   - Captures curved relationships

3. **Radial Basis Function (RBF) Kernel**
    - Most commonly used
    - Handles complex boundaries

Sigmoid Kernel

- Similar to neural networks

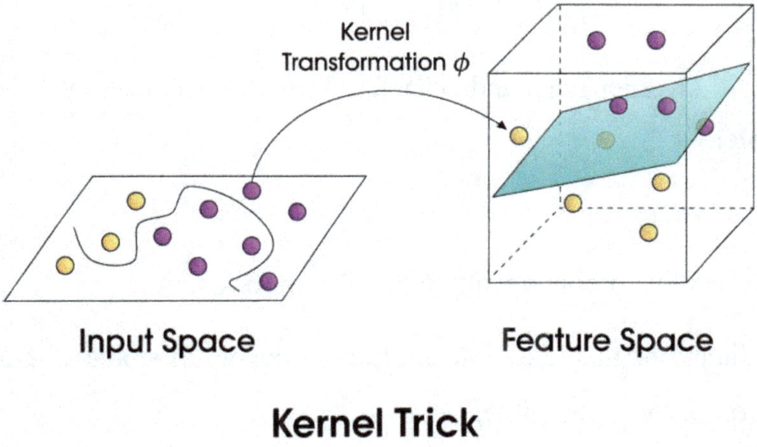

Figure 15-4: Kernel Trick

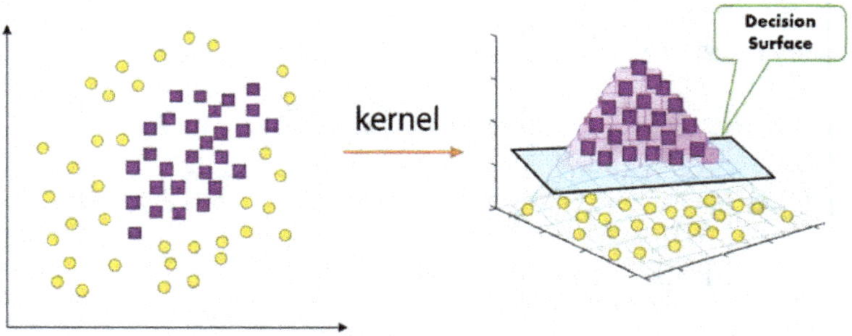

Figure 15-5

Kernel Trick and Decision Surface Visualization

Example:

Circular clusters.

SVM solves this problem using **Kernel Functions**.

Kernel functions map data into **higher dimensional space** where linear separation becomes possible.

Common kernels:

Linear Kernel

$$K(x, y) = x^T y$$

Polynomial Kernel

$$K(x, y) = (x^T y + c)^d$$

Radial Basis Function (RBF)

$$K(x, y) = e^{-\gamma||x-y||^2}$$

Sigmoid Kernel

$$K(x, y) = tanh(ax^T y + c)$$

6. Example: Customer Purchase Prediction

A company wants to classify whether a customer will purchase a product.

Features:

Age

Income

Classes:

0 → Not Purchase

1 → Purchase

Dataset

Age	Income	Purchase
25	30	0
35	60	1
45	65	1
20	20	0
30	45	1
22	25	0

Table 15-1

SVM finds a **decision boundary** that separates the two classes.

Support vectors determine the exact position of this boundary.

Many classification algorithms attempt to:

- Minimize classification error
- Model probabilities
- Fit decision boundaries

Geometric Idea Behind Support Vector Machines

Support Vector Machines (SVM) approach classification from a **geometric perspective**. Instead of simply drawing a line that separates two classes, SVM tries to find the **best possible boundary that leaves the largest distance between the two classes**.

This idea is known as the **maximum margin principle**.

In simple terms, SVM does not just focus on separating the classes; it tries to separate them **as widely as possible** so that the model performs better on unseen data.

This property gives SVM **strong generalization ability**.

Geometric Intuition of Linear SVM

Consider a binary classification problem where we have a dataset consisting of feature vectors and class labels.

Each data point is represented as:

$$x_i \in \mathbb{R}^d$$

where (x_i) is a feature vector with (d) dimensions.

Each point also has a class label:

$$y_i \in \{-1, +1\}$$

The goal of SVM is to find a **linear decision boundary** that separates the two classes.

The equation of this boundary (called a hyperplane) is:

$$w^T x + b = 0$$

where

- (w) is the weight vector that determines the orientation of the hyperplane
- (b) is the bias term that shifts the hyperplane

Maximum Margin Idea

In many cases, there may be several possible lines that separate two classes.

SVM

selects the **one that maximizes the distance between the closest points of the two classes**.

These closest data points are known as **support vectors**.

Support vectors are important because they **completely determine the position of the decision boundary**. If these points change, the hyperplane will also change.

Margin in SVM

The **margin** is the distance between the decision boundary and the closest data points from both classes.

The width of the margin is given by:

$$\text{Margin} = \frac{2}{|w|}$$

To increase the margin, we must reduce the magnitude of (w).

Therefore, the goal of SVM training becomes:

maximize the margin, which is equivalent to **minimizing (|w|)**.

Hard Margin SVM (Linearly Separable Data)

If the dataset is perfectly separable, we can construct a hyperplane that classifies every point correctly.

For correct classification, each training point must satisfy:

$$y_i(w^T x_i + b) \geq 1$$

The optimization problem becomes:

$$\min_{w,b} \frac{1}{2}|w|^2$$

subject to

$$y_i(w^T x_i + b) \geq 1$$

The term

$$\frac{1}{2}|w|^2$$

is used because:

- it makes the optimization problem **convex**
- it is **differentiable**
- it allows the problem to be solved using **quadratic programming methods**

Soft Margin SVM (Real-World Data)

In real-world datasets, perfect separation is rarely possible. Some points may lie on the wrong side of the boundary.

To handle this situation, SVM introduces **slack variables**.

These variables allow some points to violate the margin constraint.

The new condition becomes:

$$y_i(w^T x_i + b) \geq 1 - \xi_i$$

where

$$\xi_i \geq 0$$

The optimization objective is modified as:

$$\min_{w,b,\xi} \frac{1}{2}|w|^2 + C\sum_{i=1}^{n}\xi_i$$

Role of the Parameter (C)

The parameter (C) controls the balance between margin size and classification error.

- **Large C** → strong penalty for misclassification → smaller margin
- **Small C** → allows more errors → wider margin

Thus the optimization objective can be interpreted as:

$$\text{Objective} = \text{Model simplicity} + \text{Misclassification penalty}$$

Dual Formulation of SVM

To solve the optimization problem efficiently, SVM is often expressed in a **dual form** using Lagrange multipliers.

The optimization becomes:

$$\max_{\alpha} \sum_{i=1}^{n} \alpha_i - \frac{1}{2} \sum_{i,j} \alpha_i \alpha_j y_i y_j x_i^T x_j$$

Subject to

$$0 \leq \alpha_i \leq C$$

$$\sum_{i} \alpha_i y_i = 0$$

Important Insight

Only the data points with **non-zero Lagrange multipliers** influence the final solution.

These points are the **support vectors**.

The weight vector of the classifier can therefore be written as:

$$w = \sum_{i \in SV} \alpha_i y_i x_i$$

This means that the entire model depends only on a **small subset of training data points**, which makes SVM very efficient.

Kernel Trick (Handling Non-Linear Data)

Many real-world datasets cannot be separated using a straight line.

To solve this problem, SVM uses the **kernel trick**.

Instead of explicitly mapping data into a higher-dimensional space using a transformation function

$$\phi(x)$$

SVM uses a kernel function:

$$K(x_i, x_j) = \phi(x_i)^T \phi(x_j)$$

The kernel function allows SVM to compute the transformation **implicitly**, making nonlinear classification computationally feasible.

Sometimes data cannot be separated using a straight line.

Example:

Circular clusters.

SVM solves this problem using **Kernel Functions**.

Kernel functions map data into **higher dimensional space** where linear separation becomes possible.

Common kernels:

- Linear:

$$K(x, y) = x^T y$$

- Polynomial:

$$K(x, y) = (x^T y + c)^d$$

- Radial Basis Function:

$$K(x, y) = e^{-\gamma||x-y||^2}$$

- Sigmoid Kernel

$$K(x, y) = tanh(ax^T y + c)$$

Nonlinear Decision Boundary

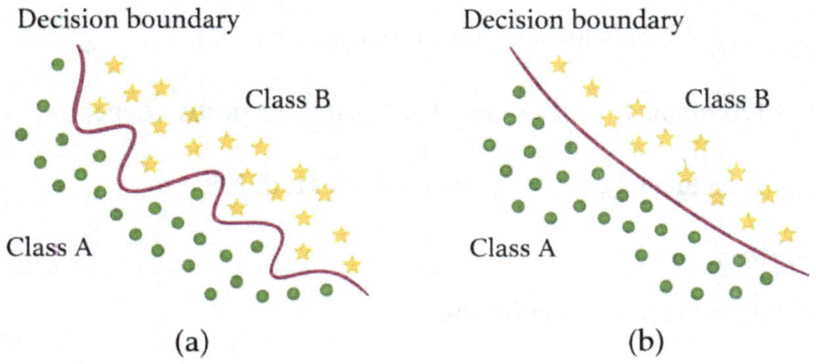

Figure 15-6 : Comparison of complex and smooth decision boundaries in classification. A highly irregular boundary may overfit the training data, while a smoother boundary captures the underlying structure and generalizes better.

The diagram illustrates two different types of **decision boundaries** used in classification algorithms to separate two classes of data points.

In this example:

- **Green circles** represent **Class A**
- **Yellow stars** represent **Class B**

The goal of a classification model is to create a **decision boundary** that separates these two classes.

(a) Complex Decision Boundary

In diagram **(a)**, the decision boundary is **highly irregular and wavy**.

Characteristics

- The curve bends around individual points.
- It attempts to classify **every training data point correctly**.
- The boundary becomes **very complicated**.

Interpretation

This situation represents **overfitting**.

Overfitting occurs when:

- The model learns **noise or random variations** in the training data.
- The boundary becomes too sensitive to small changes.

Consequence

Although the training accuracy may be very high, the model may perform **poorly on new unseen data**.

(b) Smooth Decision Boundary

In diagram **(b)**, the decision boundary is **smooth and simple**.

Characteristics

- The boundary is a **single smooth curve**.

- It captures the **overall pattern** of the data.
- It does not try to perfectly fit every point.

Interpretation

This situation represents **good generalization**.

The model focuses on the **true underlying pattern** rather than memorizing individual points.

Consequence

Such a model usually performs **better on unseen test data**.

Key Concept Demonstrated

The figure highlights an important concept in machine learning:

Trade-off between model complexity and generalization.

Model Type	Boundary	Behavior
Complex model	Irregular boundary	Overfitting
Simple model	Smooth boundary	Better generalization

Table 15-2

Connection to Support Vector Machines

In **Support Vector Machines (SVM)**:

- The algorithm attempts to find the **optimal decision boundary**.
- It maximizes the **margin between classes**.
- Kernel functions allow SVM to create **nonlinear but smooth boundaries** when necessary.

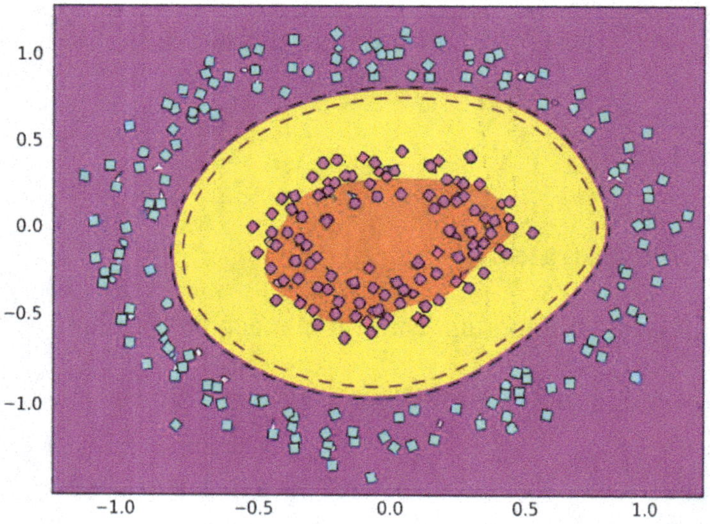

Figure 15-7: Nonlinear Decision Boundary Learned by Support Vector Machine (SVM) with RBF Kernel

The above figure illustrates how a **Support Vector Machine (SVM)** can classify data that is **not linearly separable** by learning a **nonlinear decision boundary**.

1. Two Classes of Data Points

The dataset consists of two distinct classes:

- **Inner Class (Class 1)**
    - Shown as points clustered near the center
    - These belong to one category of data

- **Outer Class (Class 2)**
    - Points forming a circular ring around the center cluster
    - These belong to a second category

Because the inner points are surrounded by the outer points, a **straight line cannot separate them**.

2. Nonlinear Decision Boundary

The SVM constructs a **curved boundary** that separates the two classes.

In the diagram:

- The **enclosed region** represents the classification area for the inner class.
- The **outer region** represents the classification area for the outer class.
- The **curved boundary** between them is the **decision boundary** learned by the SVM.

This boundary is created using a **kernel function**, which allows SVM to project data into a higher-dimensional space where separation becomes easier.

3. Classification Regions

The background color of the diagram indicates **prediction regions**:

Region	Meaning
Inner colored region	Predicted class for inner cluster
Outer colored region	Predicted class for outer cluster

Table 15-3

Any new data point falling inside these regions will be classified accordingly.

4. Margin Around Decision Boundary

The dashed curve around the boundary represents the **margin**.

In SVM:

- The margin is the **distance between the decision boundary and the closest data points**.
- These closest points are called **support vectors**.

Support vectors determine the position of the boundary.

5. Why Kernel SVM is Needed

This example shows a **nonlinear classification problem**.

If we attempted linear classification:

Inner cluster
surrounded by
outer cluster

No straight line could separate them.

Kernel SVM solves this by transforming the feature space.

Example kernels include:

- Radial Basis Function (RBF)
- Polynomial kernel
- Sigmoid kernel

The model learns that:

- Points near the **center** belong to **Class 1**
- Points far from the center belong to **Class 2**

Thus the SVM creates a **closed nonlinear boundary** around the inner class.

Comparison with Logistic Regression

Feature	Logistic Regression	SVM
Objective	Log-loss	Margin maximization
Output	Probabilities	Distance to hyperplane
Robustness to outliers	Moderate	Sensitive if C large
Interpretability	High	Moderate

Table 15-4

Hands on Real-World Implementation Project

Problem Statement

Build a **classification model using Support Vector Machine** to classify whether a customer will purchase a product.

Step 1 Import Libraries

```
import numpy as ____
import pandas as ____
import matplotlib.pyplot as ____
from sklearn.model_selection import ____
from sklearn.svm import ____
from sklearn.preprocessing import ____
```

Step 2 Create Dataset

```
data = {

"Age":[25,35,45,20,30,22],
"Income":[30,60,65,20,45,25],
"Purchase":[0,1,1,0,1,0]

}

df = pd.____(data)

df
```

Step 3 Define Features and Target

```
X = df[[ "____", "____" ]]

y = df["____"]
```

Step 5 Feature Scaling

```
scaler = StandardScaler()

X_train = scaler.____(X_train)

X_test = scaler.____(X_test)
```

Step 6 Train SVM Model

```
model = SVC(kernel="____")

model.fit(____,____)
```

Step 7 Prediction

```
pred = model.____(X_test)

print(pred)
```

Step 8 Accuracy

```
from sklearn.metrics import accuracy_score

print("Accuracy:",accuracy_score(____,____))
```

Step 9 Visualization of Decision Boundary

```
plt.scatter(X[:,0],X[:,1],c=y)

plt.xlabel("Age")
plt.ylabel("Income")

plt.title("SVM Classification")

plt.show()
```

Advantages of SVM

- Effective in high dimensional spaces
- Works well with small datasets
- Robust to overfitting
- Kernel trick enables nonlinear classification
- Uses only support vectors for decision boundary

Limitations of SVM

- Computationally expensive for large datasets
- Choice of kernel is critical
- Hard to interpret model
- Sensitive to feature scaling

Summary

Support Vector Machines are powerful machine learning algorithms used for classification and regression problems. The core idea behind SVM is to identify an optimal hyperplane that maximizes the margin between two classes. Support vectors are the critical data points that define this boundary. When data is not linearly separable, SVM uses kernel functions to transform the data into a higher dimensional space where separation becomes possible. Due to their ability to handle high dimensional data and nonlinear relationships, SVMs are widely used in applications such as image recognition, text classification, and bioinformatics. However, the performance of SVM largely depends on proper kernel selection and parameter tuning.

Exercises

1. Explain the concept of margin in SVM.
2. What are support vectors?
3. What is the kernel trick?
4. Difference between hard margin and soft margin SVM.

Practical Exercises

1. Implement SVM using the **Iris dataset**.
2. Compare performance of:

    Linear Kernel

    Polynomial Kernel

    RBF Kernel

3. Plot decision boundaries for each kernel.

Advanced Exercise

Build an SVM model to classify:

Spam vs Non-Spam emails using text features.

References

1. Cortes, C., & Vapnik, V. (1995). *Support-vector networks*. IEEE Transactions on Neural Networks, 5(2), 273–297.
2. Steinwart, I., & Christmann, A. (2008). *Support Vector Machines*. Springer.
3. Han, J., Kamber, M., & Pei, J. (2012). *Data Mining: Concepts and Techniques* (3rd ed.). Morgan Kaufmann.
4. Schölkopf, B., & Smola, A. (2002). *Learning with Kernels*. MIT Press.
5. Cristianini, N., & Shawe-Taylor, J. (2000). *An Introduction to Support Vector Machines*. Cambridge University Press.
6. Hastie, T., Tibshirani, R., & Friedman, J. (2009). *The Elements of Statistical Learning*. Springer.
7. Bishop, C. M. (2006). *Pattern Recognition and Machine Learning*. Springer.
8. Murphy, K. P. (2012). *Machine Learning: A Probabilistic Perspective*. MIT Press.
9. Vapnik, V. N. (1998). *Statistical Learning Theory*. Wiley.

16. Chapter 16: Unsupervised Learning

Learning Objectives

After reading this chapter, you will be able to:

1. Explain the concept of unsupervised learning and its applications.
2. Implement K-Means clustering and interpret cluster assignments.
3. Determine optimal number of clusters using evaluation methods.
4. Apply hierarchical clustering techniques.
5. Use dimensionality reduction methods such as PCA for data analysis.

Introduction

Unsupervised learning is an important paradigm of machine learning in which a model is trained using **unlabeled data**, that is, input samples for which no target outputs or ground-truth labels are available. In this setting, the learning algorithm is not guided by predefined answers. Instead, it attempts to **automatically discover hidden structures,**

patterns, and statistical regularities present in the data by analysing the relationships among input features.

Unlike supervised learning, where the objective is to learn an explicit mapping from inputs to known outputs, unsupervised learning focuses on **organizing, summarizing, and interpreting data without external supervision**. This makes it especially useful in exploratory data analysis, where the underlying structure of the data is not known in advance and labelled datasets are either unavailable or very expensive to obtain.

In many real-world scenarios, such as business analytics, healthcare, remote sensing, and social media analysis, large volumes of raw data are generated continuously without labels. In such cases, unsupervised learning becomes the **natural and practical choice**, as it can reveal meaningful insights that may not be evident through manual inspection alone.

Motivation for Unsupervised Learning

One of the primary reasons for adopting unsupervised learning is the **high cost, time, and domain expertise required for data labelling**. By concentrating on the intrinsic structure of the data, unsupervised algorithms are capable of uncovering **previously unknown patterns or groupings**.

For instance, when analysing customer transaction data, clustering algorithms can automatically identify groups of customers with similar purchasing behaviour. These insights can then be utilised by decision-makers to design targeted marketing strategies, customer loyalty programs, or personalised recommendations. Such applications highlight the practical importance of unsupervised learning in decision support systems and data-driven organisations.

In a typical workflow, an unsupervised model is trained on the available dataset using a selected algorithm. Since no ground-truth labels exist, the quality of the results is usually assessed using **internal evaluation measures** (such as cluster compactness or separation) and **domain expert judgement**. Based on these evaluations, the model is iteratively refined by tuning parameters, improving data preprocessing, or choosing alternative algorithms.

Types of Unsupervised Learning Algorithms

Unsupervised learning techniques can be broadly classified into the following major categories:

1. Clustering

Clustering algorithms group data points into clusters such that objects within the same cluster are more similar to each other than to those in other clusters.

2. Association Rule Learning

Association rule learning focuses on discovering **interesting relationships or dependencies** among variables in large datasets, such as frequently co-occurring items in transaction databases.

3. Dimensionality Reduction

Dimensionality reduction techniques aim to reduce the number of features while preserving the essential structure of the data, thereby improving interpretability and computational efficiency.

Clustering

Clustering refers to a broad family of unsupervised learning algorithms that **partition a dataset into subsets (clusters)** based on a chosen similarity or distance measure. The goal is to maximise similarity within clusters and minimise similarity between clusters.

Illustrative Applications of Clustering

- **Marketing segmentation**: Identifying distinct customer groups based on buying behaviour
- **Land-use analysis**: Grouping regions with similar land-cover characteristics from satellite images
- **Insurance analytics**: Detecting clusters of policyholders with similar claim patterns
- **Urban and city planning**: Grouping residential areas based on location, value, and housing type
- **Seismology**: Clustering earthquake epicentres along tectonic fault lines

Major Clustering Approaches

Clustering algorithms can be categorised into several major approaches:

1. **Partitioning methods**

   These algorithms divide the dataset into a fixed number of clusters by optimising a specific criterion. A well-known example is k-means clustering.

2. **Hierarchical methods**

   These methods build a hierarchy of clusters by either successively merging smaller clusters or splitting larger ones.

3. **Density-based methods**

   Clusters are defined as dense regions separated by areas of low density.

4. **Grid-based methods**

   The data space is divided into a finite number of cells, and clustering is performed on the resulting grid structure.

5. **Model-based methods**

   These approaches assume that data are generated from an underlying probabilistic model and attempt to fit the best model to the data.

K-Means Clustering Algorithm

The k-means algorithm is one of the simplest and most widely used clustering techniques due to its **conceptual clarity and computational**

efficiency.

Given a predefined number of clusters (k), the algorithm proceeds as follows:

1. Initialise (k) cluster centroids, usually at random.
2. Assign each data point to the cluster with the nearest centroid.
3. Recompute each centroid as the mean of the points assigned to that cluster.
4. Repeat the assignment and update steps until convergence, i.e., when cluster assignments no longer change.

Although k-means is efficient and easy to implement, it requires the value of (k) to be specified in advance and performs best when clusters are roughly spherical and well separated.

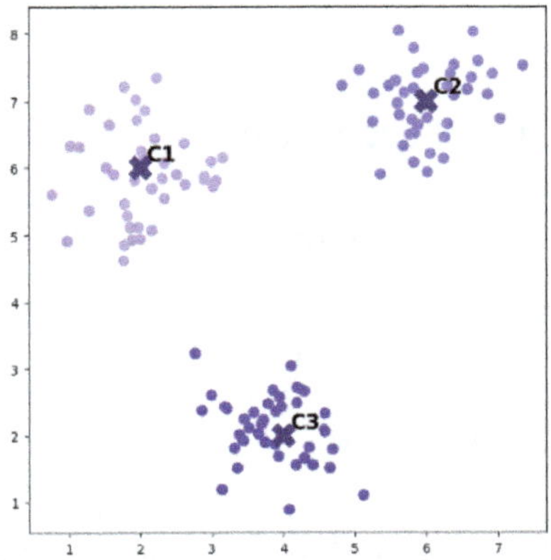

Figure 16-1
Illustration of the K-Means clustering algorithm where data points are

grouped into three clusters based on distance to their nearest centroid. The diagram illustrates how the **K-Means clustering algorithm** partitions data into *K distinct clusters*. Each cluster contains data points that are closest to a particular **centroid**.

Elements shown in the diagram:

1. **Data Points**
   - Represent individual observations in the dataset.
   - Displayed as colored dots in a 2-D feature space.
2. **Clusters**
   - Groups of points with similar characteristics.
   - Each cluster is represented with a different color.
3. **Centroids**
   - The center of each cluster.
   - Usually marked with a large **X or star symbol**.
   - Denoted as C_1, C_2, C_3.
4. **Cluster Boundaries**
   - Points are assigned to the cluster whose centroid is nearest.

Mathematical Objective of K-Means

K-Means minimizes the **within-cluster sum of squared distances**:

$$J = \sum_{k=1}^{K} \sum_{x_i \in C_k} || x_i - \mu_k ||^2$$

where:

- K= number of clusters
- x_i= data point
- μ_k= centroid of cluster k

Algorithm Steps

1. Choose number of clusters K.
2. Randomly initialize **K centroids.**
3. Assign each data point to the **nearest centroid**.
4. Recalculate centroid as the **mean of assigned points**.
5. Repeat steps 3–4 until centroids stop changing.

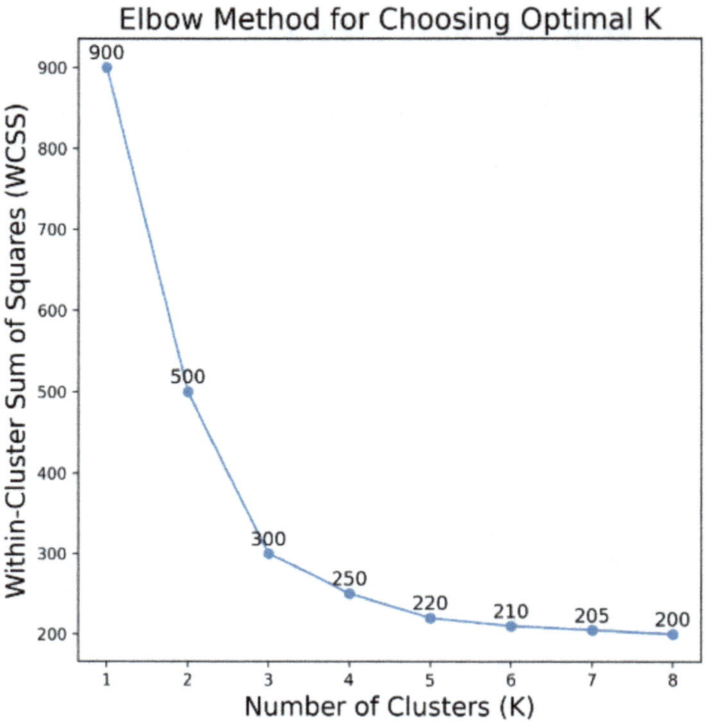

Figure 16-2: Elbow method used to determine the optimal number of clusters (K) by plotting the Within-Cluster Sum of Squares (WCSS).

The main objective of the Elbow Method is to determine the most suitable number of clusters (K) for a given dataset before applying the K-Means clustering algorithm.

How it Works:

In this approach, the K-Means algorithm is executed multiple times using different values of (K), typically in a range such as (K = 1) to (K = 10). For each value of (K), the **Within-Cluster Sum of Squares (WCSS)** is calculated. WCSS represents the total squared distance between each data point and the centroid of the cluster to which it belongs.

The "Elbow" Point:

As the value of (K) increases, the WCSS value decreases because data points are grouped into more refined clusters. However, after a certain point, the rate of decrease becomes very small. This point of change in the curve resembles an **"elbow"**, indicating that adding additional clusters does not significantly improve the clustering performance.

Applications:

The Elbow Method is widely used in practical applications such as **customer segmentation, image compression, and anomaly detection**, where identifying the appropriate number of clusters is important for meaningful data grouping.

Limitations:

One limitation of the Elbow Method is that the elbow point may not always be clearly visible. In such cases, determining the optimal number of clusters can become subjective and may require additional validation techniques.

Hierarchical Clustering

Hierarchical clustering methods construct **nested clusters** organised in the form of a tree structure known as a dendrogram.

- **Agglomerative (bottom-up) clustering** starts with each data point as an individual cluster and repeatedly merges the most similar clusters until a single cluster remains.

- **Divisive (top-down) clustering** begins with all data points in one cluster and recursively splits them into smaller clusters until each cluster contains only one data point.

Hierarchical clustering is particularly useful for **visual analysis**, as dendrograms clearly illustrate cluster relationships at different levels of granularity.

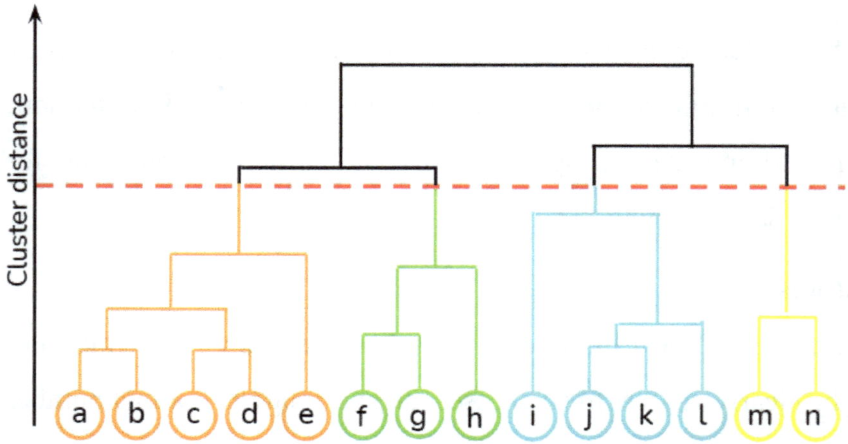

Figure 16-3

Types of Hierarchical Clustering

Hierarchical clustering methods can be broadly divided into two main approaches: **Agglomerative clustering** and **Divisive clustering**. Both techniques build a hierarchy of clusters, but they differ in the way the clustering process begins and progresses.

Agglomerative Clustering (Bottom–Up Approach)

Figure 16-4: Agglomerative hierarchical clustering where individual data points begin as separate clusters and are progressively merged into larger clusters until a single cluster is formed.

Agglomerative clustering follows a **bottom–up strategy**. In this method, the algorithm initially treats **each data point as a separate cluster**. At the start, if a dataset contains *n*data points, there will be *n*individual clusters.

The algorithm then repeatedly performs the following steps:

1. Compute the similarity or distance between all clusters.
2. Identify the **two clusters that are most similar (or closest)** according to a chosen distance metric.
3. Merge these two clusters into a single cluster.
4. Update the distance matrix to reflect the newly formed cluster.

This merging process continues **iteratively**, gradually combining smaller clusters into larger ones, until finally **all data points belong to a single cluster**. The sequence of merges forms a hierarchical structure that can be visualized using a **dendrogram**, which shows how clusters are combined at different levels of similarity.

Agglomerative clustering is the **most commonly used hierarchical clustering technique** because it is conceptually simple and easy to implement.

Divisive Clustering (Top–Down Approach)

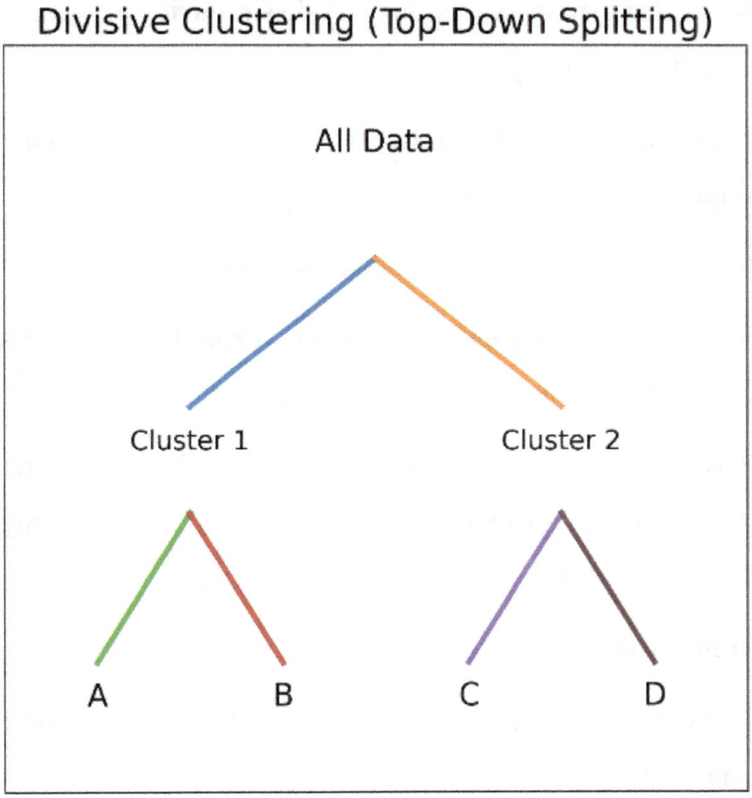

Figure 16-5: Divisive hierarchical clustering where all data points initially belong to a single cluster and are recursively split into smaller clusters.

Divisive clustering works in the **opposite direction** and follows a **top–down strategy**. Instead of starting with many small clusters, the algorithm begins with **all data points grouped into a single cluster**.

The clustering process then proceeds as follows:

1. The algorithm analyzes the dataset and determines how the

current cluster can be **split into smaller clusters**.

2. The cluster that shows the **largest dissimilarity or variance** is selected for splitting.
3. The cluster is divided into two or more smaller clusters based on similarity among data points.
4. This splitting process is repeated recursively.

The process continues until **each data point forms its own cluster** or until a predefined number of clusters is reached.

Although divisive clustering can produce meaningful cluster structures, it is **computationally more expensive** than agglomerative clustering. For this reason, it is used less frequently in practical applications.

Key Difference Between the Two Approaches

The main difference between these two methods lies in the **direction of cluster formation**:

- **Agglomerative clustering** builds clusters by **merging smaller clusters into larger ones**.
- **Divisive clustering** builds clusters by **splitting larger clusters into smaller ones**.

Both approaches ultimately produce a **hierarchical tree structure**, allowing analysts to choose different levels of clustering depending on the desired level of detail.

Hands-On Exercise: K-Means Clustering

Problem Statement

In many real-world applications, organizations need to discover natural groupings in data without predefined labels. For example, an online retail company may want to group customers based on purchasing behavior, a city planner may group regions based on traffic patterns, or a marketing team may group users based on browsing activity. These tasks require unsupervised learning techniques such as clustering.

In this lab, you will use the K-Means clustering algorithm from the Scikit-Learn library to discover patterns in a dataset. You will generate a synthetic dataset, apply the K-Means algorithm, visualize the clusters, and determine the optimal number of clusters using the Elbow Method.

Learning Objectives

Understand the workflow of the K-Means clustering algorithm

Implement K-Means clustering using Scikit-Learn

Visualize clusters and cluster centroids

Determine the optimal number of clusters using the Elbow Method

Summary

In this chapter, we explored Unsupervised Machine Learning, a type of machine learning in which algorithms learn patterns and relationships from data without using predefined labels or target outputs. Unlike supervised learning, unsupervised learning discovers hidden structures and meaningful information directly from the dataset.

We studied important techniques such as clustering, association, and dimensionality reduction. Clustering algorithms group similar data points together, while association techniques identify relationships among variables. Dimensionality reduction methods help simplify large datasets while preserving important information.

The chapter also introduced commonly used algorithms and their applications in real-world scenarios such as customer segmentation, recommendation systems, market basket analysis, anomaly detection, and pattern discovery. Practical implementation using Python and machine learning libraries demonstrated how unsupervised learning can reveal valuable insights from unlabeled data.

Unsupervised learning plays an important role in data exploration and forms a strong foundation for solving complex real-world problems where labeled data may not be available.

Exercise

1. What type of machine learning algorithm is K-Means (supervised or unsupervised)?

2. What does the parameter K represent in the K-Means algorithm?

3. What is the purpose of the cluster centroid?

4. What does WCSS represent in clustering?

5. Why does the WCSS value decrease as K increases?

6. What is the purpose of the Elbow Method?

7. In the Elbow Method graph, what does the elbow point indicate?

8. Name two real-world applications of K-Means clustering.

References

1. Hwang, K., Dongarra, J., & Fox, G. (2012). *Distributed and Cloud Computing: From Parallel Processing to the Internet of Things*. Morgan Kaufmann.
2. Hwang, K. (1993). *Advanced Computer Architecture and Parallel Processing*. McGraw-Hill.
3. Bishop, C. M. (2006). *Pattern Recognition and Machine Learning*. Springer.
4. Jain, A. K., Murty, M. N., & Flynn, P. J. (1999). Data clustering: A review. *ACM Computing Surveys*, 31(3), 264–323.
5. Xu, R., & Wunsch, D. (2005). Survey of clustering algorithms. *IEEE Transactions on Neural Networks*, 16(3), 645–678.
6. MacQueen, J. (1967). Some methods for classification and analysis of multivariate observations. *Proceedings of the 5th Berkeley Symposium on Mathematical Statistics and Probability*.
7. Berkhin, P. (2002). A survey of clustering data mining techniques.

ACM SIGKDD Explorations, 2(2), 25–67.

8. Zeng, F. (2024). A survey of unsupervised clustering methods driven by information completeness. *Proceedings of the ACM Digital Library*.
9. Dridi, S. (2021). Unsupervised learning — A systematic literature review.
10. Sarker, I. H. (2021). Machine learning: Algorithms, real-world applications and research directions. *Informatics*, PMC.
11. Grira, N., Crucianu, M., & Boujemaa, N. (2005). Unsupervised and semi-supervised clustering: A brief survey. INRIA Technical Report.
12. Gothane, S. (2023). Unsupervised learning towards hierarchical clustering. *AIP Conference Proceedings*.
13. Agrawal, R., Imieliński, T., & Swami, A. (1993). Mining association rules between sets of items in large databases. *Proceedings of ACM SIGMOD Conference on Management of Data*.

17. Chapter 17: Reinforcement Learning

Learning Objectives

After reading this chapter, you will be able to:

1. Define key components of reinforcement learning (agent, environment, reward).
2. Explain the exploration vs. exploitation trade-off.
3. Implement Q-learning for simple environments.
4. Interpret Q-tables and policy decisions.
5. Apply reinforcement learning to real-world scenarios such as game playing.

What is Reinforcement Learning?

Reinforcement Learning (RL) is a way of teaching machines how to make decisions through experience. Instead of telling the machine the correct answer, we let it try actions, observe outcomes, and learn from rewards or penalties.

Think of teaching a child to ride a bicycle. You do not give equations or rules. The child tries, falls, adjusts, and eventually learns to balance. Reinforcement Learning works in exactly the same way.

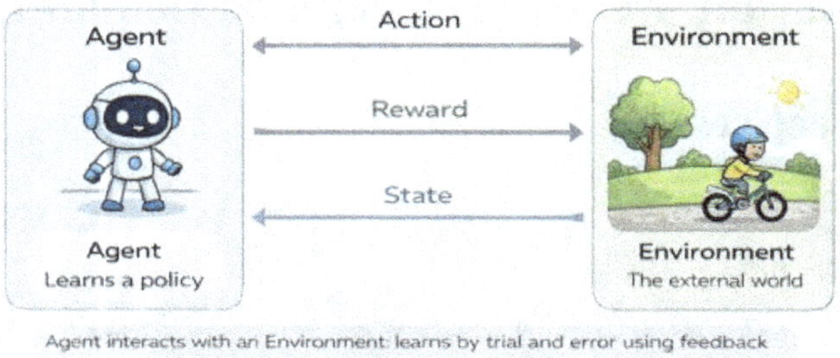

Figure 17-1: Reinforcement Learning

In machine learning terms:

- The agent is the learner (the child)
- The environment is the world (the road)
- Actions are what the agent can do (pedal, turn)
- Rewards are feedback (success or falling)

The goal of RL is to maximize long-term reward, not just immediate success.

Core Components of Reinforcement Learning

Every reinforcement learning problem has five key components:

1. Agent – the decision-maker
2. Environment – everything the agent interacts with
3. State (s) – the current situation of the agent
4. Action (a) – a choice the agent can take

5. Reward (r) – feedback from the environment

The agent repeatedly interacts with the environment and gradually improves its behavior.

Reinforcement Learning Interaction Loop

The RL process follows a continuous loop:

6. Agent observes the current state
7. Agent selects an action
8. Environment changes state
9. Agent receives a reward
10. Agent updates its strategy (policy)

This loop continues until the agent learns an optimal policy.

Reinforcement Learning Loop (How Learning Happens)

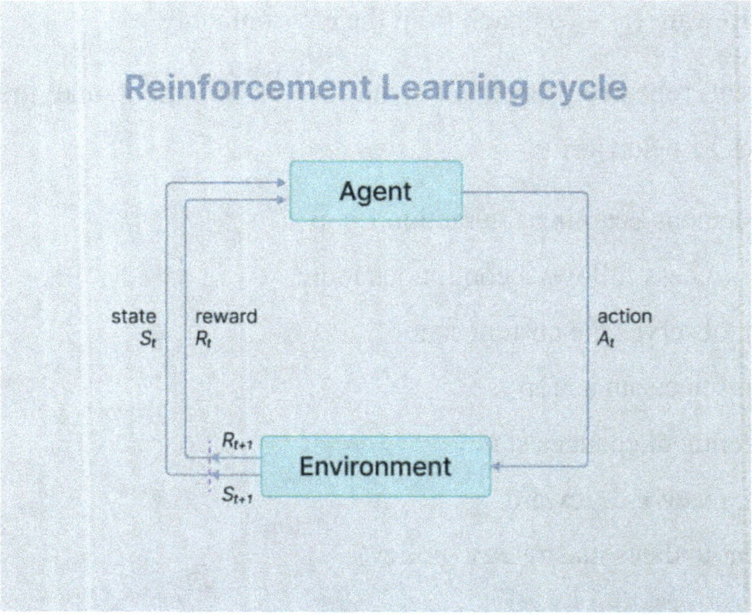

Figure 17-2: Agent–Environment interaction loop.

Above Figure illustrates the basic Agent–Environment interaction loop.

Step-by-step

1. Agent observes the state
2. Agent takes an action
3. Environment returns a reward
4. Environment moves to a new state
5. Agent updates its knowledge
6. Repeat until behavior improves

Simple Real-World Example

Example: Robot Learning to Walk

• State → joint angles, balance

• Action → move leg forward

• Reward → +1 if it stays upright, −10 if it falls

• Goal → walk without falling

The robot does not know how to walk initially.

It discovers walking through trial and error.

Reinforcement Learning vs Other ML Types

Learning Type	Data Given	Goal
Supervised	Labeled data	Predict output
Unsupervised	Unlabeled data	Find patterns
Reinforcement	Reward signal	Learn decisions

Table 17-1

RL is about **sequences of decisions**, not single predictions.

Policy and Value Functions

Policy (π)

A **policy** defines how the agent behaves. It maps states to actions.

- Deterministic policy: one action per state

- Stochastic policy: probabilities over actions

Value Functions

Value functions estimate **how good a state or action is**.

- State-value function: V(s)
- Action-value function: Q(s, a)

These functions guide the agent toward better decisions.

Exploration vs Exploitation

A key challenge in RL is deciding between:

- **Exploration** – trying new actions
- **Exploitation** – using known good actions

A popular strategy is **epsilon-greedy**:

- With probability $\varepsilon \rightarrow$ explore
- With probability $1 - \varepsilon \rightarrow$ exploit

This balance allows learning without getting stuck in poor strategies.

Model-Free Reinforcement Learning

What is Model-Free RL?

In model-free RL, the agent **does not know how the environment works**. It learns purely from experience.

This approach is useful when: - The environment is unknown - Building a model is difficult

Here's a **clear, real-world example of Model-Free Reinforcement Learning**, explained in a **simple, practical way**.

Real-World Example: Personalized Online Recommendations

Consider an online streaming platform that recommends videos or articles to users.

The system does **not** know in advance:

- A user's exact preferences
- How a recommendation will affect future behavior
- The internal "rules" that govern user satisfaction

Instead, it learns **directly from interaction**.

How model-free RL works here

- **State:** User's recent activity (what they watched or clicked)
- **Action:** Recommend a specific item
- **Reward:** User clicks, watches fully, likes, or ignores the content

At first, the system tries different recommendations. Some lead to positive feedback (long watch time or clicks), while others are ignored or skipped. Over time, the system learns which recommendations work best for different user situations.

Importantly, the system does **not build an explicit model** of user behavior. It simply learns which actions tend to produce higher rewards based on past experience.

Why this is Model-Free Reinforcement Learning

- Learning happens through **trial and error**
- No predefined model of user behavior exists
- The policy improves directly from observed rewards

Algorithms like **Q-learning** or **Deep Q-Networks (DQN)** are commonly used in such recommendation settings.

In the real world, model-free reinforcement learning is useful when system behavior is complex or unknown, and the agent must learn directly from feedback rather than from a predefined model.

Q-Learning

Q-learning is a **model-free reinforcement learning algorithm** that teaches an agent **what action to take in each situation** by learning from experience.

At a high level, Q-learning answers one simple question repeatedly:

"If I am in this state, how good is it to take this action?"

Core Idea

Q-learning learns a value called **Q-value**:

$$Q(\text{state}, \text{action})$$

This value represents the expected future reward the agent will receive if it:

1. Takes a specific action in a given state, and
2. Continues to behave optimally afterward.

The agent stores these values in a Q-table (or a neural network in deep RL).

How Learning Happens (Intuitively)

1. The agent observes the current state
2. It chooses an action
3. The environment returns:
   - o A reward
   - o The next state
4. The agent updates its Q-value based on this experience

Over many interactions, the Q-values improve, and the agent learns the best action for each state.

Q-learning Update Rule

$$Q(s,a) \leftarrow Q(s,a) + \alpha\Big[r + \gamma \max_{a} Q(s',a) - Q(s,a)\Big]$$

Where:

- (s) = current state
- (a) = action taken
- (r) = reward received
- (s') = next state
- α is the learning rate (how fast it learns)
- γ is the discount factor (importance of future rewards)

Why Q-learning is Model-Free

- It **does not know** how the environment works
- It **does not predict** next states using a model
- It learns **only from rewards and experience**

Simple Example

Think of a robot learning to navigate a room:

- **State:** Robot's current position
- **Action:** Move left, right, forward, backward
- **Reward:** +1 for reaching the goal, −1 for hitting a wall

The robot tries actions, updates Q-values, and gradually learns the best path—without ever being told the map. Q-learning is a model-free reinforcement learning algorithm that learns the optimal action-value function by updating Q-values using rewards from direct interaction with the environment.

SARSA

SARSA is similar to Q-learning but learns using the current policy. SARSA is an on-policy reinforcement learning algorithm. This means it learns the value of the policy that the agent is actually following during training. The learning process reflects the agent's current behavior, including any exploratory or cautious actions it takes.

Q-learning, on the other hand, is an off-policy algorithm. It learns the value of the optimal policy, independent of the agent's current actions. Even if the agent behaves sub-optimally while exploring, Q-learning still updates its values assuming the best possible future actions.

In simple terms, if the agent follows a cautious or risk-averse strategy, SARSA learns how good that cautious strategy really is. Q-learning, by contrast, focuses on learning the best possible strategy, even if the agent is not consistently following it yet. You can think of SARSA as learning from current habits, while Q-learning is always aiming for ideal habits.

Deep Q-Networks (DQN)

Deep Q-Networks (DQN) extend Q-learning to handle complex, high-dimensional environments. Traditional Q-learning relies on a table of state–action values, which becomes impractical when the number of states is very large.

In environments such as video games, where each state may consist of thousands or millions of pixel values, maintaining a Q-table is impossible. DQN addresses this limitation by using a deep neural network to approximate the Q-function.

By combining Q-learning with deep learning, DQN enables an agent to learn directly from raw inputs such as images, making it possible to apply model-free reinforcement learning to large and realistic problem domains.

Model-Based Reinforcement Learning

What is Model-Based RL?

Model-based RL builds an internal model of the environment, including state transitions and rewards. The agent uses this model to plan ahead. This approach is like learning the rules of a game before playing.

Key Ideas

- Transition model $P(s'|s, a)$
- Reward model $R(s, a)$
- Planning using simulations

Advantages

- Better sample efficiency
- Faster learning in expensive environments

Popular Model-Based Algorithms

- **Dyna-Q:** Combines real experience with simulated experience; a hybrid of model-free and model-based learning.
- **Monte Carlo Tree Search (MCTS):** Simulates future action sequences; used in AlphaGo and MuZero.

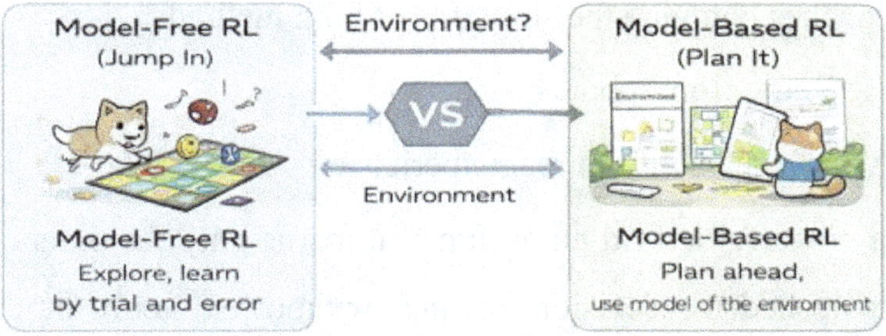

Figure 17-3 : compares Model-Free and Model-Based RL.

Model-Free RL

- Learns by experience
- No environment model
- Example: Q-Learning, SARSA, DQN

Model-Based RL

- Builds a model of environment
- Plans before acting
- Example: Dyna-Q, MCTS

Hybrid Reinforcement Learning

Hybrid approaches combine the strengths of both methods:

- Fast learning from models
- High performance from real experience

MuZero is a powerful hybrid algorithm that learns only the parts of the environment needed for decision-making, without explicitly modeling everything.

Applications of Reinforcement Learning

- **Game Playing:** Chess, Go, Atari games
- **Robotics:** Walking, grasping, and motor control
- **Self-Driving Cars:** Navigation and obstacle avoidance
- **Finance:** Algorithmic trading strategies
- **Recommendation Systems:** Personalized content suggestions

Hands on Example for Reinforcement Learning

Example: Q-Learning on a Simple Grid World

```
import numpy as np

states = 5
actions = 2  # Left or right
Q = np.zeros((states, actions))

alpha = 0.1   # Learning rate
gamma = 0.9   # discount factor
epsilon = 0.2 # exploration rate

def step(state, action):
    if action == 0:
        next_state = max(0, state - 1)
    else:
        next_state = min(states - 1, state + 1)
    reward = 1 if next_state == states - 1 else 0
    return next_state, reward
for episode in range(1000):
    state = 0
    while state != states - 1:
        if np.random.rand() < epsilon:
            action = np.random.choice(actions)
        else:
            action = np.argmax(Q[state])

        next_state, reward = step(state, action)
        Q[state, action] += alpha * (reward + gamma * np.max(Q[next_state]) - Q[state, action])
        state = next_state

print(Q)
```

Code Explanation

This example demonstrates **Q-Learning**, a classic **model-free reinforcement learning** algorithm, using a very simple environment often referred to as a *1-D grid world*. The goal of this example is not complexity, but clarity: it shows how an agent learns optimal behavior **purely through interaction and reward feedback**, without any prior knowledge of the environment's dynamics.

Environment and State Space

The environment consists of **five discrete states**, arranged linearly:

$0 \rightarrow 1 \rightarrow 2 \rightarrow 3 \rightarrow 4$

- State 0 is the **starting state**
- State 4 is the **terminal (goal) state**
- The agent can take **two actions** in each state:
    - 0: move left
    - 1: move right

This setup is intentionally minimal so that the learning mechanism of Q-Learning is easy to observe and reason about.

Q-Table Initialization

The Q-table is initialized as a **5 × 2 matrix**, where:

- Each **row** corresponds to a state
- Each **column** corresponds to an action (left or right)

Initially, all Q-values are set to zero. This reflects a **tabula rasa** agent—no assumptions, no prior experience.

The Q-table represents the agent's evolving estimate of:

"How good is it to take action a in state s, considering future rewards?"

Learning Parameters

Three key hyperparameters control learning behavior:

- **Learning rate (α = 0.1)**
  Determines how strongly new information overrides old estimates. A small α ensures stable, gradual learning.
- **Discount factor (γ = 0.9)**
  Emphasizes future rewards. Since reaching the goal requires multiple steps, valuing future reward is essential.
- **Exploration rate (ε = 0.2)**
  Implements ε-greedy exploration:
    - 20% of the time: explore randomly
    - 80% of the time: exploit the best known action

This balances **exploration vs. exploitation**, a core challenge in reinforcement learning.

Environment Dynamics (step function)

The step function encodes the environment rules:

- Moving left decreases the state index (bounded at 0)
- Moving right increases the state index (bounded at 4)
- A **reward of 1** is given *only* when the agent reaches the terminal state

All intermediate transitions yield **zero reward**, forcing the agent to learn through **delayed reinforcement**.

Training Loop and Episodes

The agent is trained over **1000 episodes**. Each episode:

1. Starts from state 0
2. Continues until the terminal state is reached
3. Updates the Q-table at every step

At each step:

- The agent selects an action using ε-greedy strategy
- Observes the next state and reward
- Updates the Q-value using the **Bellman optimality equation**:

$$Q(s,a) \leftarrow Q(s,a) + \alpha \left[r + \gamma \max Q(s',a') - Q(s,a)\right]$$

This update moves the Q-value toward a better estimate of long-term reward.

This compact example captures the **essence of reinforcement learning** and serves as a strong conceptual foundation before scaling to larger state spaces or function approximation methods.

Summary

A reinforcement learning algorithms chapter explains how an agent learns to make decisions by interacting with an environment and maximizing cumulative rewards. It is based on Reinforcement Learning, where actions in different states lead to rewards or penalties.

Key elements include agent, environment, states, actions, rewards, and policy. The framework is often modeled using a Markov Decision Process.

The chapter typically covers major approaches such as value-based methods (e.g., Q-learning), policy-based methods, and model free. It also explains the exploration vs. exploitation trade-off.

Exercises

1. Explain the difference between supervised learning and reinforcement learning.
2. What is the exploration–exploitation dilemma?
3. Compare Q-learning and SARSA.
4. Why is model-based RL more sample efficient?
5. Design a reward function for a self-driving car.
6. Implement a simple Q-learning agent for a grid world.

An agent navigates a grid:

- States: grid positions
- Actions: up, down, left, right
- Reward: +1 for goal, −1 for obstacles

Using Q-learning, the agent gradually learns the optimal path to the goal.

Problem 1 — Identify the RL pieces

Question: You are training a robot vacuum to clean a room.

1. Who/what is the agent?
2. What is the environment?

3. Give one possible state.

4. Give two possible actions.

5. Give one possible reward.

Problem 2 — RL vs Supervised Learning

Question: In one paragraph, explain why RL is not the same as supervised learning.

Problem 3 — Discount factor intuition

Question: What does the discount factor γ do? What happens when:

- $\gamma = 0$
- γ is close to 1

Problem 4 — One Q-learning update (numbers)

Question: You have:

- $Q(s, a) = 2.0$
- $\alpha = 0.1$
- $r = 1$
- $\gamma = 0.9$
- $\max_{a'} Q(s', a') = 3.0$

Compute the new Q(s, a) using:

$Q(s, a) \leftarrow Q(s, a) + \alpha \, [\, r + \gamma \max Q(s', a') - Q(s, a) \,]$

Problem 5 — On-policy vs Off-policy

Question: Explain Q-learning vs SARSA in simple language.

Problem 6 — Exploration vs Exploitation

Question: In epsilon-greedy with $\varepsilon = 0.2$, what fraction of the time do we explore vs exploit?

Problem 7 — Design a reward function (self-driving)

Question: Design a reward function for a self-driving car that must:

- reach a destination safely
- avoid collisions
- obey speed limits
- minimize travel time

Problem 8 — Episode vs Step

Question: What is an "episode" in RL? Give an example.

Problem 9 — Markov property (what does it mean?)

Question: Explain the Markov property like you're talking to a beginner.

Problem 10 — Model-free vs Model-based choice

Question: You are training a real robot arm. Each real-world trial is expensive and slow. Should you prefer model-free or model-based RL, and why?

Problem 11 — Spot the bug

Question: Your agent gets +1 reward every step and never ends the episode. What might happen?

References

1. Sutton, R. S., & Barto, A. G. *Reinforcement Learning: An Introduction*, 2nd Edition, MIT Press, 2018.
2. Kaelbling, L. P., Littman, M. L., & Moore, A. W. (1996). Reinforcement Learning: A Survey. *Journal of Artificial Intelligence Research (JAIR)*. ACM Digital Library.
3. Silver, D., Singh, S., Precup, D., & Sutton, R. S. (2015). Reward Is Enough. *Communications of the ACM*, Vol. 63, No. 1.
4. Kober, J., Bagnell, J. A., & Peters, J. (2013). Reinforcement Learning in Robotics: A Survey. *International Journal of Robotics Research*, ACM-related publications.
5. Watkins, C. J. C. H., & Dayan, P. (1992). Q-Learning. *Machine Learning*, IEEE Xplore.
6. Mnih, V., Kavukcuoglu, K., Silver, D., et al. (2015). Human-Level Control Through Deep Reinforcement Learning. *Nature* (widely indexed in IEEE Xplore).
7. Szepesvári, C. (2010). Algorithms for Reinforcement Learning. *Synthesis Lectures on Artificial Intelligence and Machine Learning*, IEEE.
8. Kiumarsi, B., Lewis, F. L., Modares, H., Karimpour, A., & Naghibi-Sistani, M. B. (2018). Reinforcement Learning Applications in Control Systems. *IEEE Transactions on Systems, Man, and Cybernetics*.
9. Sutton, R. S. (1991). Dyna, an Integrated Architecture for Learning, Planning, and Reacting. *ACM SIGART Bulletin*.

10. Browne, C. B., et al. (2012). A Survey of Monte Carlo Tree Search Methods. *IEEE Transactions on Computational Intelligence and AI in Games.*

11. Schrittwieser, J., et al. (2020). Mastering Atari, Go, Chess and Shogi by Planning with a Learned Model (MuZero). *Nature / IEEE Xplore indexed.*

12. Singh, S., Jaakkola, T., Littman, M. L., & Szepesvári, C. (2000). Convergence Results for Single-Step On-Policy Reinforcement-Learning Algorithms.
Machine Learning Journal (Springer, ACM-indexed)

13. Mnih, V., et al. (2015).
Human-Level Control through Deep Reinforcement Learning.
Nature (Referenced extensively in IEEE and ACM surveys).

14. Busoniu, L., Babuska, R., De Schutter, B., & Ernst, D. (2010).
Reinforcement Learning and Dynamic Programming Using Function Approximators.
IEEE Press.

Appendix 1

Install Anaconda and Jupyter Notebook on Windows

We are going to learn how to install Anaconda and use Jupyter Notebook on a Windows computer. No prior programming experience is required.

What Are Anaconda and Jupyter?

- **Anaconda** is a free software distribution that includes Python, Jupyter Notebook, and many useful libraries for data science and machine learning.
- **Jupyter Notebook** is an interactive tool that lets you write and run Python code in a web browser.

Why We Use Anaconda for Machine Learning

Anaconda is widely used in machine learning because it simplifies setup and helps beginners focus on learning instead of troubleshooting.

- **All-in-one platform:** Anaconda comes with Python, Jupyter Notebook, and popular machine learning libraries (NumPy, pandas, scikit-learn, TensorFlow) pre-installed.

- **Easy environment management:** It allows users to create and manage separate environments, preventing version conflicts between libraries.
- **Beginner-friendly:** Anaconda Navigator provides a graphical interface, so users do not need to rely heavily on command-line tools.
- **Industry standard:** Anaconda is commonly used in academia, research, and industry, making skills learned with it widely applicable.
- **Reliable and stable:** Packages are tested and optimized, reducing installation errors common in machine learning setups.

In simple terms: Anaconda saves time, reduces errors, and makes machine learning accessible for beginners.

System Requirements

- Windows 10 or Windows 11
- Internet connection
- Administrator access (recommended)

Step 1: Download Anaconda

Screenshot 1: Anaconda official website home page

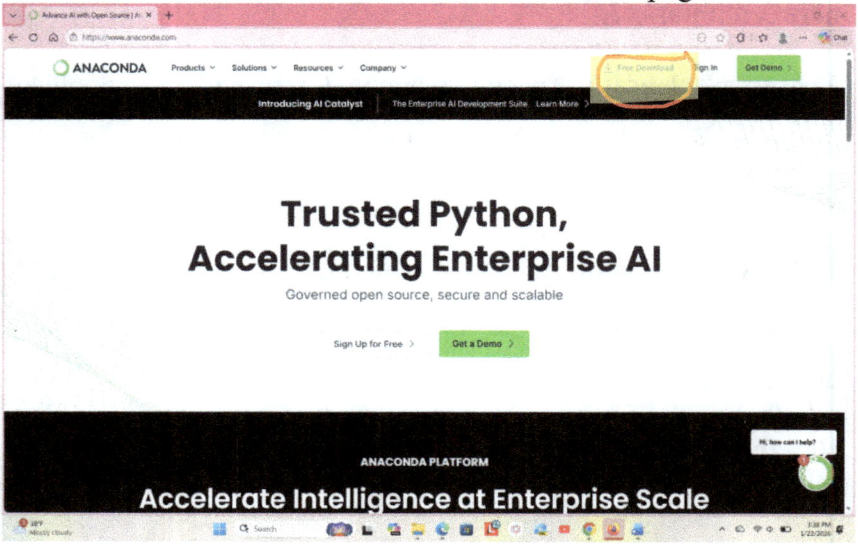

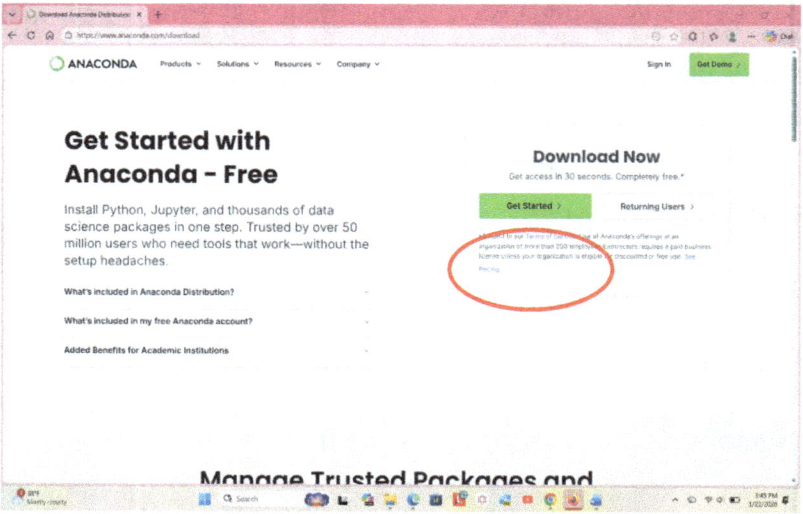

1. Open a web browser (Chrome, Edge, or Firefox).
2. Go to the official Anaconda website: https://www.anaconda.com

3. Click Download.
4. Select Windows.
5. Choose 64-Bit Graphical Installer.

Browser → Anaconda Website → Download → Windows → 64-bit Installer

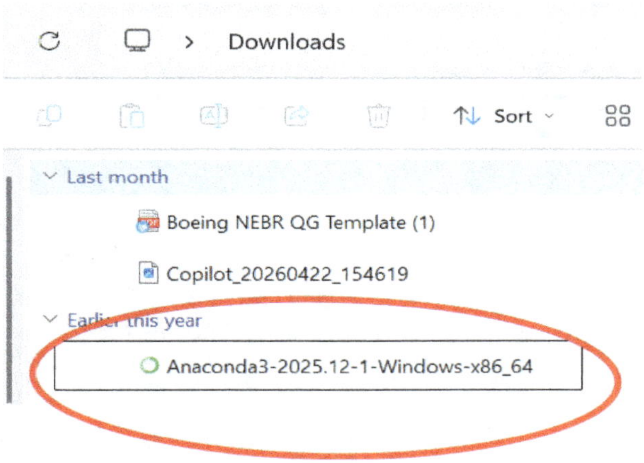

Step 2: Run the Anaconda Installer

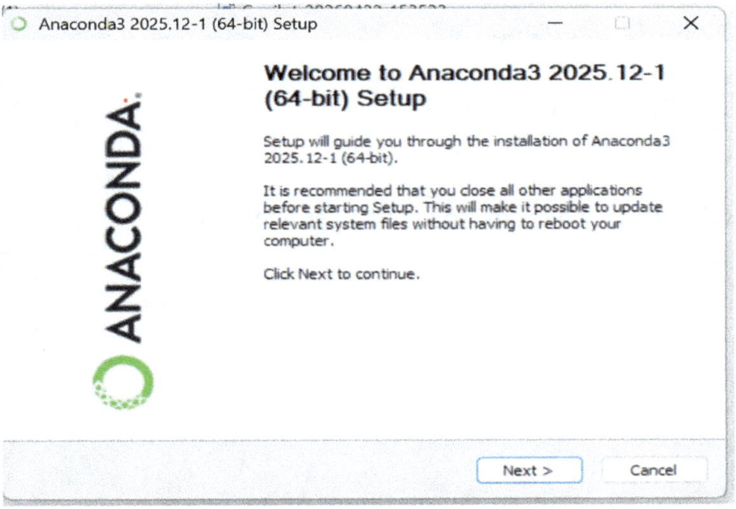

Step 3: Accept License Agreement

1. Read the license agreement.
2. Click **I Agree**.

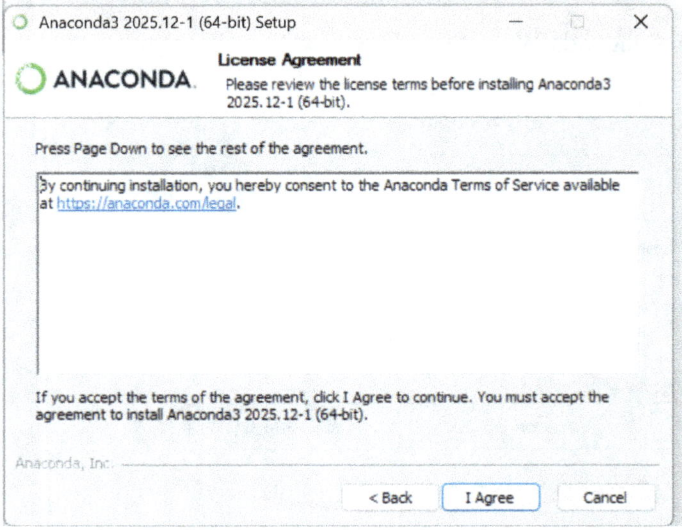

Step 4: Choose Installation Type

1. Select **Just Me (Recommended)**.
2. Click **Next**.

📌 *Tip:* This installs Anaconda only for your user account.

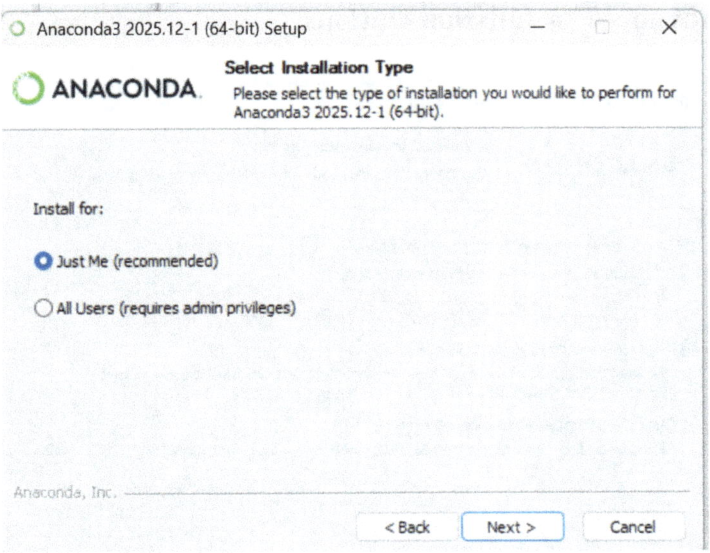

Step 5: Choose Installation Location

1. Keep the default location (recommended).
2. Click **Next.**

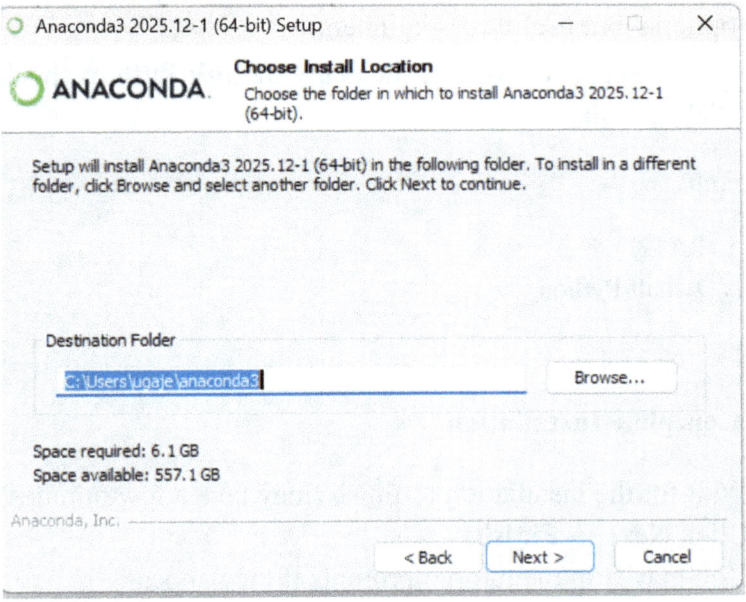

Step 6: Advanced Installation Options

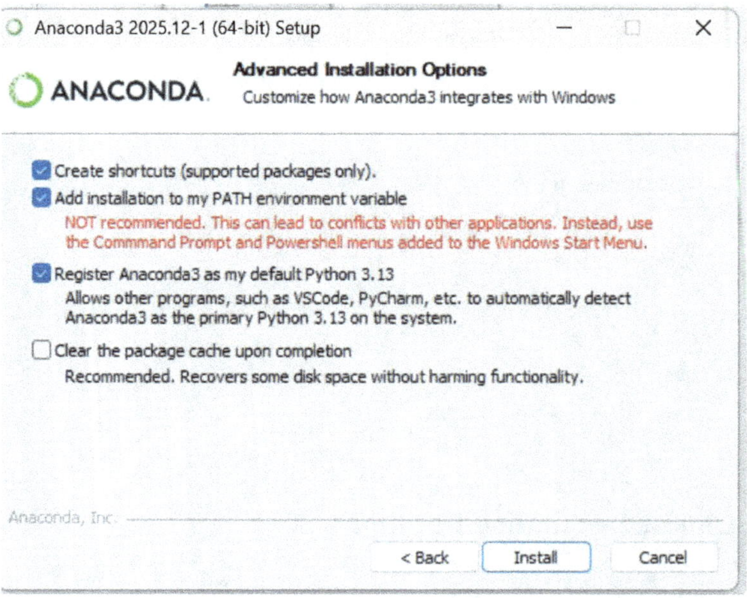

1. ✓ Check **Add Anaconda to my PATH environment variable** (optional but useful for beginners).
2. ✓ Keep **Register Anaconda as my default Python** checked.
3. Click **Install.**

📌 *Diagram:*

[✓] Add to PATH
[✓] Set as Default Python
↓
Install

Step 7: Complete Installation

1. Wait for the installation to finish (may take a few minutes).
2. Click **Next → Finish**.
3. You may skip the tutorial prompts if they appear.

Step 8: Open Anaconda Navigator

1. Click the **Start Menu**.
2. Search for **Anaconda Navigator**.
3. Click to open it.

📌

Start Menu → Anaconda Navigator → Open

Step 9: Launch Jupyter Notebook

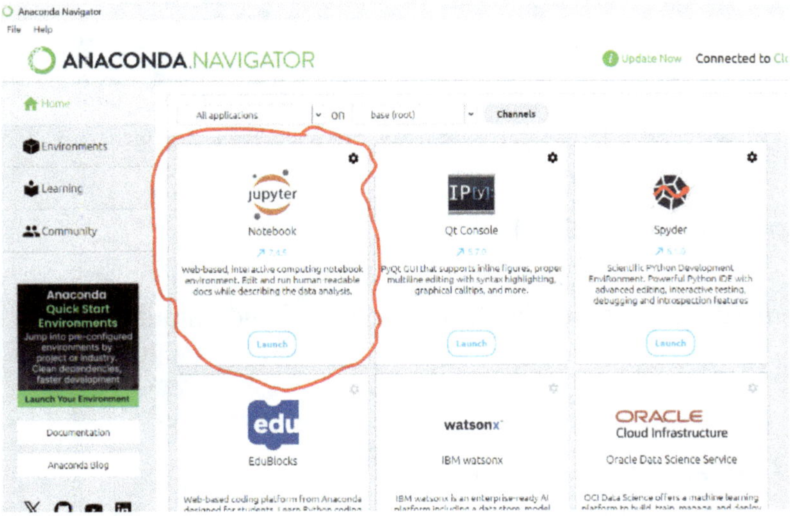

1. In Anaconda Navigator, find **Jupyter Notebook**.
2. Click **Launch**.
3. Your web browser will open automatically.

Step 10: Create Your First Notebook

In the browser window, click **New** (top-right).

1. Select **Python 3**.
2. A new notebook opens.

Jupyter Home → New → Python 3 → Notebook

Step 11: Test Jupyter Notebook

📷 *Screenshot 12:* Jupyter Notebook with code cell and output

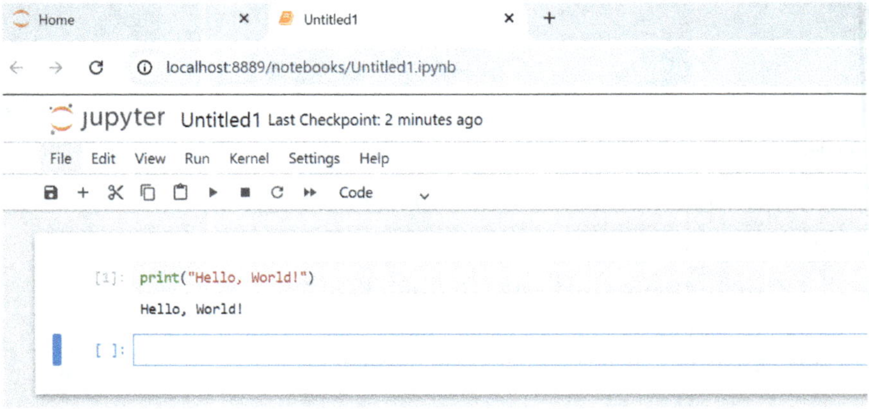

🧪 **Lab Activity:** Ask students to modify the text inside print() and run it again.

1. Click inside the first cell.
2. Type:

   print("Hello, World!")

3. Press **Shift + Enter**.
4. You should see the output below the cell.

Congratulations!

All students can open Jupyter Notebook.

You have successfully installed Anaconda and Jupyter Notebook on your Windows computer. Once the installation is done run below commands in Jupyter notebook.

Commands to run.

```
import datetime

print("  Hello and Welcome to learn Machine Learning !")
print("Current Date and time", datetime.datetime.now())
```

Troubleshooting: Common Installation Issues and Fixes

Issue 1: Anaconda Installer Will Not Open

Cause: Incomplete download or blocked by antivirus.

Fix:

- Re-download the installer from the official Anaconda website.

- Temporarily disable antivirus and try again.
- Right-click the installer and choose Run as Administrator.

Issue 2: Python Is Not Recognized After Installation

Cause: Anaconda was not added to the system PATH.

Fix:

- Open Anaconda Navigator instead of Command Prompt.
- Or reinstall Anaconda and ensure "Add Anaconda to PATH" is checked.

Issue 3: Jupyter Notebook Does Not Launch

Cause: Browser or environment conflict.

Fix:

- Restart Anaconda Navigator and click Launch again.
- Try a different web browser (Chrome or Edge recommended).
- Restart the computer if needed.

Issue 4: Permission or Access Denied Error

Cause: Lack of admin privileges.

Fix:

- Install using Just Me (Recommended) option.

- Avoid installing in restricted folders like Program Files.

Issue 5: Installation Takes Too Long or Freezes

Cause: Slow system or background processes.

Fix:

- Be patient; installation can take 10–15 minutes.
- Close unnecessary applications.
- Restart and try again if frozen for more than 30 minutes.

What You Can Do Next

- Learn Python basics
- Practice machine learning examples
- Explore data analysis using notebooks

www.ingramcontent.com/pod-product-compliance
Lightning Source LLC
LaVergne TN
LVHW022023051126
851858LV00003B/24